THE PARACHUTE PARADOX

STEVE SABELLA

emaginity.space

First published in 2016 in a hardcover limited and hand-numbered edition of 1250 + 150APs + 150 for media by Kerber Verlag, Germany.
Bestseller rating.

Second paperback edition published in 2021 by emaginity
ISBN 978-3-949392-02-3

Assistant editor & proofreader
Cécile Elise Sabella

Design
Steve Sabella

Project assistant
Henry Engelberg

Cover image
Steve Sabella, The Great March of Return 2019 (detail). A collector and a museum edition of 6 + 2APS, size 2 meter and 160 cm diameter respectively, light-jet print mounted on matt diasec. Check the video-art on: vimeo.com/336132812

The first edition of The Parachute Paradox was launched at SOAS University in London, Institute of Cultural Inquiry ICI in Berlin, Al-Serkal Avenue for Contemporary Art in Dubai, and Contemporary Art Platform CAP in Kuwait

WINNER
The Parachute Paradox won the 2017 Eric Hoffer Award and the 2016 Nautilus Book Awards, both for best memoir.

The Parachute Paradox is available for worldwide distribution in paperback, hardcover, and ebook from April 2021. Contact your local bookstore.

www.emaginity.space
emaginity™ is a registered trademark

www.stevesabella.space
www.patreon.com/stevesabella
facebook.com/SteveSabellaArtistPage
instagram.com/Steve_Sabella
linkedin.com/in/Steve-Sabella/

UPCOMING BOOKS:
The Artist's Curse
Palestine UNSETTLED
The Endings
EVERLAND
Children of the Dew
All That Remains

The supporters of the first edition of The Parachute Paradox will never be forgotten,

Margherita Berloni

Amer Huneidi

Kenneth Anderson & Andreanne Vachon

Marco Sassone

STEVE SABELLA

born in Jerusalem, Palestine, is an award-winning artist, writer, and public speaker based in Berlin using photography and photographic installation as his primary modes of expression. Sabella holds an MA in photographic studies from the University of Westminster and an MA in art business from Sotheby's Institute of Art, London.

Sabella received the *Ellen Auerbach Award* from the Akademie der Künste Berlin by nomination, leading to a published study covering twenty years of his art. His award-winning memoir *The Parachute Paradox*, published by Kerber Verlag in 2016, received international recognition winning two awards for best memoir.

Sabella's life and art have been subject to several documentaries, and his art has been exhibited internationally and is held in private and public collections, including those of the British Museum in London, The Arab World Institute museum in Paris, and Mathaf: Arab Museum of Modern Art in Doha. In 2014, The International Center for Photography Scavi Scaligeri in Verona held Sabella's first major retrospective, Archaeology of the Future.

www.stevesabella.studio

THE NEW VERSION

If you have read the first version of *The Parachute Paradox*, you will feel that every sentence, every word, every comma has been reconsidered. The stories are the same, but what changed is the style of narration. I removed the squeaks so that the words are part of a symphony where every detail matters. I was able to tune the language as the story is no longer in control of me, granting me the space to craft it to a concert without distortion. And like in my art, where I would never involve any external hands, it can only be true to my writing style. This is the only way to keep the integrity of the voice so that the story sounds right.

I created art in 2020 I usually complete in ten years, ten major projects. The night I finished an artwork was the same night I started a new one. And one series after the other was born, from *Everland* to *Endless* to *Elsewhere*. But towards the end of the year, the real magic happened. One night, I asked my sixteen-year-old daughter Cécile about the position of a comma, and when she said, "it depends," I invited her into my space. Before we knew it, we started editing the chapters of my life, the chapters of her life, together. And in the process, a whole universe revealed itself, material for a new book, *The Endings*.

The Endings are taken from the last line of every paragraph of *The Parachute Paradox*. When we put them together, they started to tell their own story.

Thanks to all the people who supported my studio in 2017 for The Patrons - Call To All Creatives:

Hani Zurob, Paula Billups, Liana Saleh, Rania Hafez, Tarik Hamdan, Amanda Tugwell, Hamodi Badarne, Reem Bader, Alex von Antje, Marco Sassone, Dagmar Painter, Hanan Awad, Ruthe Zuntz, Badar Salem, Alya Sebti, Madeline Yale Preston, Sami Alhaw, Mary Tuma, Claudia Baba, Ruven Kuperman, Hendrik Backerra, Stephi Meyer, Till Maiss, Fritz Trachsel, Ash Kotak, Lanna Idriss, Yasemin Vargi, Verena Gerlach, Simone van Dijken, Tina Zimmermann, Krista Schoening, Lee Pembleton, Angelique Abboud, Alexandra Thérèse, Alaa Mansour, João Gambino, Karin Adrian von Roques, Paul Sabella, Rafia Oraidi, Charlotte Bank, Almút Shulamit Bruckstein, Aser El Saqqa, Ursula Adrian-Riess, Elad Lapidot, Abed Abdel-Jawad, Ayman Nijmeh, George Al Ama, Peter and Beatrice Kaltenrieder, Adila Laidi-Hanieh, Léda Mansour, Linda Paganelli, Andrea Jaeger, Naila and Daoud Barakat, Anissa Salah, Ramzi Maqdisi, , Shaun Rabah, Rami El-Nimer, Haya Al-Sada, Michael Neuwirth, Maggy Berloni.

Thank you for your support in Patreon:

Gamal Abouali and Najet Hadriche
Daniela Nadira Amawi
Paula Billups
Marcia Kilmurry
Hani Zurob
David Meerbach
Hanan Debwania
Tina Zimmermann
Helmut Wartner
Nisreen Bajis
Talal Aldhiyebi
Nicoles Youness

TO

in alphabetical order

Gamal Abouali and *Najet Hadriche*, for helping me find the silence between my thoughts.

Daniela Nadira Amawi, for being part of my cosmic journey.

Mohammed Al-Asaad, for the knowledge you carry from our ancestors and for your masterpiece: Children of the Dew.

Hendrik Backerra, for spreading the light.

Maggy Berloni, for all the imagination and beauty we once shared.

Najwan Darwish, for keeping us alive with words.

Lily Farhoud, for your presence and for carrying the torch forward.

Ursula Hawlitschka and *Massimo Micucci*, for your critical eyes and for stepping in my journey at the right time.

Amer Huneidi, for your concrete support since we first met.

Claude Lemand, for your everlasting vision.

My Sabella family, *Tony*, *Fredo*, *Helen*, *Jacqueline*, *Claire*, *Peter*, *Paul*, and my mother *Espérance* for always being beside me. To my father *Emile*, who always believed that nothing is impossible.

Marco Sassone, for seeing the bigger picture.

Robert F. Wise, my first mentor and who showed me how to feel life first.

Nicoles Youness, for the clarity you share.

Hania Zawaneh and *Muin Khoury*, for the beginning of a new journey.

Hani Zurob, for your humanity.

To Francesca Sabella

the beauty of all beauties

To Cécile Elise Sabella

The One

dedicated to the power and light in you

One Heart

♥

THE PARACHUTE PARADOX

When I got home, I raced against time to pack and get to Ben Gurion Airport in Tel Aviv. I was exhausted, and dreaded the usual three hours of questioning and interrogation by Israeli airport security.

Shalom, meh eyfo ata?
Hello, where are you from?

In a Hebrew accent, while gargling the R in Yerushalayim, I said,

Ani meh Yerushalayim.
I come from Jerusalem.

She continued,

Where exactly do you come from?

If I answered with "East Jerusalem," it would be assumed I was an Arab. And if I answered with "West Jerusalem," it would be assumed I was Jewish. I replied,

Antonia Street,
The Old City.

She checked my passport, but my place of origin was still not clear to her. She asked me for my father's name,

Emile.
Your mother's?
Espérance.
Your grandfather's?
Antone.
What is the origin of the name Sabella?

Sicilian.

Do you celebrate Hanukkah?
Why not.

Do you celebrate Christmas?
Sure.

She was hesitant to ask if I was an Arab or Palestinian Arab. To speed things up, I told her I came from Jerusalem. The Arab one. All I wanted was to board the plane and close my eyes.

What is your occupation?
Artist.
I also work as a photographer for the UN.

I showed her my press card.

Where were you before you arrived at the airport?

I couldn't tell her I had just been kidnapped in Gaza. She would consider it a security threat and definitely not allow me to board the plane.

In Jerusalem.

And why are you going to Switzerland?
To have a holiday with my wife and daughter.
My wife is Swiss.

Why are you traveling alone?
Why do you work for the UN?
Have you traveled to Gaza with the UN?

Why do you live in Jerusalem?
Why don't you live in Switzerland?
When did your family settle in Jerusalem?

Why is your name Steve?

The questions were endless, and the first security guard was replaced by a second, and the second by a third, until the chief of security was called. I kept repeating the same narrative. Again and again. I had to be consistent and not make any mistakes.

Listen to me. This is my story. No matter how long you interrogate me, it will not change. Either you let me go home to Jerusalem, or you let me board the flight to Switzerland. Let's get this over with.

They gave in, allowed me to board after a conspicuous bag check and a full body search, escorted me to the plane like a VIP, and finally left me. I found my seat, sat down, and leaned back to close my eyes for the first time in two days. But every time I heard the click of a seatbelt, I woke up startled—it sounded like the cocking of the kidnappers' guns.

I opened my restless eyes and spotted a man watching me. He was black, and I imagined for a moment that he was the man the kidnappers released that morning. When he noticed that I spotted him, he unbuckled his seatbelt, walked over, and sat down on the aisle seat next to me. He spread open a newspaper and pointed to a photograph,

Is this you?

It showed a woman and me with guns and masks all around us. The bold title read, "UN Workers Freed in Gaza." I fell into my seat and said,

Sometimes, the answer is right there in front of you!

Up in the air, I traveled to the time I went skydiving in Haifa. On the tarmac, the plane looked like it hadn't flown since the 1967 War. After takeoff, the engine roared as if it could fail any second, wildly shaking as it reached the sky. When the time had come, I unbuckled my seatbelt and leaned out of the open door against the rushing wind. Without much thought, I did it. I let go. I was flying in the air. I felt light, less burdened by what was happening below. I felt identity-less, free from all the labels and classifications, free from racism and discrimination. Free from the Israeli Occupation I was born into.

But I didn't open the parachute. I was in a tandem jump, attached to an Israeli. Over the years, I have come to see this situation in the air as a metaphor for what it means to be a Palestinian born under Israeli Occupation. Life under Occupation is like the reality of a Palestinian attached to an Israeli in a tandem jump. There is an Israeli on the back of every Palestinian, controlling all aspects of life—the Israeli is always in control. This impossible reality places the Palestinian under constant threat, in a never-ending hostage situation.

On the ground, I struggled with paralyzing depression that sank to new lows year after year. But I knew my journey would have to be one of self-interrogation and liberation. With the speed of the fall, I felt Francesca's presence. Over the years, we had built our own world, rooted only in our imagination.

15

Let me take you back to 1996, when I sat alone in the back corner of Abu Shanab, a bustling hangout in the Old City of Jerusalem. I was only twenty. The First Intifada had ended three years earlier, but I was still tormented by severe episodes of depression, like aftershocks following an earthquake. Suddenly, my eyes caught sight of a face shining ethereally under a table lamp. Her bright face, blue eyes, and delicate lips, as though painted by a master, were shadowed by her long black hair. She was a sign from the universe. And I knew that my mission was to be with her.

Captured, I watched her, drowning in my own silence, mesmerized by never-fading beauty. And when the man next to her left, I snuck out and entered again. I sat down next to her and straight opened a box, pulling out black-and-white photographs I had just exposed in the darkroom. I leafed through them to capture her attention. She leaned over to look at the images. Her perfume was magnetic. I inhaled deeply, and its breeze of dewberries became locked in me forever. This dewberry never set me free. And when she looked into what I was searching for, my first words to her were,

A moment of truth.

To my surprise, she didn't turn away. She asked me what I meant, and I continued,

I'm tired of playing games. Why can't people drop their masks?

We talked, and the heavy conversation turned into a light one, where nothing mattered. Francesca was different. She didn't confront me with the origin of my name, ask whether I had changed it, or try to figure out my real name at birth. Those questions irritated me. They usually transpired within seconds of a first encounter, but when I asked people to name three typical Palestinian names, most realized the inanity of their questions.

The more I observed Francesca, the more I was falling in love with her. But how could I give her my phone number without coming on too strong? I hid my anxiety and left it for the universe to play its part. I said,

> *Here's my phone number.*
> *It's my age seven years from now, followed by the unlucky number, and the year I was born.*

Francesca never called.

Two weeks later, I was standing in front of Café Rimon, waiting for a Spanish girl who had just immigrated to Israel. It was our first date. I couldn't help but wonder what the point was. I didn't speak Spanish; she didn't speak English and hadn't yet learned Hebrew. Perhaps I preferred to date girls who couldn't ask me where I came from, about my name or religion. Such were my thoughts as I hid from the rain under an awning when I saw Francesca hurry by under an umbrella. I called out to her,

> *Francesca!*

> Hey!
> What are you doing here?

> *I'm just waiting for a friend.*

> How are you feeling?

> *I guess I'm on the wrong train, heading in the wrong direction.*
> *I'm stuck. Trapped.*

> Give me your hand. Let's jump onto another train.

I grabbed her hand, and we jumped. Over the years, I was drunk on the dewberry perfume my lips had wiped off her body. I was afflicted by a most beautiful curse. This curse still inflames my imagination. I called her Bombina with an O! She looked like Snow White, hiding in time. Once, a five-year-old-boy found her, and he couldn't wait to tell his mother that he had spotted Snow White.

Francesca was born in Switzerland. Three days before she came to Jerusalem to live with me, I flew to Bern to surprise her on her last day of work. I set up my tripod at her bus stop with a red rose. She walked down the dark street, saw it, and sat down on the empty bench on the other side of the bus shelter from where I was hiding. After a few tense minutes, the bus arrived, and just as she stepped in, I grabbed her hand from behind, pulling her close to me, and whispered,

Tonight you're not going home alone!

Francesca didn't stop laughing. On the bus, I gave her a black-and-white photograph I had created a few years earlier. Two hands and arms extend parallel to each other towards the sky, mirroring a plant stretching towards the light. Plant and arm merge and fade into each other. The effect was caused by an accidental double exposure created by improperly rolling the film. Over time, I learned that what happens by mistake bears meaning. With one arm around her, I read the words I had written under the image:

This is the World I am Looking for
A World of Love, Peace, and Serenity
This is How I Want to Live and
This is How I Love You

Francesca wore a silver ring compelling anyone who caught sight of it to remark on its exceptional presence. It was set with dark Bordeaux stone that stood out from the finger like a round Queen's signet ring. When I slipped it on my finger, I felt connected—it was a cosmic match. Francesca instantly said,

> We will wear the same ring. I will find another one for you.

She had found hers at Grass, a jewelry store on Ben Yehuda Street. We walked in, and I asked the shopkeeper if she had another one by any chance. She barely gave the ring a glance before saying "no" in harsh, accented Hebrew. I was taken aback by her attitude. Two months later, we checked again. She remembered us. While Francesca showed her the ring again, I said,

> Shalom. Did the goldsmith, by any chance, make another ring?

With a brusque attitude, she replied,

> Amarti lecha sheh lo. En li.
> I told you before that I don't have it. No.

It was infuriating, but we went back once more. This time, I interrupted her before she uttered a word,

> *Listen to me. Every time I come here, you say no. But do you know what bothers me? You have never really looked for it. Please look in the drawers. You have nothing to lose.*

She murmured a few words in Hebrew, started looking, and opened various drawers. Shortly after, her head emerged from behind the messy counter. Shining between her fingers was Francesca's ring. I knew I was the one meant to wear it. But what I didn't know then was that over the years, many forces would seek to separate us.

My first trip outside Jerusalem was planned when I was twelve. I was going to live with an American host family from Connecticut for six months, or even longer. A break meant to be an escape. My parents felt that the distance would lighten the dark depression I had fallen into since the beginning of the First Intifada in 1987 that locked us in our homes. It took me twenty years to find a close description of what I felt back then. It hit me while watching the film, *The Diving Bell and the Butterfly*, whose protagonist suffered from locked-in syndrome. I, too, had been entrapped, isolated, in endless dialogue with the voices of the self.

> *I was able to move my body, but it never moved forward.*
> *I was able to move my eyes, but they only saw death.*
> *I was able to hear, but all I wanted was not to hear the sound of bullets and tear gas every day.*
> *I felt the weather change, but my skin grew pallid from sitting in my own darkness.*
> *My home became my prison.*

As a twelve-year-old, I was aware that I belonged to a country that was not a country but a land occupied by Israel called Palestine. For the first time, I could see the enormous effort required to break free from the military occupation on the ground, and later from the Israeli colonization of my imagination.

I was impatient. I wanted the conflict to end quickly. It paralyzed me. Suffocated me. I had made plans for my future before the First Intifada, but the Occupation crippled life. The dream of promised peace that never came exhausted me. I understood then, as clearly as I do today, the impossible reality on the ground and its injustices justified by toxic amounts of ideology. At times, the exertion I needed to liberate myself took over me. Once, it found me on the highest ledge of our house in the Old City. While my eyes were drowning in the night sky, contemplating jumping from the roof, I heard my mother shouting hysterically from down below. I did not kill myself. Was it because I loved my mother, or was it because of a belief that someone in the sky was watching over me? Perhaps a bit of both.

When the First Intifada erupted, and the uprisings hit Jerusalem, Palestinians often threw resistance pamphlets over the Old City's historic wall, flying into my school's courtyard. They contained patriotic phrases and a list of rules imposed on everyone living in occupied Palestine. They also ordered all schools in Arab Jerusalem to close at midday. To compensate for the lost hours, schools started at 6:30 a.m., which was the worst in winter, when the house was freezing, and the sky still dark. My classmates from Ramallah, fifteen kilometers from Jerusalem, had to wake up as early as five o'clock. Victor, my best friend, often fell asleep during class. When we were little, we held hands during some of the breaks. One summer, he opened the cover of the water tank on the roof of his building. He took off his shoes and shirt and jumped through the narrow opening into the water. All I could see was his short spiky hair. After a few seconds, he emerged with a cheeky smile. A few years ago, I heard that Victor ended up in a mental institution.

One day, a sixteen-year-old boy I knew from my school was killed by the Israeli army, the first person to die in Jerusalem during the Intifada. His name was Nidal il Rabady, an Arabic name that means "struggle." Nidal came from a Christian family that lived between the Christian and Muslim quarters. He was shot while riding his bicycle back home. Like many of my classmates, I attended the funeral at his house. This was my first encounter with death. I was thirteen. The room was packed, and Nidal's coffin stood in the center. There were two candles placed above his head. He lay in a black coffin, which seemed suspended in air, surrounded by wailing women wrapped in black. I couldn't see his face. I took a step closer to his mother. My body still holds her grief and recalls her face swollen from countless tears. She kept touching his face. But Nidal was pale, frozen, wearing a suit that did not fit him. A morbid scene that unsettled my bond with life. I stared at Nidal and said a few words, and I left.

People die in wars, and in all wars, at one point, the enemies sit down and make peace possible. There is something distinct about the way Israelis perceive peace. I understand this because I have lived with Israelis like an Israeli. Israelis prefer revenge, to see their enemy defeated first, dead, rather than find novel ways to live in peace.

When a Palestinian was killed, people in Jerusalem and other Palestinian cities would mourn and strike for three whole days, closing all shops, schools, and institutions. Once, my school's doors were shut for three consecutive months to satisfy the agreed-upon three days of mourning per death.

This was when Brother Robert Wise volunteered to come to our house daily to teach me and my brother Peter physics, math, computer science, and chemistry. He was a scientist, a visionary at my school, Collège des Frères, and a dear family friend, who closely followed my progress. Wise wore the traditional black dress of the brothers with the white-collar. He suffered from an eye problem, incessantly wiping his leaking ducts with delicate cotton. I now see him as my first mentor, as someone who was able to see the light in me when I jumped into my total darkness.

He founded the computer department in my school when computers had just been launched into the world, teaching students BASIC and KOBOL languages. Wise later appointed my brother Fredo to run the department until he enrolled in an American University to study computer science to pursue his dreams. My first personal home computers, a Radioshack and a Commodore, were a gift from Wise who taught me how to program, design, and construct an alternate reality on his daily visits to the darkest room in our Old City house, without any windows, which he turned into a thinking lab. I found the computer syntax or codes easy to put together to make simple games and build software programs to calculate equations. He was intrigued by how I looked at problems, not magnifying them but looking at their many possible solutions.

I had many questions to ask him, and one day he gave me a book from the school's library with the title Ask Me Why. He said to me once,

> You can change the world.

When I asked him how, he said,

> Ask yourself how.

As a chemist, Wise allowed me to do some experiments with him. His clothes carried chemical smells, smells that one can never forget. I listened to him, yet Wise rarely gave me straight answers. He encouraged me to think more, to search, and to observe. On one of my special days, I asked him what happens to a mouse inside a vacuum. He brought over a mouse in a cage and locked it in a vacuum container. I grabbed the handle and did not hesitate to suck the air out. When the mouse seemed drowsy, Wise stopped me, took the mouse in both hands, and freed it in the yard. Feeling guilty, I followed to see if it survived. As the mouse sought refuge, a cat sprinted and grabbed it by its tail.

The first documentary on my life, possibly during my teenage years, was through Robert Wise by an American production company that aired the feature in the United States. They filmed me walking in the Old City, speaking on my school's rooftop, and on the stairs next to the lemon tree in our house, after my seven siblings and I did a musical performance, as we all played instruments. Wise knew the harsh effect the Intifada had on me, and it distraught him seeing my potential and future collapse. To help, he convinced my parents to send me to an American family in Connecticut for six months at the age of twelve, a form of adoption. When the situation drastically deteriorated, Wise put me on a plane to New York to meet the Larkins to live in Connecticut. He even introduced me to Yale University so that I kept my eyes open.

My eldest brother, Tony, who had fallen in love with an American girl named Suny during his studies in France accompanied me. After they had finished their master's programs, she settled in Colorado to live with her parents. His heart was broken, and he told me on the plane that he was hoping a surprise visit would bring them back together. As the plane approached New York, I kept repeating to Tony that I wanted to be the first in our family to step onto American soil. As I took the first step, I was ecstatic about the symbolic victory.

We picked up our bags, passed through security, and saw the Larkins holding a sign with my name on it. Before I knew it, Tony was gone. With their two kids in the car, the family overwhelmed me with stereotypes I had no power to deal with. Mrs. Larkin said,

I'm sure Steve hasn't seen traffic before.

Given that the Larkins had visited Jerusalem over ten times, her remark surprised me, and I replied that traffic in Jerusalem seemed to be as bad as in New York. She offered me ice cream while gesturing with her hands and tongue to make sure I got what it was for. I already spoke English well, and I had eaten ice cream before. When Mrs. Larkin showed me where I would sleep. She pointed to a bed and remarked that people slept on beds in America. Her assumption that we slept on the floor at home, or perhaps in a tent, irritated me. I had never slept in a tent before, not even at summer camps. But maybe she guessed I came from a refugee camp. Israel had displaced hundreds of thousands of Palestinians in 1948. And again in 1967. In the beginning, most refugees lived in tents, believing that in a few days, or weeks, they could return home. Israel denied them the Right of Return. Today, the number of registered refugees is over seven million. Standing in front of the bed, I wanted to clarify that I was not a refugee. I was still living at home, and I could return there whenever I wanted. The Larkins did not recognize that I wasn't a child deprived of a bed or ice cream, but a child whose freedom did not exist and was traumatized. Within two weeks, I wanted to run away—back to Jerusalem. I preferred the pain of living in Jerusalem with my family during the raging war than to suffer in a family I had nothing in common with. Then, it all ended when Mrs. Larkin announced that she had found me a place in an all-boys school. I protested,

Call Tony.

They did. I told Tony,

Come take me home. Now!

I had just run away from Jerusalem. The last thing I expected to confront in America was more segregation, judgment, and control. On the way to LaGuardia Airport, and after learning that Tony's mission with Suny had failed, I caught sight of the Statue of Liberty. As I looked at the torch in the sky, I understood that real freedom is felt, not just a scene. Its essence is beyond all symbols. In America, I became more suspicious of the power embedded in images.

Upon returning home, I was relieved when I saw the lemon and grapevine trees in the open courtyard of our house in the Old City. I looked for my parents on the upper terrace and saw them putting brown paper bags around the grape clusters to protect against bees. I rushed up the steps to hug them. As I fell into my mother's arms, I saw a snake's head crawling out. I screamed and ran to my father. He grabbed a stick and ferociously slashed the bag, beating the hanging grapes, which burst and splashed on my face. The terrified snake spiraled through the air, and as he tried to grab it, the snake lunged towards my father and was brutally killed.

The grapevine tree grew from a thick trunk that split into two long branches. One extended to an upper terrace, and the other grew towards the terrace on the opposite side of the house. The grapevine shared barely one square meter of soil with the lemon tree. These two trees looked ancient, but every year, they raised clusters of grapes and grapefruit-sized lemons. In springtime, the neighborhood air became infused with lemon blossom fragrance. I loved the lemon tree, how it flourished in the center of the house, able to survive in hardly any soil. I assumed the lemon tree thrived because its roots grew deep into the ground, so deep, they might have reached the water of our deserted house well. I was too scared to look into the well to see how far it descended into its own darkness. But one day, I did shine a flashlight inside. Its shaft looked endless, and its stone walls were covered by a mesh of roots, some protruding into the air. The roots never touched the water and seemed to absorb the humidity in the air. I became its caretaker. Once, my brothers and I accidentally bruised its trunk. I turned to Mother Veronica, a relative of my mother's who had been confined to live in a Russian Orthodox monastery at the age of five. She became a nun and has lived there ever since. Her hobby was gardening, and the convent allocated Veronica a piece of land, where I often helped plow its soil and plant flowers. She explained to me,

> Take from its soil,
> make mud with water,

plaster the wound.

From the convent rose the bell tower of the Mount of Olives Ascension Monastery, which overlooks the Old City. It's one of the few remaining places in Jerusalem where one can be alone. Upon permission, I was handed an iron key, the size of my palm. It opened a green metal door that led into a chamber at the base of the tower biblical in height, with a staircase that spiraled all the way up. I locked myself in and then started the journey up. My footsteps' echo on the metallic staircase was like the sound of drums, calling for battle. The tremors scared the pigeons, who flapped their wings and then shot through the arched windows. Climbing up felt like turning around myself. Looking down at my footsteps made me dizzy. To reach the top, I had to focus and look straight ahead. I took breaks at the first, second, and third parts of the tower. Open on all sides, I saw Jerusalem from all viewpoints. Once, I sprung all the way up until I could no longer look forward or catch my breath. At the highest point in Jerusalem, I was looking over the lowest point on earth—the Dead Sea.

From there, I was able to spot our rooftop, sitting on the lower side. As a child, I would take many people who visited my father from abroad onto our rooftop, promising them an incredible view. One could see the bell tower and the whole of the Mount of Olives from east to west. But surprise lit up their faces when they saw the large open plot of land next to our house—a sudden paradise. It belonged to the Darwish family and was where the snake came from. One half of the land was covered in grass, encircled by a ring of fruit trees, while the second half boasted a tall cypress tree that stood like a sword pointing to the sky. On one side of the garden, stone arches led to abandoned dark caves.

The trees that grew in the Darwish garden leaned against our terrace and created shade. On the morning of a scorching summer's day, my mother was sitting in the shadow as she frantically called me over to come and see something. I wish she hadn't. Our neighbor Darwish stood in front of his cypress tree. He held a torch in his hand, and when it touched the shriveled branches, flames shot up, transforming the entire tree into a rocket of fire. Snakes dropped from the tree like shooting stars. We smelled their roasted skin. I never grasped why he burned the cypress tree. Perhaps, he thought it was revealing his secret garden from afar. One day, I came home from school to see my mother sawing the base of the two-trunked grapevine tree. I was too late to stop her—the tree was dead. I asked her why she killed it. Her answer had something to do with its dry autumn leaves floating through the air and landing into our neighbors' courtyard. The tree had been rooted for centuries like an ancient widow that never failed to fruit. Instead of dying gracefully, in its one-square-meter cemetery, it was condemned to death by saw.

Our house was in the heart of the Old City, where thirty-five thousand Muslims, Christians, Jews, and many other nationalities live and, paradoxically, over the centuries, have learned how not to live together. If you have ever visited Jerusalem's Old City, you know what I mean. The almost one-square-kilometer place is walled from side to side, chaotic, bustling, in never-ending turmoil with itself. Some people even claim that Jerusalem was built at the center of the universe. They say only those born inside of its gates know when and where to find its mystical moments. I found these moments when the city was empty, deep into the night on the way to Jouret el Enab. From the valley below, the Old City wall looked like a fortress draped in shadows. Glowing city lights drew my eyes along the wall's path from the valley to the top of Jerusalem. At moments like these, I thought—this is the most magnificent city in the world. Ancient, but not ceasing to renew the spirit. Majestic, but never controlling. A city at unity with itself. At such moments we assume to know the truth. But all these moments, and the truths they reveal, might only exist in the mind.

My father, Emile, was a tour guide, and he spoke several languages, including Latin. Our livelihood depended on tourism, which crashed during the First Intifada. As a young man, he had worked for the Latin Patriarchate Church in Jerusalem. My great-grandfather was the Mukhtar of the Catholic community in the Christian Quarter during the last years of the Ottoman Empire and the beginning of the British Mandate for Palestine in the early 1920s. But the situation halted my father, like many in his generation, from completing high school. The 1948 War, which came in response to the creation of Israel, fragmented Palestinian life, the trauma of which is still lived today. My father substituted university with self-study, a habit he cultivated all his life. My memory sees him sitting in a wooden chair facing the lemon tree, reading, as if in conversation with the ideas buried in his treasured leather books. I learned from my father how to follow a path of knowledge when no path seemed possible.

My father regularly took care of his plants and brought many home to my mother, who liked to spread them on the far right side of each of the twenty-three steps that connected the lower terrace to the upper one. I remember how he would water them with a cup and a silver tin bucket, intuitively knowing the right amount of water to sustain them throughout the heat of the day. He raised chickens, pigeons, rabbits, and even ducks. Every morning, he would wake up early, drink coffee with my mother, and then shave with a brush and a razor blade. Once in a while, he cut himself and took care of the wound using a silver stone that stopped the bleeding. Afterward, he would put on his suit and tie, something he did till the day he passed away. Yaba, as I called him, had hazel-green eyes, which I wish I inherited. For many years he wore black-framed glasses with thick lenses. When he was a child, he fell from a rooftop onto his face, an impact that permanently twisted his vision. He also broke most of his teeth, forced to wear dentures, which led to an extreme gag reflex, something I for sure inherited. This made it impossible for him to enjoy food, and our attempts to help him were in vain. The injustices of life have always irritated him. He believed a quick solution would only come with the end of the occupation of the Holy Land. When he talked about the 1948 War, Al-Nakbah, he condemned the Arabs, the world, and the United Nations. He has never come to terms with the way Palestine was divided—the partition was wrong. There was no justice.

One winter, Jerusalem witnessed a massive snowstorm. Most people I have met think Jerusalem is in the desert, hot and dry, but it lies almost nine hundred meters above sea level. Because it borders the Jordan Valley, the pressure difference triggers strong winds. The day began with a sandstorm and temperatures over twenty degrees Celsius. In Jerusalem, each person lives within fixed categories. I was labeled the Christian, the Arab, the Palestinian, and even a Jew. I could live with all four, and many more. But these labels have never really defined who I am. I struggled to fit in when almost everyone lived in the past, with a faith contaminated by deadly ideology. In Jerusalem, I sailed and navigated between religious stories to avoid becoming locked into the vision of others. I realized my task was not to find my identity but to get rid of it. I wanted an identity of my own, embroidered with my own life philosophy and stitched with my own threads.

The entire city was washed in yellow, becoming invisible. At night, temperatures dropped below zero, and another storm hit, leaving a knee-deep blanket of snow. At moments like these, I felt a mystic love for Jerusalem, when nature, rather than people, took control of its air, land, and narrative. I got a fever, hallucinating as

I murmured,

> *Jerusalem groans under the weight of prophecies. There is a secret channel between Jerusalem and God. Words are biblical signs. God built Jerusalem in the heart of the universe. My mother sacrificed the grapevine tree she adored by severing its trunk to cleanse her contaminated faith. The well leading to nowhere exists beyond time and darkness. The fight between my father and the snake is an eternal battle of good and evil. The snake comes from the paradise next door and is witness to this prophecy. The cypress tree points to the hidden land of The Third Temple. Darwish, the hand of God, burns all evil that reveals his sacred sanctuary. My Father, The Son, and The Holy Tree.*

The prophecies are endless. If God gave The Promised Land to the Jews and sacrifice everyone else, who can argue with God? This is what God wants. End of the story.

Since time immemorial, Jerusalem has been denied to reinvent itself. Jerusalem became a sign, an image from the past. And the image became a reality based on fiction, shattering the lives of people.

To set myself free, I sacrificed everything I loved about Jerusalem. I suffocated the lemon tree with my own hands: I cut off the circulation of its moist air. I filled the well with rubble and dirt. The tree suffocated, with no choice but to die slowly until it inhaled its last breath. I killed the lemon tree. From that point on, Jerusalem was in exile. The island of serenity Francesca and I had built on the remains of the grapevine tree vanished. I dragged myself into eternal exile. I destroyed my temple with my own hands.

Francesca is not my lemon tree. She is like the well, which was deep and had a mystery that was never revealed. No one knew how deep the well was and where its clear water came from. Francesca's charm and presence are a mystery, even to me, and I am afraid to search for their origin.

Francesca became my Jerusalem.

14

When I asked Francesca if she would marry me, she said without hesitation,

YES!

That summer's night, in 1997, we sat on a bench looking over the Old City of Bern. Almost a year and a half earlier, we had jumped on our imagined train. Even though Francesca flew back to Switzerland three months after we had met, our train kept moving. We defied its speed and discovered many stations along the way. I made frequent surprise visits to Switzerland, and after a while, Lisa, Francesca's flatmate and best friend, became familiar with the way I rang the doorbell and would answer in response,

Yes, Steve. Come up. Francesca is here, waiting.

Once, I called Francesca and Lisa picked up the phone. She slipped and said Francesca had flown to Jerusalem to surprise me. In anticipation, I lit a path from the entrance hall, up the twenty-one stairs, to the rooftop with candles. A table for two, surrounded by light, was waiting for us. As the night progressed, the air became thick with dewberry. The more time we spent together, the more intoxicated I became. There was something about her that ignited me. I could not live without her. Every time we said farewell, I felt a piercing pain that lingered until the distance between us disappeared again. Her presence formed me, gave sense to my life when it had lost all meaning. But the powers of earth were sometimes more powerful than our free imagination. After another enchanting surprise visit to Switzerland in 1996, we decided to part ways. The physical distance between us had become a barrier. At times, it seemed impossible. Flying was expensive, and back then, EasyJet only had two routes. The internet had just become available, and Skype didn't exist yet. Making calls cost three dollars per minute, and we talked at least once a day.

After our farewell in Zurich, I headed to Austria. A day later, Francesca surprised me in Vienna. We gave the farewell a second thought, delaying it until her departure. The end would come when we reached the train station. On our last day together, I promised her,

> *Before you depart, I'll tell you ten times:*
> *I love you.*

Throughout the exciting day, I asked random people to help me fulfill the promise. In the evening, I asked the DJ at a dancing bar to announce into the microphone,

> And by the way,
> Steve Sabella says he loves you for the sixth time.

Later, I asked a waitress to bring the bill, and on it she had scribbled,

> Steve Sabella loves you for the seventh time.

The ninth time, closer to Francesca's departure, and while she was browsing the train station's bookstore, I asked a police officer to stop her,

> Hey.
> Steve tells you he loves you for the ninth time.

Even though we dreaded departing, Francesca was amused by the strangers woven into our tale. But now, her train was about to leave, and as we counted the moments, we understood less and less how and why we were in this position again. We were both in tears. Shattered. I embraced Francesca, and I let the dewberry penetrate me. I kissed her parted lips, knowing I was leaving the most beautiful woman in the world. Her presence was magnetic. Her absence was torture.

Francesca boarded the train to return to her reality. I watched her find her seat, and as I waved the final goodbye, the train slowly departed. I walked with it until I reached the end of the platform. And then, she was gone. It was over. Her presence completed me, or more precisely, her presence was like a sedative, an injection—a drug that worked. Later on the journey, a man found Francesca still in tears, sat down next to her, put his arms around her, and whispered to her,

> Francesca.
> By the way, Steve says he loves you for the tenth time!

I took the night train to Prague, and as I was strolling through its vibrant streets alone that night, I felt enchanted by its lights and dim alleyways. Prague looked like a city for lovers. And my lover was gone. I called Francesca from a payphone and asked her to join me. Later, she revealed the promise she had made to herself after she got my message from the mystery man on the train,

> If Steve calls me tonight and asks me to go to Prague,
> I will.

Francesca had just graduated and was also broke. She asked her father to cover the trip and boarded the night train to start the next day together. To celebrate, we rented a rowboat on the river at sunset. Francesca and I loved acting in our imagination. We dressed elegantly, in black, as if going to the theater. On the boat, we made a small mountain of different berries we could find in any color. As Francesca leaned back, holding a glass of red wine, the street lamps of St. Charles bridge lit up behind her. It happened under the arch when a ray of sunlight hit Fracesca's glass and glittered on her face. I don't know what possessed me, but I took off my clothes, down to my black underwear, becoming Francesca's own stripper on the boat. All of a sudden, flashes of light bombarded us from above, like lightning on a stormy night.

Look! A naked man.

It started with a woman pointing her finger at me. Then, a group of tourists began flashing their cameras off the bridge. In that moment, I secretly felt,

I want to marry her.

I had been anti-marriage all my life. I rejected the ceremony and the commitment and philosophized and preached against them. I was so vocal about it that even Francesca believed it would never happen. But I thought,

If I change my mind by a miracle and decide to get married in twenty years, I'll find no one like Francesca. So why waste my time if I have already found the one?

When Jeremy Jonathon, the teacher of my color photography class, saw Francesca for the first time, he turned his head to me and disclosed,

Now I understand why you photograph so beautifully.

Jeremy is an Israeli artist and was a teacher at the Musrara School of Photography, an Israeli art school where I enrolled to delve into photography for three years. He was an American immigrant who backed Israeli settlements in Palestine, always carrying a gun with him when he came to class. He was a religious Jewish man, with silver-white hair, a father of three, who had down-to-earth spiritual beliefs.

Jeremy justified the Occupation, and I rejected it. Despite our inner conflicts, we were able to connect by staying open. He could identify with the Palestinian struggle for liberation. His ability to switch from one consciousness to an opposing one was unexpected—rare among Israelis back then, and even more unusual today.

I learned many things from Jeremy. He spoke a language of life that defied the aim of the gun he wore. I accepted him, but I preferred to meet in my world—gun and death free. Once, we traveled to the Jordan Valley for a photography expedition. At sunrise, I woke up and saw Jeremy tightening the black straps of his *tefillin* in preparation to pray. As he nodded his head back and forth, I approached him to ask a question. He didn't answer. But later, he explained that observant Jews keep the silence before the morning prayers. I apologized. His face brightened, and we carried on as we always had. It was that simple. There were no temples involved, no ideologies attached, no signs to decode—just an unorthodox recognition of the other living in both of us.

In the desert, I conveyed to Jeremy my frustration with not being able to see color in Jerusalem. I only saw Jerusalem in shades between black and white. He looked at me and replied,

Steve.
It's about time you open your eyes.

Jeremy's answers were often more abstract than my questions, and they left me wondering about their essence. He inspired me to look beyond the surface. He pushed me until he felt I was on the right visual track—a search for self through photographic light. I now realize that Jeremy never came to my world. I probably visited him in his vast desert. And yet, we shared a secret language, even though there has been little possibility of honest dialogue between Israelis and Palestinians, Israelis and Arabs, or Arabs and Jews, or whatever label people choose to use. I referred to him in the text for my first exhibition, *Search*, which ended with whoever wants to see the invisible has to penetrate more deeply into the visible. When I asked if he had looked at it, Jeremy said,

I read it to my children.

I was baptized at the age of ten, a sin for any Christian family living in Jerusalem. My Father, a Catholic, disagreed with the Latin Patriarchate over remuneration and unfulfilled promises. He worked for the priests for over twenty years. He threatened that he would not baptize his last two children, Paul and me, as Catholics. The priests ignored my father, even though he served them loyally. Years passed, and Paul and I became labeled. The Unbaptized. Eventually, my father caved in, but to inflame the Church, he had us baptized Greek Orthodox. This was how Paul and I ended up at the Nativity Church in Bethlehem one early Sunday morning. I did not want to be baptized, stripped naked, and thrown into a basin, the orthodox way. Neither did Paul. We slipped away from the priest. He chased after us from behind the altar, missing us through the narrow pews, out of the church door, up the stairs to the inner courtyard. My mother, father, and family members I hated, also rushed after us. We ran in circles, escaping everyone's hands, till they cornered us. When my mother tells the story, she always describes the stressed priest who rolled up his shirt sleeves when he lost us. They forced Paul and me to strip naked, down to our underwear, like a sacrifice at the altar.

My parents went even further, re-baptizing all my six other siblings, Greek and Russian Orthodox. Up to then, they had been Catholic. Most people lived and died with one label of religion. My brothers and sisters had two or three versions of the same religion. The baptism was intended to save my soul, and maybe it did—it liberated me from religion. It was a blessing I was baptized so late, an event that happens in a Jerusalem Christian family only once, or in this case twice, in a thousand years.

Still, whenever I traveled to the Dead Sea, I sought my own spiritual journey. I plunged into salty water. Despite its name and nature, the sea didn't kill me. One might wonder how a sea of total death, where nothing survives, renews the spirit. It seems like a spiritual paradox, a mistake, but this mistake and my reflection on its essence transformed my perception of life. To survive, I confronted all the toxic labels and images planted in me. I faced them, questioned them, and let them go. We dread this self-confrontation because the self prefers to survive on sweet water.

When Francesca gave birth to our baby girl, Cécile, we baptized her. After all, I am my father's son, from Jerusalem. But this baptism had to be different. We baptized her in nature, in the sweet and serene water of Lake Tiberias, where the Jordan River ends. Or starts.

I was born behind the Old City gates and lived in a house bestowed on my father by an old man. In my faint memory, I recall him wearing a worn-out black garment with a sash tied around his waist multiple rounds, where he kept his documents. He had a pyramid-like hunch, a beard like a wizard, and spent his days tending to his forest of plants on the terrace, neighboring the Darwish land. Moving to this out of place and out of time old house was the best decision my parents ever made. Leaving the Christian Quarter for the Muslim Quarter displaced us from the Christian community, and by the Old City's logic, we didn't belong to the Muslim community either. This gave us independence. My siblings and I grew up in a house that was an oasis of light. From the front door, one walked through an arched cave, and after ascending six steps, encountered the lemon tree, whose branches reached the roof. The grapevine tree next to it spread leaves that covered the two terraces in summer. The shade and the light streaking through the leaves created a feeling of life as if somewhere else, a retreat, away from the charged atmosphere in Jerusalem.

Over the years, we took care of turtles, cats, hamsters, pigeons, chickens, ducks, a parrot, an eagle, fish, and even a goat. But, I mostly remember the dogs I grew up with. Ringo, a white puppy with brown spots and long curls on her neck, was the first dog we sheltered. My brother Fredo found Ringo wandering in the neighborhood on a cold, rainy night. He took her in, and shortly after, white Lassie was born. Later, Lassie gave birth to a long-haired Puchi. A Diva. Those three were the only dogs allowed to sleep in our beds. I also remember blonde Rocky, stern Mukless, who appointed himself commander-in-chief of all the dogs, and terrified everyone in the neighborhood, black Lucky, and dozens of puppies through the years. Ringo's dynasty ended with Toska, who had black lines around her eyes, like thick eyeliner. After days of suffering, when she died, Francesca and I buried her next to Mukless, her companion. We took a shovel and carried her in our arms, from Lions Gate to the Mount of Olives. We buried her in a grove of olive trees under the teardrop church of Dominus Flevit. Facing home.

Inside, our house had many rooms painted in various colors. Every summer, we painted the walls, and by autumn, the paint would start to peel, creating shapes, fragments, and contours that puzzled the most sophisticated of eyes—a Pollock painted by many at different times. As each loose fragment took flight, its absence exposed visual palimpsests, stories buried beneath many layers of paint.

Our house stood like a watchtower, overlooking all others in the neighborhood. Climbing up the worn-out wood ladder my father built to get to the roof, the first thing that would catch the eye was an old church with a low tower squeezed between houses.

To its left, the Dome of the Rock lies quietly in its place. At sunset, before darkness, the golden dome blends with the sky, and the blue of its base slowly turns deeper and deeper until it dissolves. Looking further to the left, the main minaret of Jerusalem rises up in the air, echoing "Allah Akbar, Allah Akbar," reminding the birds resting on its arches to fly around it in circles. Further along, the panoramic view of the Mount of Olives starts with the Jewish cemetery, which occupies a third of the mountain's slope. At its top, the Seven Arches Hotel built during Jordan's rule is visible, followed by the pencil tower of the Church of the Ascension at the center of the horizon. The Augusta Victoria Hospital, the heart of the German Protestant community in Palestine during the Ottoman Empire, stands at the far left. On the mountain's slope, one can also see the Dominus Flevit, known in Arabic as the church of the Tear Drop, the church and convent of St. Mary Magdalene with its six golden Russian domes, and the Church of All Nations next to the Garden of Gethsemane. The Old City Wall leads to the courtyard of St. Anne's Church, owned by France. A French flag flies there every year on the fourteenth of July. To the very left of this panoramic view, one can see Mount Scopus, the Hebrew University, and the Rockefeller Museum, formerly known as the Palestine Archaeological Museum. This tableau caught everyone by surprise, and I've always been gripped by it. It condensed thousands of years of Jerusalem's history into one view. Today, the center of the Mount of Olives is no longer marked by the church of the Ascension's bell tower, but instead by a vast, blue-and-white Israeli flag, stretching meters long, celebrating the Occupation of a Palestinian house at the highest point. To me, it seems like a visual error. A stab in the eye. And no matter how much I tried to make it fit into the view, I failed.

But I was able to blend in—in all of the divided Jerusalem—and pass freely through Israeli checkpoints, partly because of my fluent Hebrew. I liked speaking Hebrew, and I perfected the R in Beseder by repeating it while gargling water. Over time, the R echoed with the right ring.

Shalom. Hakol beseder?
Shalom. Is everything all right?

As I grew older, I realized I was living in Palestinian culture as an observer and experiencing Israeli culture as an outsider. I had to go through an identity check and started my exploration through my mental wilderness. One of my stations was the Musrara School of Photography, where I lived invisibly among Israelis for three years. My invisibility put me into situations where I saw Israelis take off their masks and have conversations they otherwise would only have behind closed doors. When they asked for my name, I said Steve Sabella. That was enough for them to assume I came from somewhere else, anywhere in the world, but definitely not from Jerusalem or Palestine. In their minds, I fit the category of a Jew who came from Italy or France, not their stereotypes of Arabs. Through the years, I would dare people who confronted me with labels to describe what a Palestinian looked like.

After printing sessions in the darkroom, Zvika and I, along with other classmates, would meet for tea or coffee. Once, Zvika laughed as he recalled scaring a Palestinian by pointing a gun at him. On another occasion, Nurit complained all day long about one Israeli student who had identified the Israeli name of a military base to our guest lecturer, a Palestinian photographer. The army base looked over the photographer's village, Al-Issawiya, and he was consoled to discover the real name of the base that had controlled his life for years. Nurit considered this to be classified information that shouldn't have been leaked to the enemy.

Amir was the classmate I interacted with the most during my three years of studying at the Musrara photography school, probably because he reminded me of my brother Fredo, who was living in exile. They had similar faces and mannerisms, and they both taught me martial arts. Amir liked that I compared him with my brother, who "lived in America." We often sat next to each other in class. On the day we took our class trip with Jeremy, Amir and I drove together in his fancy car to the Dead Sea when I spotted a hitchhiker stranded in the middle of nowhere. I asked Amir to stop. But he swiftly reacted,

> No. He's an Arab.

I asked him,

> *How do you know he's an Arab?*

He answered,

> I can smell an Arab from three kilometers away.

Amir's remark shocked me. It penetrated me like the first time I inhaled Francesca's dewberry. Only this time, the smell didn't make me dizzy. It woke me up. What was wrong with my smell? Was I wearing an anti-Arab perfume that made me smell better? Why did I not smell like an Arab? What did an Arab smell like anyway?

13

In her dreams, Francesca saw herself on her wedding day, dressed in white, standing on a high cliff looking over a sea of sunflowers. The light breeze brushing her face whispered: her prince on a black horse was on his way. She nicknamed me Prince. I didn't come to her on a horse. But on a rickety plane, with a ticket bought with borrowed money. I was twenty-two, a student, and broke. We had decided not to plan a classic wedding—there was no time. The task of finding the perfect dress seemed impossible. Francesca's beauty exceeded any hand-tailored dress made in Paris or Milan. Her silk hair and deep blue eyes were embroidered with cosmic threads.

I flew to Switzerland to propose to Francesca, carrying my wedding suit with me. I secretly worked in concert with Doris, one of her best friends, who handled civil marriages at the mayor's office. On that night in 1997, sitting on a bench in Bern, Francesca and I set our wedding date for a month later. When she called to tell her parents the next day, they both felt they were losing their daughter. But we were young, and we fell in love with our story. We fueled our relationship with imagination, which kept it free throughout the years to adjust and adapt to the demands of life, creating a bond based on change.

Francesca fancied traditional wedding rings. I didn't want to replace our ring. But we rushed from store to store in Bern until we bought an identical pair made of shiny gold, cut at the top, and each fitted with a diamond. To me, the diamonds looked fake. I glanced at my ring, but because I loved Francesca, I forged a smile and agreed to wear both on one finger.

We scoured the city hunting for Francesca's wedding dress. At the point of frustration, we spotted a boutique in the Old City, run by a peculiar woman dressed in black, who wore several silver chain necklaces. After a striking chat, she became enamored with our story and asked her assistant to drag an antique chair from the parlor into the large dressing room and bring two glasses of dazzling wine. I sank into it and watched Francesca alter from one look to another until she found the one in the shade of her blue eyes. At the mayor's office, we asked for a ceremony in English, and as I was filling out the documents, the restless secretary wondered,

> Where do you come from?

I replied,

> *I come from Jerusalem.*

Palestine did not exist on the map; it was not formally recognized as a state, and it had no international legal status. Jerusalem was under Israeli Occupation, and I had no choice but to write "Jerusalem, Israel" on my marriage form.

When the secretary spotted it, she quickly remarked,

> Oh. I love Israel. I love the Jews.

She thought I was Jewish.

> *Great. I love the Jews too.*
> *But please don't write that I'm Jewish on the certificate.*

She did not register what I had said and continued,

> I really love the Jews!

I got concerned, and I emphasized,

> *I get you. And I am happy for you. Just please don't write that I'm Jewish because I'm not. Israel won't recognize our marriage paper unless my religion is stated inside. Please write,*

I am Christian.

I worried when the secretary grinned as she said,

I'm gonna give you a super special present for your wedding.

Later, in the presence of Francesca's family and guests, the registrar pronounced us: husband and wife. Then he said in a spirited tone,

My secretary prepared a gift to honor this wedding.

The registrar, God save his soul, took a few steps backward, reached for the tape player resting on the bright windowsill, and pressed play. At full volume, the traditional upbeat Jewish wedding song "Hava Nagila" echoed across the stunned room.

That autumn, Francesca moved to Jerusalem to start a new life. In December, we drove to the beach of Jaffa to celebrate Paul's 20th birthday. We arrived before midnight, drifting along the shore until we were far from the city lights. The night was pitch black, clearing the view to the stars. In the far distance, the old mount of Jaffa resembled fire embers. At midnight we popped open a bottle of champagne and made a toast. We took off our shoes and stepped into the sea, which felt unusually warm. We waded further out till the water reached above our knees. Out of nowhere, a strong wave engulfed and separated the three of us. Not knowing how to swim at sea, I panicked. Francesca reached for my hand as we dragged ourselves to shore. My rings disappeared. When I felt Francesca's tears, she sank into my wet arms. After catching our breaths, Paul and I went back into the sea, desperate to find them. Paul waded deeper while I searched in the shallow waters watching Francesca pace back and forth by the shore. I kept urging Paul not to give up.

I found one!

Paul yelled and rushed over to us, and there it was again—Francesca's ring—the one we found at the jewelry store in Jerusalem. Over the years, the ring and I became inseparable.

Only a few months earlier, I had almost drowned in the same spot. I was with Paul and Issam, a friend of ours from Jerusalem's Old City. It was midday, scorching hot, and the beach was empty except for the lifeguard sitting in his booth. We made the mistake of going straight into the sea after having a heavy lunch under the boiling sun. When Paul alerted the lifeguard that I was drowning, he yelled in Hebrew over the loudspeaker,

Atem. Sham. Ma koreh?
You. There. What's going on?

Was he expecting an answer from a drowning man? Waves kept pulling me away from the shore as I fought my way desperately against them. Issam rushed to the rescue, but the waves intensified, and he couldn't reach me. Instead, he started kicking me towards shallow waters. But another wave dragged me downward. Near surrender, weightless, with silence in my ears, I saw my life flash before my eyes. Francesca and the ring were the last images that passed before me when a wave forced me up. I flailed my arms at the lifeguard. This time, he shouted in the loudspeaker,

ARAVIM TETZ'UH MISHAM!
ARABS GET OUT OF THERE!

My toes found the sandy seafloor for a precious moment, and I pushed myself up to scream in Hebrew,

HATZILUH! HELP! HELP!

At last, I saw the lifeguard jump into his motorboat to save me.

It is astonishing how people in Israel and Palestine contemplate on life and death and how they mediate between both. Palestinians quickly become aware that Jewish Israeli lives matter more than theirs, compelling many Palestinians to learn to survive on their own terms.

In 1991, the First Gulf War in Iraq stormed from the desert to the Mediterranean Sea, hitting Tel Aviv. I was sixteen when I took command of the house to protect it from chemical weapons. I took no risks. Paranoia guided me in my quest to protect the family. We were not going to die from sarin or mustard: two lethal gases I didn't learn about from Robert Wise, but from the Israeli army.

That year, both Jews and Arabs thought they were going to die from chemical weapons. The Israeli media bombarded us for the entire year with reports about secret weapons of mass destruction in the hands of Saddam Hussein. It aired incessant campaigns on what should be done in case of an attack. This continued in early morning school drills that began with students practicing putting on their gas masks, which we were obligated to bring with us every day. At home, I took on the responsibility of retrieving gas mask kits for the entire family. The Israeli army had a limited supply, so everyone had to queue for hours with no guarantee of getting any. On local school playgrounds, Israeli soldiers lined up people in rows to measure their heads. I handed the soldier ten ID cards and gave an explanation for the absence of my family members. He asked me to guess their head sizes by pointing to all kinds of heads around me. I carried home ten boxes, and since my brothers, Tony and Fredo, were studying abroad, we had two spares. Each box also contained the dreaded yellow and red antidote injections. Both were to be thrust in the body with fist force in case of exposure to certain gases, one into the heart and the other into the thigh. People found it hard to remember which needle was for which gas. Injecting the wrong needle into the wrong organ would be fatal. The thought of this horrified everyone to the extent that when the first sirens rang out in Jerusalem, there were many reported cases of people panicking and mistakenly injecting themselves. Some grimly joked about imminent death,

> What's the point in knowing which injection is for what?
> If Saddam gases us, we will die anyway.

They built all new flats in Israel with an additional airtight, fortified room, like a bunker, to protect against chemical gases and rockets. Army experts warned that the safest rooms would be the highest, since chemical gases settled on the ground. People living in older, unequipped houses like us had to make tough decisions. We were mainly afraid of the rockets, so we instinctively sought shelter underground. Now they were telling us to find safety in the sky. Everyone was confused, but most people chose an upper-level room. Our room had an uninterrupted view towards the Mount of Olives, from which one could follow the flight path of the missiles coming from the east. I alerted my parents,

> *Israel distributed masks to all the Jews here and to Palestinians living under Occupation in Jerusalem. But they didn't give masks to Palestinians in the West Bank or Gaza. A chemical attack by an Arab army would be the perfect way to get rid of all those Palestinians. What if I am right?*

Even though the Israeli government was responsible for the lives of Palestinians, they would not be held morally accountable for their deaths because the rockets would have been launched by Arabs. This was before the signing of the 1993 Oslo I Accord, which gave Palestinians limited autonomy, relieving Israel of many duties regarding the protection of all Palestinians under Occupation when faced with a national threat.

During the war, we locked ourselves into the two rooms upstairs, cooped up like chickens in a factory farm. Eight people and two dogs lived on top of each other for at least three weeks. This proximity offered us a sense of solace, but it also generated tension. We had insomnia from the snoring at night and fought over which channels to watch on TV, even though we only had three back then. This was the last year my family was physically close.

The army distributed a list of food to stock up on. To avoid death by contamination, they advised us to buy canned goods only. Like maniacs, people began buying all the cans they could find. The shelves in my neighborhood stores were quickly cleared out, and people even snatched up the cans with years of dust on them. I bought food that I had never heard of. I made a buffer zone in our upstairs bunker to mark my territory. Every time I found a new can, I made my wall higher and higher until it hit the ceiling. I collected them as if they were stamps, looking for all the imported meatloaf I could find. I turned into an obsessed can collector, living among paranoid Palestinians and Israelis.

To prevent gas from entering the two rooms, I applied plasticine to all the stone cracks outside and inside the house. I also bought rolls of transparent plastic wrap and permanently covered the front windows and all the doors. I left one door open, though, which I would seal from inside by rolling down the plastic wrap I had attached above the door's frame. People rushed to buy all the plastic wrap and scotch-tape they could locate. Prices soared. Street vendors at Damascus Gate gave the tape a nickname, still in use today, *Tape Saddam*. People asked each other,

How many rolls of Tape Saddam you managed to find?

The answer was usually none, one, or at most two. The rolls became the most sought-after commodity in the city, commanding up to twenty dollars apiece, as Israelis and Palestinians consumed kilometers of them, long enough to reach Iraq and ask Saddam if he really did intend to gas us.

On January 17, 1991, day one of the war, the streets of Jerusalem were silent like a desert on a cold night. We were all confined, restricted to the upper rooms, anxiously waiting, but nothing happened, and no rockets were fired towards Israel. The next morning, there was a sigh of relief across my neighborhood. One neighbor arrogantly claimed,

> I told you.
> It's all a joke.
> The war is fake, a game.

At three a.m. on the second night of the war, I heard a beeping coming from my mother's radio, which she kept on at low volume. I was lying on my mattress at my mother's feet.

> *Ma, wake up!*
> *Did you hear the beep?*
> *Is this the war alarm?*

My mother jumped, startled, stared at me, and turned on the TV. News reports confirmed that Israel was under attack by missiles containing gas. She shouted,

> Everyone.
> Get up!

Suddenly, sirens screamed out everywhere, breaking the eerie stillness of that doomed night. The sound everyone dreaded became a reality. The End. Rockets were fired from Iraq, exploding in Tel Aviv, shivering windows in Jerusalem. I had to collect my thoughts to remember the sequence of tasks. I dashed down the steps, jumping the last ten to quickly grab the two dogs on the other terrace. There, I spotted my next-door neighbor in a total panic, pouring liters of liquid chlorine onto her floor because it was rumored it absorbed mustard gas. After locking the dogs in their shelter, I hurried back up, almost falling down the stairs. Alarmed, I covered the door with plastic sheets and also found myself pouring chlorine on the outside floor.

> *Come on. Wear your masks!*

Everyone was struggling. Paul panicked the most,

> Goddamn it! Mine isn't working. I tested it yesterday. Quick. Give me Tony's or Fredo's.

My father wrestled in trying to wear his mask and threw it saying,

> Leave me. I want to die alone!

Confused whether he was serious about our imminent deaths or whether he thought the whole ordeal was a bluff, I begged him to wear the fucking mask. I didn't want to see him suffocate,

> *Yaba, mishaan Allah. Ilbiss-ha!*
> *Father, for the love of God. Put it on!*

The sirens screamed incessantly, echoing through the darkness of the night, gripping us in fear; we were facing our last seconds of life. But after a few days, Palestinians and Israelis climbed out onto their rooftops, not to watch shooting stars, but rockets on their route to Tel Aviv. During the five or six weeks that followed, nobody took the threat seriously any longer. Saddam fired forty-two missiles at Israel, and none of them carried any gas. We all woke up from the excessive paranoia that had been injected into us by Israeli politicians. We had been poisoned, not by Saddam's chemical weapons, but by the human gas locked for weeks into our crowded, airtight rooms—a splendid exercise to prepare for the next war. And if nothing else, I treated the dogs with canned meatloaf for six months.

Still, a decade later, during the Second Gulf War, dark memories came flooding back of the paranoia, the horror, and the end of days. Both body and mind remembered and relived the trauma. But this time, I could distinguish between the psychological war and the real war in Iraq. The apocalyptic scenes on television conflicted disconcertingly with an American pilot's raving descriptions of how he lit up Baghdad's night sky like fireworks. Was that something to be proud of? I remember the UN Security Council sessions. High ranking military officials, dressed in uniform, pointed to fuzzy satellite images, claiming that intelligence sources had confirmed the presence of weapons of mass destruction in Iraq. Colin Powell, the US secretary of state, whom I nicknamed back then "Colon Power," justified the war based on images. Many trusted these images, took them at face value, and barely questioned their authenticity. But then, during the sessions, Dominique de Villepin, France's minister of foreign affairs, confronted Colon Power, arguing, reasonably, that the search for weapons should first start on the ground. Ultimately, though, the Iraqis had no choice and paid the price for images and the realities they created.

In 1992, during the end of both the First Gulf War and the First Intifada, I was close to graduating from high school. I never fell for fighting, but sometimes we become hostage to the moment and are confronted as if without a choice. Four guys at my school, who dressed in a uniform of black and white, bullied everyone. They abused their role as political activists in the First Intifada to enforce their own school rules. They were power drunk. During one lunch break, I was queuing at the school shop when one of them came up and pushed me sideways. The break was only twenty minutes long, and everyone was in a frenzy to grab anything to eat. I gently said to him not to cut in front of me. He turned to look straight at me, pressed his hands on my shoulders, pushed down hard, and then left me in suspense as he skipped out to fetch his three friends over to teach me a lesson. The four showed up swiftly, walking like guards, surrounding me, as if in a Roman arena fight. To them, I was spaghetti-sized. I knew I had to hit the strongest one first—the one who had just bullied me. I punched him right in the face with all my power, knocking him backward—flat on the floor. He was later taken to the emergency room because of non-stop bleeding. His nose had been broken in half. I hit the second cocky guy in his stomach with my elbow, bending him like a banana, kicked the third one in the center of his balls, freezing him like a Roman statue, and the fourth never knew what struck him. They were all flat on the floor, groaning, defeated within seconds. Not any one of them touched me. Escorted to Frère Rafael, the school director, the first thing he did was check my hand, stare at my fist, holding it as if it was a boxing match victory,

Show me the hand that hit them!

He suspended me for two days to calm their family clans down, but when I returned, my entire class applauded me. I had earned everyone's respect—even the respect of the four.

By the time I completed high school, I had thought little about my future since we had all been preoccupied with living through the troubled period. I felt lost, couldn't see any direction. I spent many evenings at the video arcade, turning into an expert at a shooting game. I was one of the few players who could beat it, attracting kids who watched me fight the final stages. The remarkable thing at this Israeli-run arcade, located around the corner from Ben Yehuda Street, was not the many games it had to offer, but the huge man who managed it. He looked like the Incredible Hulk. His arm was the size of my waist. If any Israeli boy bullied other Palestinians or me because we didn't speak Hebrew, or if they figured out we were Arabs, he would jump to our rescue. He was so big, able to lift older boys, hanging them up in the air, their legs dangling far from the ground. Scared, the boys would run away, cursing in Hebrew. It took me a while to discover that this man, Anwar, was also a Palestinian from Jerusalem. Years later, he was picked as a bodyguard for strong-man Jibril Rajoub, the head of the Preventive Security Force in the West Bank set up by Yasser Arafat. I spotted him one late evening in front of a restaurant in Jericho, carrying a gun with unusually long straps. He opened the door of a black car as Rajoub was stepping in and then speeding away into the darkness. A few years later, my Hulk was shot in the legs at close range, disabling him for a long period.

I couldn't wait to turn eighteen to check out the bars on Jaffa Street. Life on the Palestinian side was still recovering from the Intifada. I didn't speak Hebrew back then and only spoke with Israelis in English. Few Palestinians born in Jerusalem spoke Hebrew, even though it was taught in Israeli-run public schools for Arabs. Collège des Frères, the private school I attended, did not include Hebrew in their curriculum.

To get into the clubs or bars in Jerusalem or Tel Aviv, Arabs had to play the game. Some faked an American English accent by speaking with twisted lips. But those who spoke French, especially the Palestinians who studied at the French school in Jerusalem, were the best game players. French was like their native tongue. I remember one guy who pretended to be an American with the fifty words he had picked up. I spoke to him in Arabic one Saturday night, but he kept replying in English, uttering words I didn't understand. Apparently, he was from New York. A "French" Palestinian we knew, who did not speak English, entered the conversation. The American and the French avoided speaking to each other in Arabic. The language they shared sounded Scottish and could only be understood after a joint and two or three whiskies. The system we grew up in forced us to feel ashamed when we spoke Arabic in Israeli areas, requiring us to whisper. Many times, Israelis tried to pass laws to drop Arabic as an official language even though over six million Palestinians live under Israeli rule. And in 2018, only Hebrew became the official language of Israel.

Zion Square had many clubs and bars, and some Palestinians faked international driver's licenses or university ID cards to convince bouncers they came from abroad. They corrected the bouncers when they suspected them,

Hey man. Wassup.
What're ya talkin' about?

I'm from the US of A!

Zion Square was filled with tourists, Israelis, and soldiers in uniform whose job was to spot Arabs and register their IDs. Many Palestinian guys dressed like Israelis, wearing tight white T-shirts, tucked into jeans to avoid being stopped and humiliated. Saleem wore blue contact lenses that looked scary and didn't match his dark complexion. Yasin was a phenomenon. His Hebrew was perfect, and he could clear a club's dance floor with his Michael Jackson moves. He even styled his hair like him. Wassim drove the flashiest convertible Golf in town, a hit among young Israelis. He optimized its engines with dual exhausts that roared like a lion in front of clubs and bars. He always got in swiftly. Fady grew his hair long and wore an eye-catching Hai necklace, a potent Jewish symbol that literally means "Alive." He justified it by saying,

I also want to live.

Jeffrey flattened his hair by dipping his comb in a gummy gel, which he carried in his jacket. His hair was incredibly stiff—not even puffed by the wind. It defied nature, remaining intact, whereas my hair after a stormy night would look like that of a biblical whore. Jeffrey's Palestinian identity dissolved when he was among Israelis, that he had no issue wearing a Star of David necklace. This sign alone ensured that no Israeli Jew would doubt his identity. Jeffrey also suffered from a speech impediment that affected his pronunciation of the letter "R," a peculiar blessing that granted him a perfect Hebrew accent—he didn't need to rehearse by gargling water. He panicked when Paul and I surprised him one day at Pizza Hut, where he worked in an Israeli mall. We sat at a table, waiting to say hi, waving. He deliberately ignored us. After ten minutes or so, he approached the table when no one was looking and urged us not to speak Arabic at all. We all played the game because we knew that if Israelis found out we were Arabs, they wouldn't leave us alone. Nobody liked Arabs. We lived with self-hatred, triggered by a system that degraded Arabs and rated them inferior. But we wanted to break free from these constraints in Israeli clubs, or at least pretend to. Only a few Palestinians got past the Israeli bouncers without a problem. I got into Arizona and The Underground clubs a few times. When denied entry, my mood slumped for days, avoiding going there at all. But it repeatedly happened when I hung out with tourists I met in the Old City who wanted to dance. The bouncers would let them in and then point at me,

Ata.
Ata lo nichnas.
You.
You're not getting in.

In 1993, my brothers Peter and Paul and I opened our own club, the Sabella Underground, so we wouldn't have to bother getting into the clubs on Jaffa Street. We rented a former barn in Bethlehem, shaped like a maze. Our friends who wore the Hais, the Stars of David, and the clip-on earrings, picked up brooms and spent an entire week sweeping out animal feces. We poured tons of bleach into the holes of the barn's unplastered walls to extract the funky stink that had seeped into the cracks. The effervescence and fumes choked us, and we joked about getting cancer. This would have been the right moment for us to wear the gas masks. A friend gave us his refrigerator, which we filled to the top with beer. We dimmed the atmosphere and hung strobe lights behind the music station. Above the middle of the dance floor, a disco ball reflected rotating stars. For our grand night, we invited a long list of friends. Entering was free. And although we had bouncers, their job was not to select people but to protect the door in case we were raided by independent Palestinian factions dominant during those years. These groups had gained their strength during the First Intifada, which had ended a year earlier. Palestinians were ruled by opposing factions that ordered society and often set up their own laws in the absence of law. Parties, or any kind of fun, were seen as a distraction from the national struggle for independence. Until 1993, Israel had ruled the West Bank under military administrative law with a disregard for social order, so the factions sprang up to enforce the local civil rule. Only when Arafat landed in Gaza and the West Bank, he managed to unite all these factions under his control and channel their power into organized civil and military forces to maintain order. This included the "Jeep People," as most of us referred to them, the self-organized authority of the streets in the West Bank.

For the Sabella Underground opening night, my special guest was Grace, a Palestinian girl from Bethlehem. Grace was the sister of my best friend, Sami. It's because of her I like freckles. When she smiled, the freckles lit up like stars. Grace was delicate, like a spring leaf. She was my first love. We could have been happy together, but William, a jealous guy, made it his objective to break us up. William called the shots for Grace and Sami, making it impossible for me to see her. The few times we could speak in private were through secret phone calls or at random parties.

But Grace defied William, fought with her brother, and came to my party. The DJ played Grace's favorite song, Please Forgive Me, and set off the smoke machine as I pulled her chest to mine—she did not resist. Her hands stroked my hair, and then she wrapped her arms around my neck. The distance between my body and Grace dissolved. This was the first time I had been that close to a girl. When I heard her breathe into my ear, I wanted to tell her I loved her. But I couldn't. I had never told anyone I love you and didn't know how to say it. The song finished. Grace and I looked into each other's eyes and squeezed hands. Please Forgive Me was the last song played in The Sabella Underground—ever. One of the bouncers rushed in to alert us that two jeeps filled with armed men were at the door. They ended the party and warned us not to open its doors again. It was all over. The only thing that remained was the lingering odor of manure.

William had tipped off his buddies, the Jeep People. Later, he threatened to kill me if I stepped foot in Nativity Square to see Grace during the celebrations on Christmas Eve. I couldn't tolerate being threatened, not because I was afraid to die, but because someone denied me access to a public square in my own country. That night, enraged, and despite the risk, I drove to Bethlehem in defiance. William spotted me, called over the armed Jeep People, and accused me of being a traitor publically, urging them to deal with me. Luckily, they quickly realized they were being called upon over a love affair, letting me go. On the crowded square, I found Grace to give her a photograph of a rose on piano keys. It must have been the kitschiest image I had ever made. We spoke on the phone a day later, and then we broke it off. My last words to her before she went silent,

I love you.

On many occasions, Palestinians settled personal conflicts by accusing one another of collaborating with Israeli intelligence. Some lost their lives for the wrong cause. And mine could have been lost over a tragic love story. It became clear to me that dating a Palestinian girl would be next to impossible. We lived on the same land, yet I found it very hard to relate to Palestinian social constructions limiting relationships and forbidding intimacy between couples before the marriage.

Like many of my friends, I was not interested in Israeli girls, knowing Zionist ideologies prohibited Jewish women from even attempting to speak to Palestinians. Today, Israeli anti-assimilation groups, like *Lehava*, oppose marriages between Jews and Arabs, going as far as beating Arabs and burning down institutions that promote Jewish-Arab cohabitation. As a result, some Palestinian men pursued relationships with women from abroad who often hung out in the Old City and Zion Square.

Zion Square was also where I met Juda, an Arab Orthodox Jew whose family had originally immigrated from Morocco. He played a *darbuka* drum in front of a crowd on weekends. His fingers were hard like stone, a sign that he played daily. Impressed with his drumming style, I carried my *darbuka* to the square one weekend and sat down next to him. We drummed in harmony as if we knew each other. The audience grew, and Juda's earnings doubled that night. He asked me to play with him again, offering to split the pot. After a few performances, we joked about creating a duo named "Elvis & Chocolate," based on our two obsessions at the time. Juda knew I was Palestinian, or an Arab as most Israelis referred to Palestinians. Arab-Jews, like all Jews who came from elsewhere, made Judaism the first reference to their nationality. Many Israelis perceived themselves as Jewish first. Israelis second. Religion defines their national identity. Immigrants from Morocco labeled themselves in this order: Jewish, Israeli, Moroccan. But they were never Arabs. One night, Israeli soldiers stopped our show, pulled me from my chair in front of the crowd, and took me with them. I looked to Juda, but Juda looked away. The soldiers dragged me to an empty street corner and threatened to beat me if they ever saw me step foot on Jaffa Street again. One of them, with his fist pushing on my face, said,

> You dirty Arab!

I was furious. How can a soldier deny me the right to live freely in my own city? Of course, I rambled my way to Jaffa Street again, but this time, I happened to be with a girl whom I had just met, Francesca. When we reached Zion Square, where the soldiers were usually stationed, they saw me and rushed over. Again, they forced me into the same dark corner across from The Underground. Francesca got worried and followed us from a distance. The soldiers were getting amped up,

> We told you never to come here again.
> Now you're going to get it!

I knew the soldiers were serious, but I was serious too. In defiant Hebrew, I said,

> If you beat me, I'll report you.
> What are your names?

They laughed. Francesca had witnessed soldiers harassing Palestinians before for no reason. She shouted from a distance that she had already called the police. The soldiers backed down, cursed at us, and threatened to get me the next time.

I learned Hebrew at the age of eighteen. I liked the resemblance between Arabic and Hebrew, both having Aramaic roots. It seemed natural to speak the other language of my city, but mostly because I chose to study photography at the Bezalel Academy of Art and Design in Jerusalem. I enrolled in an Israeli ulpan, an institution that taught Hebrew to new Jewish immigrants. Palestinians enrolled too because the teaching methods proved useful. When I registered for the course a week late, I had difficulty catching up. After two or three weeks, I knocked on the director's door and asked Ruti to temporarily suspend my enrollment. After she agreed, at home, I nailed the entire study book in two weeks, seizing the opportunity to catch up with the rest of the class. I also bought a newspaper published in easy Hebrew for new Jewish immigrants. As I read it from front to back, I circled every word I didn't know and looked it up in an electronic dictionary my father had bought for me. I told myself if I managed to understand every word in the newspaper, my job was done. After four weeks of studying day and night, I returned to the ulpan to continue my beginner's course. I knocked on Ruti's door again,

Shalom Ruti. Zocheret oti?
Hello Ruti. Remember me?
I would like to continue the course, please.

Ruti asked me to close the door and sit down, and we spoke in Hebrew for several minutes, jumping from one topic to another. Impressed by my progress, she wondered,

Why do you need to study here?

To double-check, Ruti asked me to read a passage and write a few sentences. Afterward, she took out a certificate and a pen and noted that my Hebrew was equal to a student who had finished class Hey, the second-highest level, which usually takes a year and a half to complete.

I did apply to Bezalel and took the entrance exam, and got an interview. But they did not select me. The photography school in Musrara was my second choice. In time, I picked up an Israeli accent that allowed me to mingle among Israelis with ease. I liked speaking Hebrew. It came out naturally, almost like my mother tongue. While I was a student, I worked as a waiter at an Israeli café. I had a job interview at Café Rimon, and Ronen, the owner, liked me straight away. My recent marriage to Francesca intrigued him. He was also in a relationship with a European woman and wondered if it would work out. My opinion mattered to him, and we regularly sat down talking about life. Café Rimon was popular, with a large outdoor seating area just off Ben Yehuda Street and Zion Square. On a busy Saturday night, I saw my brother Paul and his friend Mahdi rushing towards the café. Paul looked tense, and I asked him what the matter was. While Paul and Mahdi had been sitting on a bench in Zion Square, an Israeli settler wearing a kippah harassed them, demanding they clear the whole bench for him. Paul was fuming, but to avoid an unnecessary fight, he told the settler in English,

> I can give you my seat if it's necessary.
> All you have to do is ask politely.

The settler yelled for his friends, one of whom was an off-duty Israeli soldier. A fight was about to erupt. Paul and Mahdi were worried, but Mahdi came from a fearless Jerusalem family. He called his brother Ehab, who happened to be only minutes away. In those few minutes, the settler gathered a crowd and approached

Café Rimon, looking for Paul and Mahdi. As they began to surround us, Ehab and his friends burst through the crowd. Ehab shouted to his brother,

> TELL ME WHICH ONE OF THOSE THUGS WANTS TO BEAT YOU?

Mahdi pointed,

> THAT ONE!

BAM! Ehab hit the Israeli guy with the *kippah* in the face with everything he had, knocking him flat on the floor. A fistfight broke out, triggering a bigger fight, forcing diners from all the restaurants on the square to flee. All of a sudden, the off-duty soldier kneeled down, took his gun out, and pointed at Ehab. Out of nowhere, a chair from Café Rimon knocked him out. People swung chairs, were blocking and ducking, throwing plates at each other. Some chairs were found later a block away. Paul, Mahdi, and Ehab and his friends escaped, and I got stuck inside Café Rimon with the rest of the waiters and some guests. Aggressive Israelis kept banging on the door, shouting "Death to Arabs"—an expression I grew up with, still used without repercussions to this day. They demanded that Ronen hand over the Arabs he employed. Ronen refused to open the doors until the police came and dispersed everyone. An hour later, Paul called and asked me to pick him up from where he was hiding, a few streets away. In the car, Paul got a phone call from another friend who asked for a ride home after finishing work at a hotel near Zion Square. He had no idea what had just happened, and against my better judgment, I returned to the square to pick him up. He sat in the front seat, whereas Paul hid in the back. At the traffic light, I saw an Israeli guy check my car from all sides, and when he spotted someone lying on the back seat, he shouted,

MATZATI OTAM!
I FOUND THEM!

Fists and legs raged on the car, smashing all the windows. We were sandwiched between two vehicles. I slammed on the horn with both hands, but the traffic light was red, and the drivers in the front or back didn't move. A girl on the street banged on the window of the first car and yelled,

> Zuz! Zuz mepo!
> Move! Move away!

The driver caved in, but a second too late. They dragged Paul's friend from the seat out of the car's front window. He was in their hands, and when I looked back, he was already under their feet.

These incidents happen regularly in Israel. When I visited in 2012, fifteen years after the fight at Café Rimon, another attack occurred, with very similar details. Sergeant First Class Shmuel Shenhav defined the attack as a lynching and was quoted in Haaretz, Israel's oldest daily newspaper, as saying,

> The victim lost his consciousness and was thought to be dead until a Magen David Adom crew arrived and resuscitated him. He was anesthetized and on a respirator in the hospital for days. This was an extremely severe crime. Only a miracle saved him from death.

The teenage suspect involved in the attack said,

> For all I care, let him die. He's an Arab. He cursed my mother.

> He can die.

The same suspect was quoted in The Jerusalem Post as saying,

> So I caught him and beat him. I hit him and I hope he gets it again. I hope he dies. You can't go by Damascus Gate without getting stabbed. So why do they come here? I beat him and I'd beat him again.

The Haaretz journalist reported,

> A police representative told the Magistrate's Court that hundreds of people watched the event without helping the victims. . . . The suspect's brother, who was also present at the scene, said outside the court that it was the four Arab youths who had provoked passersby and "made passes at Jewish girls".
>
> He added:
>
> "Why should an Arab make passes at my sister? They shouldn't be here, it's our area. For what other reason would they come here if not to make passes at Jewish girls?"

In the 1990s, we played the game of not speaking Arabic because we knew the price we would have to pay. When I visited Jerusalem in 2010, I went back to the square to check out the nightlife. I waited in line to get into the Irish Pub behind a bunch of young people. When I finally got to the door, the bouncer said,

> Ata lo nichnas.

You're not getting in.

I got in his face and said in Hebrew,

Is it because I'm an Arab?

With a smug laugh, he said,

I thought you were underage. But now that I know you are an Arab, you are definitely not getting in.

On a visit in 2014, Jakub, a friend, warned me not to go to Zion Square because of an Israeli gang that hunted Arabs each night. But I wanted to take that risk anyway. So he insisted that we only speak Hebrew when going through the Jewish crowds. But I didn't care. In the twenty years since that Saturday night at Café Rimon, Ehab had been shot dead by the police, but the arcade around the corner from Ben Yehuda Street was still there, and the identity games were most likely still being played. Observing the crowds, I could hardly spot any Palestinian. Either they had learned their lesson not to step foot in Zion Square, or they had managed to look and speak like Israelis, becoming invisible.

12

On the morning of Francesca's first birthday in Jerusalem, I snuck out of the house, while she was still sleeping, after leaving some words I had drawn on the mirror with her lipstick:

Café Hillel - 11 am

At our night and day café in Jerusalem, my plan was to disappear from the table. When I found the moment, the waitress delivered a clue to Francesca on a piece of paper,

Remember the snow words and the sticks?

I followed Francesca while she received clues on the way from people I involved in advance. The aim was to pass through Independence Park to find the last clue to get to the last spot. A station of three payphones standing side by side. I had asked all her friends and family from Jerusalem and abroad to call these public numbers starting at two p.m. sharp. They received a tight schedule so that each could speak with Francesca for five minutes. She made it on time, and the first payphone rang. Francesca figured out the call was for her. It was Lisa, her best friend. After five minutes, the second phone rang. Francesca picked up the receiver while still speaking on the first phone. It was her mother. Then the third phone rang. Every time she hung up, one phone rang again, and more voices traveled down the lines. For the next two hours, I stood there like a guard at a scene, explaining and directing the anxious people around to look for other phones.

For Francesca's twenty-seventh birthday, I planned the day with Lisa to start at noon, at Café Hillel. I had flown her in for the occasion and arranged with the owner to employ Lisa for fifteen minutes. What better gift than have Francesca spend her birthday with her best friend, whom she would spot working at her daily café. I vanished for the rest of the afternoon and joined them later at the Mount of Temptation in Jericho.

When she turned thirty, I focused on the number. Francesca woke up in the morning to a tug on her arm pulled by a thirty-meter long thread tied around her wrist. She followed the thread from the second floor on the upper terrace, down the stairs, around the lemon tree, to the cave room on the ground floor. On the other end was a black box I had made for her, brightened by thirty silver stars. She opened it, and inside were thirty letters. Each of her friends sent her thirty words. Looking for light, she went back upstairs and sat on the windowsill with her knees pulled to her chest. On the stone, she read them, one by one. When I heard a tear drop on one of the letters, I waited to give her the next gift,

> How to Be Thirty

We cuddled, and once she cheered up,

> *We're going out!*

In the car, I gave her the keys and reset the odometer,

> *You're going to drive thirty kilometers from here to the Dead Sea. See it as the journey of your entire life, year by year, station by station. When the meter hits thirty kilometers sharp, you stop the car. There, no matter where we are, we will sit down and have breakfast.*

I hid a tablecloth and a bottle of Prosecco. I was curious about her journey into the unknown. I brought a Polaroid to record the various stations. Just before ignition, Francesca said,

> Year zero.
> I was born.

At kilometer fifteen, she recalled,

> My fifteenth birthday was so boring that I said to myself, I have to find an escape. This was when I decided to leave home.

At kilometer twenty-three, Francesca glanced at me,

> This is the year I met you.

We stopped the car in the middle of nowhere. The road to the sea was empty. She got out, and as she reached the middle of the highway, she stopped. I shot a Polaroid. When the image appeared, it showed Francesca standing where the white line dividing the street ends. Her shadow intersected with the line. It looked like Francesca was at a crossroads, and when we drove away, she reflected on this coincidence.

> Kilometer twenty-five.
> The year we got married!

Francesca stopped the car again. We got out, and I snapped another Polaroid. In this image, Francesca stood still, her arms behind her back, with a thin shadow next to her, surrounded by the desert. It looked as if she was dissolving into her shadow. On our way to Jericho's main intersection, the odometer turned thirty. She stopped. We were stunned to find a picnic table right there in front of us. And next to it was a wall, with a mural of camels, one after the other. I set down the tablecloth and opened the prosecco. This is what I remember, but images have a memory of their own. When Francesca showed me the Polaroid years later, there was no trace of the prosecco on the table. But we did see two bottles of iced tea.

After breakfast in the desert, we drove up to Jerusalem. On the empty road, Francesca received a phone call from her friend Beatrice in Switzerland. She told her to go to a bookstore in the city center to discover the time for her next surprise. In the bookstore, Francesca had to look for a specific book. She didn't see me as I watched her leaf through books, one after the other. I worried she would not find it. But, she found the one. She held the book in her hands and jumped straight to page thirty. At first glance, she didn't find the clue. But then she discovered it after counting thirty words from the top left where it was written,

. . . at one p.m. . . .

Francesca arrived at the next station to just receive a text message,

Look up!

I had asked Shlomy, a friend, to lower a basket from his flat on the fifth floor to the sidewalk. When it reached Francesca, she pulled it towards her to find thirty roses, thirty chocolates, and an invitation to go upstairs. I hadn't planned for this invitation, but Shlomy, leaning out the window, insisted that we come up for a surprise. He had baked her a cake.

I took Francesca to play the lottery with thirty numbers. Of course, we never won. At night, our closest friends came for a party in the Old City, lit with thirty candles I had placed around the arches. When the evening ended, or had just started, Francesca received half an hour massage, promising her a gift. She was shocked when she got the book,

What to Expect When You're Expecting

She flipped to page thirty to find a message,

I know this may surprise you. Maybe one day, we will create life. I can hardly imagine anything more beautiful than our baby.

As she read those words, I captured the moment with my last Polaroid.

A couple of years after we got married, Francesca and I were called to model as bride and groom in Tel Aviv for a fancy limousine service. Francesca would have a magical chance to dress in white as she had always dreamed, a misfortune I always felt guilty for. But on the day of the shoot, she was in Switzerland visiting family. Instead, I was destined to see in white a new Israeli Jewish immigrant from Russia.

On the morning of my wedding day, I slept in. I had nothing to worry about. The producers handled all preparations and arrangements. A car picked me up from Lions Gate and drove me to Tel Aviv. They took me to a boutique where the tailer laid out three suits on the counter: white, blue, and gray. I chose black. Then, I was taken to a hairdresser who turned my hair from Elvis Presley into James Dean. I asked for a bit more gel. When I was almost done, I looked through the glass door and saw a black limousine arrive. The first thing I noticed was my bride's high heels as she stepped out of the limousine, dressed in white. For a moment, I imagined our night together. Picking up the hem of her dress, she entered the salon, and we shalomed each other. She came over to the chair where I was sitting, threw me a smile, sat down next to me, and introduced herself.

As the video shoot started, Israelis on the streets kept congratulating us,

Mazal tov!

The importance of the arabic language.

I replied back with a grin, immersed in the scene,

Todah. Todah rabah.
Thanks. Thank you very much.

En route to the hill of Jaffa, towards the sea-view, the limousine broke down at a busy intersection. The driver panicked when the engine couldn't start. He then looked at the aggravated producer and me to quickly push the car. Embarrassed, I buttoned my jacket, asked my bride how my hair looked, put my sunglasses on, and snuck out. Onlookers nearby offered their help, feeling sorry for me, as I pushed my own wedding car. I kept my head down, and when the engine started, I hurried back inside the limousine.

On the hilltop in Jaffa, I took my bride's hand to step into a garden with a sea view. We wandered around as the sun was setting and the clouds looked lit from behind, a scene out of this world, the moment to be with Francesca. As I felt this, the producer looked at me,

Kiss her on the lips!

As her lips touched mine, three guys from Bab Huta, my neighborhood in the Old City, who knew Francesca, appeared out of nowhere, interrupted the scene, and asked me in loud Arabic,

Walak Steve. Shou saar? Itjawwazet Israeleeyyehhh?
Steve. What happened? You are marrying an Israeli?

Later, to escape judgment day in Bab Huta, I had to explain to them that I had no secret Jewish or rich life in Tel Aviv.

After the clouds dispersed, the producer had planned to end the wedding shoot in a real Jewish wedding that was happening on that day. As we stepped out of the elevator, he rushed us into the festive banquet hall, which had real guests lined up to clap and cheer for us while playing a wedding song. And before I knew it, I was pushed onto the packed dance floor. This time, I found myself not only listening to a Jewish wedding song but also dancing to one.

When Francesca returned from Switzerland, we searched for a jewelry store to buy new wedding rings, especially because I had lost mine in the sea. The new ones were white gold, engraved with an olive tree branch, a tree close to our heart. But these rings disappeared in the blink of an eye. One day, I called a technician to fix the heating in my studio. The ring Francesca found me, the one found in the sea, and the one with the white gold were the only things on my studio table in direct sight. I left the studio to grab him a drink from the counter. But how often do we fail to trust our intuition? When I returned, only the wedding ring was gone. I didn't accuse him because I had a one percent doubt that I might have been wrong. I let go. Soon afterward, Francesca lost her wedding ring while sitting in Independence Park after putting it right next to her. It was gone. We both came to the awareness that our real wedding rings were always shining on our fingers.

During these years, I met two people I developed a powerful bond with, poet Najwan Darwish and artist Kamal Boullata. I met Najwan during the opening night of *End of Days*. I searched for dark spaces to install light boxes suspended in the air at varying heights. The Cave Art Gallery in Bethlehem was unreal. Its darkness, and how its void was lit from the light boxes, drew explorers to wander in my imagination and theirs. It was there where I encountered Najwan, and in the cave, we delved into images of art and life.

Najwan is like the foreign man in a photograph, without a past. He conceals his address—only a few friends know where he really lives, and it's not on earth. Up to this day, I don't even know when his birthday is, but we are about the same age. For many, his gender is unclear, as his name is often mistaken for a woman's. It took me a long while to dissociate it from the feminine ring it seems to bear. Najwan is nocturnal, awake every night. If I ever saw him in the morning, that would be a sign that something extraordinary had happened, like a star falling out of the sky. He travels at night, always shaved, perfumed, wearing cologne, exuding elegance. He reads a lot and retains a lot. His mind is encyclopedic, divided into categories, yet his poems are beyond all categorization. He is intelligent enough to know when to challenge his thoughts and wise enough to know when it is time for new thoughts. Najwan is,

A lawyer by the book.
A poet by the word.
A thinker by the letter.

It took an immense effort to satisfy his intellect, and I embraced the challenge. He awoke my thoughts. We became like cellmates in prison built in the center of Jerusalem, surrounded by a centuries-old stone wall, and later fortified by an eight-meter-high concrete Separation Wall. We lived in Jerusalem in exile. And when we thought we broke out, we found ourselves lost in deeper exile. Najwan found his way out through words, but I decided to plunge beyond my realities to find mine.

Najwan knew that my life in Jerusalem had an expiration date. On September 4th, 2007, I boarded a plane and made my exit from Jerusalem. I grabbed several newspapers to mark the events coinciding with the departure. As the plane ascended into the unknown, I browsed through their pages. A headline written by Najwan set in boldface jumped out at me,

He wrote that the moment I stepped foot out of Jerusalem, the price would be an exile, with no return. His words broke me, melted the drops of frost on the plane's window next to me. But I defied this truth. I vowed to return to Jerusalem the following year. I wanted Jerusalem to be the eternal capital of my imagination. Jerusalem, a star in my mind. On the plane, I lost my ground to find myself, castaway at sea. My communication with Najwan continued, and he often came to the rescue via a Skype line. Some calls lasted for hours into the darkness of the night. Our collision, and its impact, resulted in a bond—hard to break, challenging to change, and solid enough to endure the shocks of life.

Najwan often claimed that his insomnia was a biological disorder, but I have a different theory. It's nearly impossible to maintain sanity living in Jerusalem, a place that drives everyone to the edge. To avoid falling off, he worked at night, when no one else did. He made his moves when only a few cars lined the dark streets. Most of them were driven by lovers or by those tired of their daily struggles, impatiently searching for home.

Francesca and I had been among those drivers. The longer we drove, the more we found ourselves lost in our own city. We couldn't keep up with the unnatural speed of change as Israeli settlements spread throughout it. We had to stop and ask for directions. I would ask in Arabic or Hebrew,

'Afwan.
Slicha.
Excuse me.

Fein ana?
Eyfo ani?
Where am I?

I lost my way in the Old City more than once. I perceived it as a maze, with dead ends and locked gates. I tried to find my way home but always took turns that led me away from it. When I asked for directions, the people directly inquired,

> Minain inta?
> Meh eyfo ata?
> Where do you come from?

I answered as the locals would,

> *Ana ibn il-balad.*
> *Ani yalid ha eir ha'atika.*
> *I am a son of the Old City.*

I was not as wise as Najwan, who realized when it was time to let go. It took me a lot of effort to construct a new reality, a new home, a new Jerusalem. But one day, a man showed me a different path—difficult, long, but well worth embarking upon. I met Kamal during an interview by the jury of an art competition in Palestine. The title of the work I worked on was *Identity.* When the jury asked about the story behind my images, I said,

> *This is the way I see Jerusalem.*

Kamal provoked me,

> You speak of Jerusalem constantly, but I do not see it anywhere in your work. Where is it?

Agitated, I replied,

> *Do I need to photograph Jerusalem to see it?*

Do I really need to depict the Dome of the Rock or the city gates? Jerusalem is just a perception.

He liked my answer and congratulated me. I won Kamal in that art competition, and it felt like the first prize.

In interviews, I was often asked,

Which artists inspire you?

For many years, I answered: Kamal Boullata. He radiates light, although some people perceive his brightness as a threat. I see it instead as an invitation. The sparkle between us flared not only up when I saw his magnificent artist book *Twelve Lanterns for Granada*. Rather, Kamal moves me with his words. They rang in my ears for years, and with each echo, they struck new meaning within me. His words interrogated me—pushed me to my limits. He compared me to hermits, who move to the desert to live in seclusion and even gave me the book, *The Wisdom of the Desert,* which he signed,

To Steve—Journey to the Unknown.

When I met Kamal, he knew my story without me telling him. I lived in mental exile in Jerusalem. Kamal lived in real exile, and it pained him to see me suffer, living in our city of birth, a city to which he was denied The Right of Return. We became friends in exile.

One spring, Francesca and I visited Kamal and his life partner Lily at their home in the south of France. Driving on the winding roads of Menton, I sighed as I told Francesca how upset I was for them, living there, far from major cities in a dull town, alone. We drove uphill, looking out for their waving hands.

We entered their house and found ourselves in a living room. It looked down-to-earth, a retreat in a hermitage, for introspection and revelation. When they opened the windows to bring in more light, an endless sea mirrored a crystal blue sky. Kamal's home rested at the center of the mountain, looking over almost every other house. It took me straight back to the view of our rooftop in the Old City. For Kamal, maybe the view of the sea looked like that of Haifa. The trees were like those in Palestine, resilient. The air was like how it was once in Jaffa, infused with orange peels. And the houses, one behind another, were built with golden stones, recalling those in Jerusalem. Kamal was not in exile. He had found a home—a space—that enabled him to live in all of Palestine with its borders set to reach infinity. I felt sorry for myself. His words echoed in my ears again. Kamal had invited me to embark on the rewarding path into the unknown. I was there. But I still hadn't found a way out. I was living in a permanent state of exile, while Kamal had found a way to live free, on top of the world.

As we descended from the balcony towards the seashore of Côte d'Azur, Kamal pointed to delusory house windows that overlooked the sea. He explained how Italians had mastered this painting technique to give the illusion that some houses had more windows than they really did. Kamal painted windows in my mind overlooking free lands. It was up to me to figure out how and when to open my windows of exile to see a real path towards liberation. But first, I had to deal with the earthquake that had shaken and split open the ground under my feet in Jerusalem. Kamal kept pulling me out of the cracks. When I got stuck again, I found myself dialing his number. His words were always to the core, just like the words of Mother Veronica.

Mother Veronica was my refuge when I was a child, and I often ran to her when I sought retreat. She often read me stories from the Bible, from Russian and Greek theologies, highlighting the moral of the story. I learned a lot from her about the philosophy of faith.

When I was seventeen, I struggled to study for my high school final exams living in the Old City house. I was suffocating there during the first Intifada. I wished to isolate myself and focus. Then I remembered that the seminary at St. Anne's Church, located four rooftops from our home, reserved a few rooms for visiting scholars. One day, I approached a priest with whom I was friends and asked if the church would make an exception. He said,

No. It's impossible.

But I believed in exceptions. After I spoke with Mother Veronica, she inquired, and against all odds, the convent agreed to provide me with a room for several weeks. Many trees surrounded my hermitage, and during the harsh winter of 1992, the trees danced in strong winds, creating free concerts late into the nights. When the morning light appeared, the winds settled down, and only the whispers of the leaves remained, calming my wicked thoughts. And if the leaves didn't, I would ask for the iron key to climb up to the bell tower.

Mother Veronica painted Christian icons, a tradition she had learned from Russian monks. As a child, I asked her to teach me about this process. I remember her saying,

Lesson one: We do not paint icons. We write them.

When I asked her about the colors, she explained how the powders were extracted from earth and stone. I was intrigued, considering how the minerals crystallized over thousands of years and then transformed into visual stories that carried a lot of essence. The minerals came from earth to become painted light. With her thin brush, she refined shadows and brightened auras. She showed me how to prepare the icon's wood surface from scratch. After the pinewood was cut and smoothed, I filled the visible cracks, coating the surface with a white plaster primer called *lifkas* in Russian. *Lifkas* is set from carefully measured ingredients. After adding several thin layers, I smoothed them down with fine sandpaper until the surface was flat and even. To inspect, I lifted the panel to eye level. Veronica explained that the *lifkas* was the icon's foundation of which without, any icon would later crack. While listening to recorded prayers from Russia, she withdrew from her surroundings. Her attention to the tiniest details would bring the icon to life.

Veronica's bond with icons is unshakable, and this is the connection I developed with Michael—my very best friend in Jerusalem. Like a rare mineral, he pulled me back to earth when I got lost in the sky.

Of all the people I have known, I find writing about Michael the most difficult. He was tailored intricately into my life while I lived in Jerusalem. The threads of our friendship were spun in every color imaginable and flexible enough to withstand any changes. He was the only person with whom I shared all the details of my life. We met at school when I was twelve. He was a bit younger than me, had blonde hair and freckles, wore striped shirts, open sandals with socks, carrying a brown leather bag. He is one hundred percent German by birth but has never lived in Germany. He was born in Amman, Jordan, and grew up first in Istanbul and then in Jerusalem. Nobody questioned his Palestinian "origin". Later, after becoming close friends, when we would walk the streets of the Old City together, people often greeted him in Arabic and asked,

> Minain sahbak?
> Where is your friend from?

Either Michael had decoded Palestinian culture, or he simply learned to adjust or assimilate himself into it. He adapts quickly to different environments and speaks many languages, a true cosmopolitan. His mother is a prominent academic on Islamic culture and the Holy Qur'an and was a cultural diplomat in the Arab world for many years. But, like me, Michael was baptized Greek Orthodox, something rare for a German. So I called him *Michos*.

The two of us frequently played chess at his house. Once, during an extended power outage, Michos grabbed an antique lantern from a shelf and lit it. In the dim light, he showed me his cherished, five-hundred-year-old Qur'an. The light and shadows flickered on its handwritten pages. Captivated, we later shot a double exposure of the open Qur'an merging with the glowing lantern. This time, the double exposure was not a mistake. We turned the image into a poster and printed thousands. We dreamt that this unique visual would cross borders and even become profitable. We held regular meetings at Abu Shanab hangout, along with my brother Peter who I had involved as a business partner, to plan international marketing and strategize about how we would manage the influx of orders later.

The dream died when the first gift shop owner we approached at Damascus Gate—the main entrance to the Old City where locals and tourists flock—spotted a word scratched out in one of the holy verses. Promoting a Qur'an with a mistake in its scripture was a sin and could have led to a great deal of controversy. We dropped the initiative and subsequently stored thousands of posters. Strangely, not long afterward, Michos's house was robbed, and the Qur'an and the lantern disappeared.

A couple of years later, we came up with a better idea. I photographed the Dome of the Rock, the Wailing Wall, and the Church of the Holy Sepulchre, Jerusalem's most recognizable landmarks and the holiest of sites representing Islam, Judaism, and Christianity, respectively. We designed a poster where we arranged the iconic images one on top of the other and titled it,

It was a catastrophic failure. These religions couldn't even be united on paper, not next to each other, or on top of one another. Most of the shop owners we approached told us that combining the three religions in one space would never sell, and many questioned which religion should be on top, or in the center. After Michos mailed ten or fifteen to his mother as a gift, I stored over ten thousand. Like our first project, the Jerusalem poster didn't cross borders as we had imagined—its circulation hardly passed our doorsteps. We concluded to leave religion alone, and every now and then, we learned to laugh when the topic was brought up.

A few years later, Michos went abroad to study. When he didn't hear for weeks from his brother, Ismael, he asked a friend to check on him. For several days, the friend knocked at the door with no answer. Michos asked his friend to break in to find Ismael hanging from the chandelier in the living room. His decaying body had been left to rot for weeks.

Here and there, I felt Michos was also lost within himself, but that was not the image he conveyed to others. Perhaps, that's why we stayed friends for so long in the course of life—so I could watch over him. Or maybe, it was the other way around, and he was watching over me.

Kamal and Michos first met in Jerusalem. In 2003, Kamal worked on a research venture requiring photographs of historic Christian icons stored in sealed archives of monasteries or displayed on church altars in Palestine. When he hired me to photograph the works, I asked Michos for assistance. It took no time for them to sit down together in the Old City and catch up, like native Jerusalemites.

Before I left Jerusalem in 2007, I collected twenty stones from land threatened by political annexation for one of my art expeditions. These stones had existed in the same location for thousands of years and were witness to rapid changes on the ground. I revealed images of what they might have seen onto their surfaces, capturing the unnatural erasure of Jerusalem's identity in recent history. I realized that people, and not stones, give a place its character and identity. An instant connection happened when Kamal met Najwan and when Najwan met Michos. The three became the pillars of my life in Jerusalem. As for Francesca, she was the foundation, strong, yet delicate, invisible like the *lifkas*. But her aura always shines like an icon.

11

One summer day, I received a message wishing me,

A fragrant morning
like the smell of homeland soil
after a long rain

I have never had a homeland or known the smell of rain on its soil, but I found a home with Francesca that no land has given me. Just a few weeks earlier, while Francesca was in Switzerland, I painted the walls of the courtyard orange to blend with the green leaves of the vine tree. I also painted the pots we hung everywhere dark green and added many new ones on the stairs to the courtyards. There were so many plants you could almost get lost between them. When she returned, she felt as if she entered the countryside of Tuscany with an outdoor bathtub under the lemon tree. We let ourselves go, smoked and drank, and when it got dark, the scattered candles exposed a forest of shadows.

On one of these nights, she handed me a letter stamped from France from a girl named Claire. Claire was a promise from the past. I knew what it was about and hesitated to open it, saying that I was going to break my promise.

Francesca looked confused. I told her my story. When I was eighteen, on my first drumming tour in Europe, jumping from one city to the other to feel the rhythm of the world, I found myself on the train to Montpellier to visit friends from France I had met in Jerusalem. They invited me to a summer camp. On the bus, I saw Anne Gaëlle, and we hooked up in a flash. During the camp, Claire, who was fourteen back then, spent a lot of time with us, and me, talking about life. By the end of the summer camp, her soul got entangled in mine. And mine in hers. On our last day, we embraced each other in front of the waiting bus, knowing that it was our last time. But her timeless tears directed me to say,

I promise that when you turn eighteen, I'll fly to Paris and find you at the train station. I'll be dressed in black. And you'll be dressed in red."

Claire turned eighteen. The words she wrote carried four years of anticipation. They were floating in space, drawn, from the heart. I passed the letter to Francesca feeling tense and disappointed. After she saw its beauty, she said that such beauty calls upon a response. But I let it be.

Six years later, Claire found me again. She sent an email written in French, with words that lingered in my soul. It arrived when Francesca had just given birth to Cécile. I took a deep breath and picked up the phone. Claire was on the other end. I started with an apology, for breaking my promise, for not meeting at a train station. I told her about Francesca being the one, but she still enticed me to live in the moment and meet her in Paris. When I said that I really couldn't, she revealed that her wedding was in four weeks.

I called Michos straight away to help me understand where I was. Maybe Claire was looking to see if she had not missed out on our promise. We speculated that perhaps she wanted to see if there would be a flare between us. Despite the temptation and the mystery of Claire, I remained with Francesca and Cécile and didn't fly to Paris.

The weeks passed, and I received another letter from Claire. Inside, I found a photograph, ripped in half, with her husband cut out, showing her dressed in red on her wedding day.

Four years passed after this misfortune, fourteen years after our promise for me to contact Claire to see if she was in Paris. She instantly replied. Perhaps we were both looking for closure. Or not. Claire was an artist, a painter of the soul. Our meeting point was in front of the Grand Palais. We spoke about the past while looking at many works of art. Then we roamed the streets of Paris, crossed several bridges, and sat on a bench to rest. Only then did she reveal why she agreed to see me. She had received my email on the same day she signed the divorce papers from her husband. This gave us something to ponder on as we watched the sun set in Paris.

I was late for my train. At the Gare du Nord station, on the second platform, looking over rows of trains, the moment had come for Claire and me to depart. I took her hands just as she leaned forward to give me a fleeting kiss on the lips. Then she left. I watched her disappear down the escalator—she never looked back.

We stayed in touch via email but have not seen each other since. When I lived in London and she was there, I was in Dubai, and when I traveled to Paris again, she had moved to Beijing. From there she wrote me,

> It would make a nice drawing on a map: our dance around the world. Materialized by a red line for my moves, a black line for yours . . .

Living in parallel realities, our lines have still not crossed, neither in the sky, nor on the ground, or anywhere in between.

My reality was held hostage in Jerusalem under Israeli Occupation. I defied it whenever possible. I grew up in the rough neighborhood of Bab Huta, but I disliked its name that rang in the ear as if telling someone to avoid you. It easily gave away where I came from on my identity card, which in some situations could threaten my life in case Israelis were hunting Arabs. Having it neutral was also perfect to cross Israeli checkpoints, which I wanted to pass without let or hindrance. In those years, a court ruling also ordered the Ministry of Interior to replace the race category with stars. For years, I had been passing my neighborhood street sign written in Arabic, English, and Hebrew. Apparently, Arabic and English didn't suffice—I had to learn Hebrew to know where I came from. And when I did, I read the sign, and it didn't say "Bab Huta Street" in Hebrew, but instead, "Antonia Street." I rushed to the Israeli Ministry of Interior and filled a form to get a new identity card. At the counter, the clerk declined my request, got upset, and said with a raised voice,

> Adoni annie lo yechola. Ata hai beoto beit.
> Sir, I can't. You are still living in the same house.

I challenged her, certain that the neighborhood was listed in the ministry files in two different names. And since Hebrew was the recognized language of the state, I insisted she speak with the director. When she went up to check that this change was not breaking any laws, she came down the steps bothered. On the spot, my identity card looked like this:

Name:	Steve
Family Name:	Sabella
Father's Name:	Emile Antone
Mother's Name:	Espérance
Race:	*****
Address:	Antonia Street .

In 2005, psychological defeat swept over all of Occupied Palestine. Neither the land nor the self was liberated. It was the fifth year of the Second Intifada, and Israel had asserted control of all areas in Palestine. The solution was the Separation Wall, to divide Arab Jerusalem, to snake around every Palestinian town and city, from hill to valley. The hundreds of demeaning checkpoints that appeared everywhere made life very difficult, many times, impossible. During this period, I was working on Kan Yama Kan. Once Upon a Time was a vision to liberate the Palestinian story held hostage in the minds of Palestinians. To free it from the collective narrative, which left little room for any individual thought or any chance to revive a dead dream. Given the intensity of the task, I asked five known artists from Palestine, from five different cities, to join hands with me. I created five wonder boxes made of wood, sarcophagus-like, to deliver and transport the story. I placed in each a photo strip of surreal images I had taken all over historic Palestine, which one could roll by turning a handle on the outside while peeping through a round hole I had cut on the upper surface of each box. Leaning on the box to look inside, a tunnel of light directed people to see another Palestine, resurrected, from one reality to another, but I left part of the image obscure, in essence requiring people to imagine the rest and complete the story. The loop was like a time machine. People queued to view the stories, adults before kids, primarily because each of the painters drew all over the outer surfaces of each box, down to the six legs that carried each, creating a celebration of colors, attracting viewers to delve into a new experience.

That hot summer, Francesca and Cécile flew to Switzerland, and I was going to join them a few days later. I was immersed in unfolding Kan Yama Kan, studying, and wrapping up photography commissions for the United Nations to make it for my booked flight to Switzerland. I couldn't wait to leave. Two days before my flight, I had a work meeting with Sawsan, a poet I didn't know, to find out later that her parents were from Palestine, but she was born and raised in the United States. She had come to Jerusalem to seek collaboration on a cultural project, and having seen my work online, she contacted me. We set the meeting at Aska Dinya restaurant, named after the mythical loquat tree, which translates in Arabic to The Tasty Life or The Most Beautiful Universe. Aska Dinya was built on the remains of a garden, where only the loquat tree was kept, now standing inside. I arrived early and sat under its leaves. Given the heat, I asked for a freezing beer and waited for her, keeping my eye on the door. The moment Sawsan entered, her eyes twinkled in mine. For the first time since being with Francesca, almost ten years after being together, I felt shaken. This was the trial I feared the most. I called Michos to rush to Aska Dinya right away and keep an eye on me.

When he walked in, he sensed our electricity from the door. Sawsan and I were having a blast and couldn't keep our voices down. We never even talked about art. We were in it, and our vibrations were about to cause an earthquake, and there was nowhere to hide. From nowhere, Sawsan asked me,

Is it safe in Gaza?

I answered,

If there is a place where I feel safe in Palestine, it's in Gaza.

I wondered how to tell Sawsan I was married, and when I found the chance, I did. The smile on her face melted away. But we picked up our spirits again, and our vibe continued until Aska Dinya shut its doors. We were aware of our last date. As we stood under the tree, I made no promise for the future this time. I let her go, and we departed with a bitter aftertaste.

The next day I woke up beaten, heavy, not wanting to make it to burning Gaza in the early morning. I was on duty with Zoi Constantine, a friend of mine in her mid-twenties. She was newly hired as the Focus magazine editor to work on a special edition for the next UN issue: *Focus on Gaza*. The situation had drastically deteriorated, falling to a new low every day. After a long ride to the hotel at the seashore, I strolled to the sea to find an escape from my feelings for Sawsan. As I battled myself, massive waves relentlessly struck me.

In the middle of the day, we interviewed Mohammed Dahlan, the powerful security chief of Gaza. Dahlan had many enemies. His political posturing, his work with Israel and the US on security, and mostly his aim to succeed Yasser Arafat, put many on alert, thinking twice before they targeted him. The photo session and the interview took place in his office, on the third or fourth floor of a heavily guarded building. The elevator didn't work, so we had to walk up to be met by armed men sitting around on every floor. Diana Buttu, the legal and communications adviser to Arafat's successor, Mahmoud Abbas, was already sitting in Dahlan's office to greet us. When Dahlan came in, he sat us down on the couches facing his desk. I sat to his left, a good place to capture him gesturing in profile. I made a few shots and then placed my camera on the table. After a few minutes, I picked it up again and took a few more shots. Dahlan looked irritated the second time. And when I did my third shoot, he turned his head to Diana, not knowing I understood Arabic, to tell her he didn't like being photographed and asked her to tell me to stop. Not in the mood, wanting to hang myself anyway, I surrendered and put my gear down.

Later on in the afternoon, Zoi and I met with artists who were to be featured in the magazine to highlight their hardships. After taking a few photographs of the group, I apologized and excused myself, saying that I didn't feel well and sought seclusion in my room. While gazing at the sea from my window, I dialed Gina's number, a close friend of mine and Francesca,

Gina. I can't breathe. Where are you?

She took me to the UN private club, the only place in Gaza that served alcohol to foreigners only. We sat at the bar, ordering whiskey, one after another. I vented to her about Sawsan, and she listened. I expected her to be on Francesca's side, as she usually was, but her response surprised me,

You didn't act on it. You are only human. These things happen. The question is what you do about them.

And the thought of what to do about it kept me awake another whole night. In the morning, I felt even more depressed, and on top of it all, a double hangover. The hours of the day passed slowly. I had no desire to work and even fought with Zoi. All I could think about was Sawsan and how to tell Francesca the next day in Switzerland, not knowing where to start.

Before noon we had an interview with Dr. Eyad Sarraj, a known psychiatrist. I wondered about the coincidence. While Zoi was interviewing Dr. Sarraj, I made a few shots, and then laid back on the chair for patients, drained by my thoughts. Seeing me wasted, Dr. Sarraj even said that I could close my eyes. But I kept staring at the spinning ceiling fan, feeling my eyes getting heavier and heavier when I heard the doctor say,

A third of Palestinians in Gaza are within the normal range.
A third show severe symptoms of depression.
And a third is a lost cause, beyond treatment.

Then Zoi, a bit alarmed, inquired,

How do you recognize those beyond treatment?

Dr. Sarraj continued,

There are several indications, and they have to do with how one relates to reality. When I hear people speak as follows, I get worried,

"We are shit."
"We deserve what is happening to us."

"The Jews are better than us."

"We have nothing to lose."

I closed my eyes again, sinking deep into my own shit. In between worlds, I felt my phone vibrate, bringing me back to no reality. The UN office in Jerusalem was calling to inform us of a sudden change of plans, and they could only reach my phone. We had to cut our meeting with Dr. Sarraj short and drive back to Jerusalem right away. Zoi and I were ready to go. We had already put our bags in the jeep's trunk that morning since we were supposed to leave in the evening to make it for my morning flight. But first, we stopped to pick up two colleagues staying at separate hotels traveling with us to Jerusalem. Given the urgency, I called them to meet us in front of the hotel. When we arrived at the first hotel, we waited for a few minutes. When she finally came out, I looked at my watch. 1:20 pm. I was sitting in the front seat and noticed that my bulky camera bag was occupying the backseat. I jumped out and fetched my bag to make room for her when out of nowhere, masked men with guns surrounded me. They cocked their guns, pointed them, repeatedly shouting in Arabic,

DITCH THE BAG AND GET IN THE CAR!!

The car they were pointing to with their guns was, to my shock, in front of our jeep, as if they were already stationed waiting for us. In that second, the awkward photography session with Dahlan struck me. I didn't want to let go of my camera and ditch it on the street. Not this time. With them still shouting at me, I fired back in Arabic to at least safeguard the bag in the car. But I didn't feel they understood one word of what I was saying. They were maybe five. To shut me up, they got louder, and when I saw them coming closer to me, I ditched the fucking bag. They grabbed my arms and pushed me into a small car, sandwiched between two men with their guns pointed at my head. The one in the front was wearing a Palestinian police uniform. The car sped away, and in the first few seconds, I thought of Nabil Razouq, a friend of mine from the Old City who had been kidnapped in Iraq the year before and held captive for seventeen days, with a threat to behead him when they found a card in Hebrew letters in his wallet, a sign they caught an Israeli spy. He had traveled to Iraq to work for a US firm, forgetting to take out his membership card for an Israeli supermarket.

As the car raced down the street, I saw the second colleague we were supposed to pick up waiting in front of the hotel. He looked stunned at how fast the car was driving, but he didn't see me. Inside the car, the kidnapper in the police uniform turned around and spoke to me in broken English. I replied back in perfect Arabic. I didn't say I come from Jerusalem, as I normally would. Instead I stressed,

> *I AM Palestinian.*

He replied in Arabic, startled,

> You speak good Arabic for a foreigner.

I interrupted,

> *NO. I AM PALESTINIAN.*
> *If you don't believe me, look at the Al-Ayyam newspaper from a few days ago as it says, "Palestinian artist Steve Sabella unveils Kan Yama Kan."*

Not convinced, he asked for my ID and phone straight away. Just as I handed them over, his eyes caught sight of my ring, triggering him to also say,

> The ring too!

I was sure that the last thing a kidnapper wanted to hear was a ring and a love story, so all I said,

> *Please take care of this ring.*
> *It's very special to me.*

He snatched it from my hand, looked closely, and then he started checking my identity card. The text was in Hebrew, as is the case for every Palestinian living in Jerusalem. He struggled to read the names loud but still managed:

> Steefe—not Arab.
> Sabeela—not Arab.
> Amil—not Arab.
> Esss-pee-rance—I've never heard this name before.
> You are not Arab!

I had to clarify,

> *These names are very common in Christian Palestinian families from Jerusalem.*

The car driver got impatient as he, too, wanted to know the identity of the person they just abducted. He interrupted, asking to check my address whether I am Arab. Or not. I interjected,

> *WAIT. WAIT.*
> *I DON'T LIVE ON ANTONIA STREET.*
> *I AM FROM BAB HUTA!!*

I said Bab Huta with a strong B and a felt double T. Now, for sure, I felt I had a problem. Not knowing where I was being taken or why, and aware there was no escape, after a few minutes, I asked the kidnappers next to me if they could lower their guns. But they didn't respond. Hearing me, the kidnapper in the front seat wearing the police uniform turned around and instructed them to do so. On the route to the unknown, the kidnappers were nervous, sweaty, kept turning their heads to the back to see if anyone was following us. At one junction, when the car slowed down, I spotted the UN jeep fast behind us. For a second, I was relieved that someone was following the car to see where they were taking me. But then, I caught sight of Zoi, in panic, crying in the back seat, with a man right next to her. And the kidnapper who was driving the jeep was swerving it like a maniac in euphoria. Disturbed, I turned to the kidnapper in the police uniform and asked him from all my heart,

> *I am aware I have been kidnapped. And I'm going nowhere. Look how nervous the girl is. Can she just sit next to me?*

My words reached him. He took his phone out and called the maniac driver to tell him,

> When I stop the car, you bring the girl to me.

Soon afterward, both cars swerved and stopped. Zoi's abductors jumped out of the jeep with their guns pointed in the air, dragged her over, and pushed her in next to me, between the two who were holding the guns on my head. She was shaking. I took her hand, held it tight, assuring her not to worry,

> *I spoke with them. Everything will be okay. Trust me.*

The UN jeep driven by the maniac rolled its wheels away. Zoi caught a breath or two and felt better. While going through a refugee camp, the car got stuck in the sand. The driver pounded the gas pedal again and again, and the more gas he gave, the deeper the car sank. In stress, he asked the three kidnappers to push the car. They got out, but they told Zoi and me to stay inside. The driver, sweat dripping down his face, kept pressing the gas, now burying all four wheels. Because of the weight, he turned to us, and in frustration, said,

Get out of the car!

We stood by a wall, watching them struggle under the burning sun. I don't know why, but I felt compelled to help. I moved away from the wall and found myself pushing my kidnapper's car with them. My quick action didn't give them the chance to say no, quickly accepting that the faster we unstuck ourselves, the safer it was for everyone. When the wheels got freed, they rushed us back into the car and raced away.

On the road, I drew a map in my mind to trace the path we had driven. It was already several kilometers. I recognized some streets as we were there earlier on that day. I kept my eyes open for any signs, specifically street names. Francesca knew how claustrophobic I was, but I was doing well, aware of my surrounding.

In another moment of panic, the nervous driver leaned closer to his right mirror to warn,

I saw the Jeep of Death.
They spotted us.
Get ready to shoot!

Dahlan was in command of these jeeps, which were part of the Palestinian National Security Forces. As the driver slowed down to blend in with other cars, the kidnappers cocked their guns. I squeezed Zoi's hand, and I looked back to see if the Jeep of Death was behind us, and seeing it take a turn to the left, caused a moment of relief. After what felt like a long drive, the car stopped in front of a house in a remote area, where armed men were waiting for us. They opened our car door and grabbed Zoi and me, pulling us straight to the house, down the steps, to a dark cellar room where we remained for a short while. Stepping inside was like entering a furnace. Gaza was boiling hot that day, and this room had no windows. They sat us on the floor, close to each other, with our backs to the wall keeping the door open, bringing in some light. Zoi and I could barely breathe. I was in that state before, finding myself joking to Zoi,

If we're going to die, it will probably be from this heat.

Zoi found my joke out of place and asked me to be quiet so that we didn't attract the attention of the people guarding the place all over. After a short while, the maniac driver, with a gun strapped to his shoulder, came in to greet us, his own way. He said a few things to me, but it was hard to put them together. Zoe and I still did not know why they kidnapped us.Then he took out a grenade from his jacket, spoke while playing with it, to see him extend his arm down to my face where I was sitting, telling me to hold it. I wondered why it didn't already explode from the heat in the room, asking him,

Is it secure or not, and what to do with it?

He said,

Just hold it. Check it.
It's made in Gaza.

I took it in my hand as he wanted, looked at its army green color,

It looks well made.

He kept it in my hand as he stepped in and out of the room, talking to armed people guarding. I couldn't help but whisper to Zoi,

> *This is the first grenade I have ever held, and it had to be made in Gaza? Why not Germany?*

Somehow the irony made Zoi smile, even though everything around us was serious. The maniac then came back, grabbed it from my hand, and to scare me, he fiddled with its safety lock, and then left. From where we sat, I could see the kidnapper in the police uniform in a narrow corridor, speaking on the phone. I overheard him say he had kidnapped an Australian and an Israeli. I raised both hands to correct him from where I was,

> *Falastini, Falastini!*
> *Palestinian, Palestinian!*

Knowing the fate of abducted Israelis during the Second Intifada, I had to react. But he didn't respond and made another call, stating in a strong voice,

> We demand the release of Jihad Abed immediately.
> Or we are going to execute them in three hours.

I didn't know what to tell Zoi, but just as she asked me to translate, they moved us to another room, a much cooler one. I saw two kidnappers lounging on a mat under a ceiling fan with their guns lying on the floor beside them. The Oprah Winfrey Show was playing on TV. They turned it off, picked up their weapons, and left, replaced by others. We were seated in the corner, and this room had a door open to a garden with trees. It looked like a farmer's house. Not long after, a young barefoot boy entered the room carrying a black plastic bag.

He came straight to us, and the bag was full of ice cream. It seems this was his task. We were happy to pick up one each, just like every kidnapper around us.

As I was staring at the fan's spinning blades hanging from the ceiling, the maniac driver showed up again, still in his euphoria. He came in with a butcher's knife to tell me in Arabic that he would cut Zoi's head if the demands were not met in three hours. It was hard to know if he was serious or not. For a moment, I imagined the next Focus on Gaza issue printed with a tribute in our memory, with both of us pictured on its cover. When Zoi asked me what the knife was for, I translated,

He's ranting, asking if he should kill a chicken for our dinner.

He continued lecturing us about life and politics while gesturing with a rifle held in his other hand, almost hitting the ceiling fan. We would have been sprayed with bullets, triggering me to say,

Watch it! The fan is up there.

He didn't care. He finished his rant, rested the gun on his shoulder, and strolled out of the room again. When I found a chance, I asked the kidnapper in the police uniform, the one who agreed to bring Zoi to sit next to me, why we were being kidnapped. He opened up about the corrupt and brutal Palestinian Authority in Gaza and how he was convinced that Dahlan was behind the kidnapping of Jihad Abed, his uncle. In response, the family vowed to abduct foreigners to use them as a ransom to negotiate the uncle's release, who was a high-ranking security officer, a rival to Dahlan apparently. I thought it was in Zoi's and my best interest not to mention our meeting with Dahlan the day before. I asked him why he said over the phone that I was an Israeli, explaining that Palestinians living in Occupied Jerusalem are forced to carry Israeli identity cards.

He told me how a crowd had grouped in front of his uncle's house, cheering for my death, because he spread the news he caught an Israeli. This led to a clash with shots exchanged between the one hundred and fifty armed members of his family and the Dahlan forces in the Palestinian Authority. But then his shoulders slumped, and in a voice filled with self-pity, he said,

> We are shit.
> We deserve everything that's happening to us.
> The Jews are better than us.

I thought of Dr. Sarraj—the kidnappers had nothing to lose, just like I felt about the maniac driver, alarming me that anything could go wrong at any moment. I asked him for his name, and he said it was Firas. To win his heart, I told Firas I was married, had a child, and about to take my flight to Switzerland in a few hours. I hardly stopped talking—this is my thing, not knowing when to shut up. I was curious about how the kidnapping was planned. Firas explained how they had targeted a black man in the morning, assuming he was a foreigner. When they reported they had abducted a black man, they were told to ditch him and look for a white foreigner. He narrated how they drove for several hours, nervously scouting the empty Friday streets until they spotted me. He said that my long hair, sunglasses, and red shirt made them speculate I was spot on an Italian.

Firas and I were connecting, making it easy to ask him to reach out for my photography jacket to give him my business card. I pointed out the link to my art website, suggesting he look at Kan Yama Kan and the Palestinian story. I spoke about my experience of the Occupation, understanding where his anger and frustration were coming from. I couldn't blame the kidnappers for their circumstances–they had also been held hostage, bruised by a long history that failed to grant them real freedom or any felt justice.

Firas confessed he was actually an on-duty policeman with the Palestinian Authority, which explained his uniform and why he kept lying about his whereabouts to the police commander over his walkie-talkie. He warned me that if the police stormed in, he might have to threaten my life with a knife, but he wouldn't kill me. I told Zoi not to panic if we ended up in such a situation as she was now part of the play. After thinking about it, I realized a better scenario to save all of our lives was if Firas pretended instead that he had just arrived on the scene. We bounced around possible scenarios to pass the time. Almost two hours went by, and I kept joking with Zoi, who chuckled here and there.

The young boy with the bare feet came in again, now carrying a tray with cups of tea on it. As I took my first sip, the maniac driver was in the room, turned to me and asked,

How do you know it's not poisoned?

I answered,

I have no choice but to trust you.
And I love tea.

I didn't die. We kept chatting with Firas until the maniac entered the room again and shouted that they had made a deal. Everyone was now on the move. Zoi and I were put back in the car, and as they started driving, they handed our IDs and phones back to us. After around twenty minutes, we stopped on one side of a major roundabout. A line of police cars and many Jeeps of Death had positioned themselves on the opposite side. Firas pointed his gun at Zoi and me, as he told me he would, and said,

GO NOW!

We got out of the car to walk to the other side, caught between guns, those of the kidnappers, and those of the police. A policeman across the roundabout held a car door open for us. He signaled for us to walk towards him. When we finally made it, I let Zoi get in first. As I was climbing in after her, I heard Firas shout,

> STEEEEFE—CATCH!

I looked back and saw my ring flying through the air. It landed straight in my hand. I put it on my finger right away, feeling the presence of Francesca. I got in; the policeman followed and shut the door. He identified himself in English as the police chief of the northern section of the Gaza Strip. I thanked him in Arabic for arranging our release. In response, he asked,

> Btihki 'arabi?
> You speak Arabic?

I said,

> *Taba'an. Ana Falastini.*
> *Yes, of course.*
> *I am Palestinian.*

He reacted instantly,

> I swear to God. Had I knew you were Palestinian, I would not have worked for your release.

He informed us that we had to stop at Abed's house, where the negotiations had taken place, and everyone was waiting for us, including our UN colleagues. As we approached, I saw a horde of journalists waiting for our arrival. My smile dropped when I realized I wouldn't be able to hide this story from my mother, who had always warned me not to go to Gaza. As the car doors opened, Zoi and I were pulled into the crowd. Hundreds of flashes separated us. We greeted the Abed family, and then the police chief escorted us back to his car, and we drove straight to the presidential palace.

When we arrived, an officer escorted us inside. Zoi asked to go to the bathroom right away, but he told her to wait until after meeting the president. She argued with him and went anyway. Meanwhile, the police chief escorted me to the presidential lounge. There, I saw Dahlan, and he remembered me. We shook hands, and I said to him in fine Arabic,

> *You didn't really need to kidnap me because you don't like being photographed.*

He laughed, and the ordeal ended with a group photo with Zoi and me sandwiched between Dahlan and the Palestinian president Mahmoud Abbas. Leaving Gaza was a whole other ordeal. Our only way out was in the UN jeep, which the kidnappers had returned to the Palestinian police. Around midnight, at Erez Crossing between the Gaza Strip and Israel, the Israeli army conducted a thorough search of the vehicle in suspicion that someone could have tampered it with by Palestinian factions. After nearly two hours, they had found nothing, and let us go. Back on the road, I checked my voicemail, listening to over seventy messages, ten from Gina and Michos. And, of course, Francesca.

At home, I raced against time to pack and get to Ben Gurion Airport in Tel Aviv. I was drained, three nights now without any sleep, and dreaded the usual three hours of interrogation by Israeli airport security. Even though I had an Israeli ID, to them, I was nothing more than a Palestinian Arab.

Shalom, meh eyfo ata?
Hello, where are you from?

In a Hebrew accent, while gargling the R in Yerushalayim, I had to say,

Ani meh Yerushalayim.
I come from Jerusalem.

She continued,

Where exactly do you come from?

If I answered with "East Jerusalem," it would be assumed I was an Arab, and if I answered with "West Jerusalem," it would be assumed I was Jewish. I replied,

Antonia Street, the Old City.

She checked my passport, but my place of origin was still not clear to her. She asked me for my father's name,

Emile.

Your mother's?
Espérance.

Your grandfather's?
Antone.

What is the origin of the name Sabella?
Sicilian.

Do you celebrate Hanukkah?
Why not.

Do you celebrate Christmas?
Sure.

She was hesitant to ask if I was an Arab. To speed things up, I told her I came from Jerusalem. The Arab one. All I wanted was to board the plane and close my eyes.

What is your occupation?
Artist.
I also work as a photographer for the UN.

I showed her my press card.

Where were you before you arrived at the airport?

I couldn't tell her I had just been kidnapped in Gaza. She would consider it a national security threat and definitely not allow me to board the plane.

In Jerusalem.

And why are you going to Switzerland?

To have a holiday with my wife and daughter.
My wife is Swiss.

Why are you traveling alone?
Why do you work for the UN?
Have you traveled to Gaza with the UN?
Why do you live in Jerusalem?

Why don't you live in Switzerland?
When did your family settle in Jerusalem?
When and where did you meet Francesca?
Why is your name Steve Sabella?

The questions were endless, and the first security guard was replaced by a second, and the second by a third, until the chief of security was called. I kept repeating the same narrative again and again. I had to be consistent and make no mistakes.

Listen to me.
This is my story.
No matter how long you interrogate me, it will not change.
Either you let me go home, or you let me board the flight.
Let's get this over with.

They gave in, allowed me to board after a conspicuous bag check and a full body search, escorted me to the plane like a VIP, and finally left me. I found my seat, sat down, and leaned back to close my red eyes for the first time in three days. But every time I heard the click of a seatbelt, I woke up startled—the clicking sounded like the cocking of the kidnappers' guns.

I opened my restless eyes and spotted a man watching me. He was black, and I imagined for a moment that he was the man the kidnappers had released that morning. When he noticed that I spotted him, he unbuckled his seatbelt, walked straight over, and sat down on the aisle seat next to me. He spread open a newspaper and pointed to a photograph,

Is this you?

It showed a woman and me with guns all around us, and the bold title read, "UN Workers Freed in Gaza." I fell into my seat and said,

Sometimes, the answer is right there in front of you.

When I returned from Switzerland, I went straight to cut my long hair at a salon close to Zion Square. A customer was watching the news while sitting under a hairdryer. She commented, with angry hands, how they ought to hang Yossi Beilin in the city center. Beilin, an Israeli Knesset member, was a radical leftist against the Occupation. I remarked to her in Hebrew,

Lama at omeret et zeh?
Why are you saying this?
What's so bad about a person working for peace?

She was Israeli, a Jewish woman from Jerusalem. We argued back and forth, and then my hairdresser interrupted us to ask me,

Steve. Why do you care?

I said,

You already know I am Palestinian. The Occupation must end.

He looked at me in the mirror and said,

You can't be Palestinian. I don't believe it.
You look like a Jew.
You speak like a Jew.
You dress like a Jew.
Be honest with me, Steve.
You must at least feel like a Jew.

Maybe there is a Jew in me, but just as much as there is a Christian, a Moslem, and a Buddhist. And, Nothing. Two years earlier, Israel went through a wave of Palestinian suicide bombings; some were just hours apart. Because buses were the primary targets, Francesca and I never used public transportation. The explosions became routine. In one incident, an Israeli couple was interviewed because each had survived a suicide bombing attack at opposite ends of the city on the same day. After one big blast, a friend of mine found a dismembered hand in his garden ten days later.

Yet, it was during those hard circumstances that Francesca and I conceived our baby. And it mattered to have Cécile born in Jerusalem, a place whose roots stretched into the distant past when humanity was still at the very dawn of finding words to express itself. When Francesca got pregnant, she wanted to take childbirth classes. Based on a friend's recommendation, we ended up attending a course run by an Israeli midwife. We were the last couple to arrive at the first session. The midwife, Rachel, warmly invited us into her home, where the class was held, touching Francesca's belly and then patting me on the shoulder. We made our way into the living room, and to my surprise, only ultra-Orthodox Jewish couples had signed up. All the men, including me, were dressed in black. The midwife asked us to share where we came from, and when it was my turn, to avoid any confusion, I said,

> *Ani meh Yerushalayim, Falastin.*
> *I come from Jerusalem, Palestine.*

When she smiled, I saw it as a sign she accepted where I came from, especially when she said that her father was from Palestine. Over the weeks, we became friends with Adam and Hadar, a couple from Canada and Holland. When the course was over, they invited us for a Sabbath dinner. We accepted the invitation with pleasure. When we got home that day, I remarked to Francesca how strange it was that I had never been invited to a Sabbath dinner before, given that Judaism has always been part of Jerusalem's identity. But after the creation of Israel, people from different religions locked themselves into their own ghettos. I had lived in Jerusalem for over thirty years and thought of the advantage of getting to know more about the other side.

On Friday night, we joined Adam and Hadar in their home in the orthodox Jewish neighborhood of Har Nof, along with two other couples. Before dinner, Adam picked up a kippah from a set of Jewish hats resting on the bookshelf and passed one to me. I was caught by surprise, but out of respect, I put it on and said,

If you want me to wear it during prayer, it's fine.

His eyebrows scrunched as he began the *netilat yadayim*, the ritual washing of the hands before the Sabbath. I remembered Jeremy and the silence observed by Jews during their rituals, and I didn't open my mouth. After he blessed the food, he came over, sat next to me on the couch, and asked me why I hesitated to wear the *kippah*. I answered,

Because, as you know, I'm not Jewish.

He said,

What do you mean?

I clarified,

I thought you knew where I came from.

He said,

> Hadar and I thought about it. We were one hundred percent sure you were Jewish and that Francesca was a goy.

I assumed I had made it apparent that I was Palestinian in Rachel's class. Apparently, he and Hadar thought I was a Jew with an extra dose of religious ideology, referring to the land of Israel as Palestine, as some traditional Jews do. When we sat down at the Sabbath table, Adam struggled to explain to his bewildered friends where his unexpected guest suddenly came from. The dinner became awkward, served by frozen silence. If someone spoke, the topic remained on the Second Intifada and the Palestinian suicide bombers. I emphasized that I represented my views only that I was not an ambassador of any state. I insisted that the only solution was the end of the Occupation.

After dessert, Francesca and I excused ourselves. At the door, Adam seemed eager to tell me something,

> Steve. I want to tell you something.

With a smirk crawling out of his face, he said,

> My father was a Christian and converted.

I patted him on his shoulder,

> *I knew there was something good about yo*u.

Francesca and I stepped out of their house, and we never saw Adam and Hadar again. Five years later, however, I did hear back from Firas:

عزيزي ستيف

اتمنى ان تكون بأحسن صحة و أفضل حال ,لقد بعثت لك رسالة أؤكد فيها اعجابي الشديد بمعارضك وصورك التي هي غاية في الجمال.

ثم ها أنا أعيد لذاكرتك حادثة الاختطاف المؤسفة لك و الأنسة كونستنتين التي تمت قبل ما يزيد عن ثلاثة سنين في غزة و أنا كنت احد مدبريها.

فمنذ ذلك اليوم و الاحساس بالذنب ينتابني, على الرغم من تفهمكم السبب وانكم لستم المقصودين فبكم تم انقاذ حياة انسان .

ومن هذا المنطلق اقدم لك و كونستنتين بالغ اعتذاري عن الحادثة واطلب منكما مسامحتي عن اي لحظة مزعجة سببتها لكما.

ارجو منك ان تنقل اعتذاري لزوي كونستنتين اذا لديك طريقة اتصال بها
كما ارجو منكما مراسلتي وقبول اعتذاري لأنكم وان سامحتموني يوم الحادثة

يراودني احساس انكم لم تسامحوني من كينونة قلوبكم

المخطئ

F. Abed

Dear Steve,

I hope you are in the best of health and in excellent condition. I sent you this letter to confirm my deep appreciation for your exhibitions and photos, which are very beautiful. And here I am, bringing back to your memory the kidnapping incident, a tragedy for you and Miss Constantine, that happened over three years ago in Gaza. I was one of its masterminds.

Since that day, I have been feeling guilty, even though you understood the motives and that you were not the target. Because of you, the life of a person was saved.

Having said that, I offer you and Miss Constantine my utmost apologies regarding the incident and ask for your forgiveness for any annoyance I have caused you both. I urge you to convey my apologies to Zoi Constantine if you have a way to contact her. I'm asking both of you to correspond with me and accept my apology because even though you forgave me during the incident, I have a feeling you did not forgive me deep inside your hearts.

The one who made an error,

F. Abed

10

Despite the insanity, Francesca and I remained in Jerusalem. We renovated the Old City house, beginning with the upper terrace, where the grapevine leaves and branches covered it once like a blanket in the sky. There, we built an extra room that joined two others, creating an intimate space, a retreat—a faraway island from the bleak everyday reality. On our remote island, we exposed stone walls and arches to look over the lemon tree, whose branches and lemons reached the new windows, almost growing inside. We kept the front space open with panoramic windows to always see the gold of the Dome of the Rock and the entire Mount of Olives. At each twilight, this scene told another story, set against a sky exploding with color and clouds until they faded away to darkness. Many nights, we watched the stars and drifted to other distant shores. We got lost in space, but we would find our way back to our island in the morning light.

But the Jerusalem I lived in was in a constant state of alert, like an electric pulse with a disturbing rhythm, always charged, ready to explode at any second. To change this reality, I wished I lived in the past, or far in the future. Knowing this was not possible, I traveled there in my imagination. This was where I met Francesca—she was from a different place and time. We have been together since we met during my search for unseen light. Francesca is the unseen spark in all my art, hidden under many layers. I know the difference between image and reality. Francesca became an image to me, detached from all realities. We roamed our world, but the reality was grounding, incessantly interrupting our dreams.

Our first kiss was in 1996 at The Underground club. We got in and danced all night. At dawn, drunk, we dragged ourselves out and continued kissing on a bench at the very beginning of Jaffa Street. We lost track of time, and when her bus arrived, I couldn't stop kissing her and insisted she wait for the next one. Two more buses passed before she boarded one, and we continued kissing on its steps until the doors folded. I waved a last goodbye and strolled home. Just as I opened the front door, I heard an explosion in the distance. I turned on the TV and saw breaking news. A Palestinian suicide bomber blew himself up on bus eighteen at the station where we had flirted.

Six years passed, and Francesca and I were driving home on Jaffa Street as one traffic light just turned red. I had run red lights before, but I waited, breathing air out, restless as usual, and as the light turned yellow, I pressed the gas to a BOOM! My heart dropped. Falling down by the pressure. In that silence, the car drove itself. I looked around. Everything was motionless. Dead silent. As if someone had pressed the mute button on the remote control. What remained was a misty scene, with bodies scattered on street corners. Francesca and I were not injured. We later heard that a Palestinian suicide bomber had detonated herself. We had escaped death again, but the explosion still vibrates, echoing that hollow feeling in the heart.

To our remote island, the neighbors called in a specialist to kill the tree that shaded our terrace, where my mother used to sit, where the old man with the beard like a wizard used to tend to his forest of plants. I watched him insert an injection into its veins. Without warning, the tree withered, died. The neighbors chopped it down and tiled over its soil to cover their crime. Two years later, Darwish's next-door neighbors plundered his land by unforeseen force, and to uphold it, they erected a building taller than the cypress tree he had burnt down. In the meantime, another building was constructed, but this one was glued to our rooftop, to that place where I took my father's guests to the view that dazzled and caught everyone by surprise. The houses were built and inhabited in a few weeks, like a story from a thousand and one night. The visual pollution of Israeli settlements was now at the center of our house. It concealed the celestial view of the Dome of the Rock. Only a slice of its crescent remained. Our night sky was covered. Francesca got pregnant then. Our retreat was no longer, and we began our escape from our island. Cécile was conceived there, under its skies, but she was not born under the lemon tree.

I was born at home, on a May day, on Via Dolorosa in the Old City, Latin for The Road of Suffering. I had always felt tortured, occasionally believing that my fate was determined by where I was born. As a child, I would be tormented after fights with my parents, and as a consequence, I was scared to go into their bedroom to find them dead under their sheets. What if they died before we sorted it out? The question of how to live with guilt and the death of loved ones haunted me. This feeling intensified when I hit thirty, after my encounter with my aunt Mary.

Aunt Mary lived in the heart of the Christian Quarter in the Old City, in the house where she was born until she died eighty-two years later. She only ever traveled to the cities surrounding Jerusalem. When I asked her why, she said she never had a chance, often dependent on others. That was her world, restricted by certain cultural traditions from the past that never made things right. She couldn't see change. I often heard her blame others for her misery, all of which seemed beyond her will.

When I was a child, Aunt Mary was often in our house. I liked to listen to her tone of voice. Her accent was typical of the old generation of Jerusalemites, rich with expression and proverbs. I often observed her reach into her handbag, hold up a tiny mirror, and powder her cheeks. I wondered how she could see anything through her glasses, with lenses as thick as those of telescopes. I teased her a lot. And when she was out of sight, I crept to her handbag to snap its clasp again and again. Aunt Mary was a hypochondriac, always complaining about headaches and backaches. She grew old, gained weight, and her knees failed her. From then on, she could no longer walk the short distance from her house to ours. The few times I did drop by with my father to see her, she asked me to visit her more often and help. I never did. But deep inside, even though I always felt sorry for her, I truly loved her.

I always thought I would be dead by the age of twenty-five, and when that didn't happen, thirty became the promised date. I never liked the heavy day of my birthday. It often dragged me deeper into myself, made me silent, more lost in the doomed self. But Francesca lightened those dreaded days by arranging spa escapes, massages, by always being there.

On the morning of my thirtieth birthday, I woke up to find myself still breathing. Cécile's fever was over forty degrees, hotter than the Dead Sea temperature, where Francesca felt would help me transition from my twenties to the afterlife. Cécile's fever cooled down by night, and after she dozed off, Francesca made a fancy dinner on our terrace, lighting the table with candles. We sat down in the summer breeze to finally relax, and as she was pouring the wine, my phone rang. It was almost ten-thirty. I didn't recognize the number and did not pick up. But somebody was insisting, and to stop the nagging, I answered. It was my uncle Yousef, whom I avoided whenever I could. As we spoke, I wondered how he had got my number. He asked me, or more likely, he ordered me to drive and pick him up from his house because of an emergency, but it didn't feel urgent enough. I asked him what the crisis was, but he couldn't say as he wanted us to find out. His home was on the other side of the city, and none of my brothers or my father were available. I left Francesca, furious with myself, cursing the day I was born. After speeding over, and who knows if I crossed red lights, I made it to the other side of Jerusalem in twenty minutes. As he stepped in the car, he passed on a small piece of paper where he had written on it the name of a hospital I never heard of.

The nurse I spoke to at the information desk had a sticky note on the window with my uncle's name in case he showed up. She guided us to sit down in the waiting room. Not long after, a doctor came in asking about our relationship with Mary Sabella. Uncle Yousef showed him his ID to prove that he was related to her, being her brother, and explained that he had not recently checked in on her. Maybe he wanted to say never. Aunt Mary was in the hospital for days. The doctor patted my uncle's shoulders to tell us she had died. They looked for anyone from the Sabella family to identify her body in the morgue. This was not how I wished to spend the last hour of my thirtieth birthday.

I froze at the door when I saw her body. I stood a few feet away. I could tell it was Aunt Mary by the shape of the white drape covering her. I approached her. The room was bright with fluorescent lights. Cold. Mary lay on a table in the corner. Her cheeks were not powdered pink. She looked pale. Beaten. Silent. Mary had lived alone. And died alone. I looked at her and felt guilty for all the mean things I had done to her as a child, those she knew about, and those she never found out. I felt guilty for not finding the occasion to visit her every now and then. I asked her to forgive me countless times. But we all have to live with our mistakes from the past. Since that birth day and death night, I continue to see Mary at least once a year.

Being born in Jerusalem as a Palestinian is entering life as an immigrant to become a foreigner at home, unlike the mass of Jewish immigrants who automatically receive their Israeli citizenship in envelopes as they disembark their planes in Tel Aviv to become the natives from abroad. Israel's Law of Return applies only to Jews. Palestinians have to live with the Law of No Return. Many Jewish immigrants settle in Palestine to gain incentives and tax breaks to make their life easy. Meanwhile, Palestinians born and living in Jerusalem remain stateless, subject at any moment to live the end of their birthright. It's a paradox that these Jewish immigrants can return to a place they have never been in or seen before.

Fredo, my brother, lost his birthright when he traveled to the United States in 1988 to study on a six-month scholarship coordinated by Brother Robert Wise. He could only return to visit family years later, on a tourist visa, after he had received his green card, which took many years. Fredo told us how he sold his blood when he had no money in his first years in exile. Paul, my youngest brother, flew to America at the start of the Second Intifada in 2000, a break, also meant to be a retreat. The Israeli authorities revoked his identity card and canceled his right to return home shortly after. Paul had to wait long till he found his way to getting American citizenship before he could travel home ten years later. But only on a three-month visa. The annexation of Jerusalem in 1980 stripped native Palestinian Jerusalemites of their birthright by issuing them permanent residency status that was anything but permanent. Subject to endless conditions. Over the years, Israel revoked thousands of residencies, uprooted families—often without warning to make Jerusalem predominantly Jewish. Two-thirds of Jerusalem is now Jewish, whereas the whole Jewish population in all historic Palestine was less than nine percent at the beginning of the twentieth century.

B'Tselem, a dedicated Israeli organization for human rights, has reported that between 1995 and 2000, Palestinians who had not lived in the city for the last seven consecutive years had lost their permanent residency status, even if they had returned periodically. Those who went abroad kept their status, provided they returned to Jerusalem within three years to have their exit permits extended by the Ministry of Interior. If you failed to remember like my brother Paul, your destiny was to remain abroad.

Israel extends the foreign land for Palestinians to include the same land they lived on, where they were born. Most revocations have been executed because people lived in the West Bank, around Jerusalem, including Bethlehem or Ramallah, next door cities to Jerusalem, where family members lived or studied. In reality, Palestinian Jerusalemites live in a suspended state. They are neither here nor there. If they wish to travel, they must apply for a travel document called a laissez-passer, meaning Let Pass in French. In practice, to border police, laissez-passer means: Stop This Person. What happens next is the opposite of without let or hindrance. A visa is required to go anywhere, including one for the way back home. And if it expired, you lost the right to be home.

Foreign embassies complicate the visa procedure, asking for many absurd forms, including exorbitant bank guarantees, money only a few people have. These frustrating applications last months, anticipating their arrival is like the anxiety of passing a final exam. Or not. Making these procedures easier could have been an opportunity for the world to ease the suffering of all Palestinians. But instead, they get repeatedly punished. Cornered. To Israel, Jerusalem is its eternal unified capital, but the Ministry of Interior has two famous branches: one for Jews and another for the Arabs. The one on Jaffa Street applies the Law of Return to every Jew in the world. The one off Damascus Gate uproots native Palestinians to throw them all over the world.

I wanted to return home. A way out was to apply for Israeli citizenship. Only then could I escape life in exile. I was eighteen when I filled the application, and when the clerk asked me to write why, I drew on all the white paper two words:

Lama Lo
Why Not

She double-checked with me whether this was what I really wanted to state on my application to her shock or amusement. In a few weeks, the passport was in my hand. I always wanted to travel the world, but never leaving permanently. Jerusalem was my home.

Once I married Francesca, Israeli citizenship would secure Francesca's residency. Or so I thought. Becoming an Israeli citizen never gave me, or Francesca, equal rights to Jewish Israeli citizens. When I proposed to Francesca in Bern, I promised her a great life in Jerusalem. After our honeymoon in Venice and Rome, we flew back to Jerusalem for a fresh start.

When she applied for residency, we had no doubt that she would get permanent status given my Israeli nationality and her Swiss passport, which would lead to Israeli citizenship within three years, as we had been initially informed. But the ministry only allowed her to remain on a three-month tourist visa, which had to be renewed every quarter. After strenuous endeavors, we succeeded in having the visa upgraded to a six-month permit and then to a one-year permit.

Meanwhile, the ministry limited Francesca's traveling out of Israel, counting the number of days she was allowed to be out if she ever wished to be on track of getting Israeli citizenship. She was denied the right to work, and when we fought for one, they gave her one three years later on the condition that they approved the employer. Francesca's offer was from Berlitz, the international school of languages with the main branch just off Jaffa Street. The ministry rejected the application with no explanation. We battled till we reversed their decision.

I hired a Palestinian lawyer. Maybe two. And when I consulted with Jeremy, he referred me to a Jewish lawyer who specialized in family reunifications, even though Francesca and I lived together. He said that I could settle his payment with art. But the family unification, specifically applicable to Palestinians, was applied to our case regardless of our nationalities. My argument was that Israeli law should be equal to all its citizens. We were being discriminated against, mainly because our friends Marianne and Bezalel had a completely different story. Bezalel, a fellow student from my photography school, was an Israeli born to Jewish immigrants from France. He married Marianne in Switzerland in the same month as Francesca and I did. Like Francesca, Marianne was Swiss but not Jewish. But Marianne started her life in Jerusalem without worry about any formalities, receiving her Israeli identity card, national and health insurance within the first two months of her landing in Tel Aviv. She even got financial assistance and prepaid Hebrew classes, along with many other benefits. I only had one session with the Jewish lawyer, and it did not involve any art. It ended when he explained how the right of entry and settlement was only extended to people of Jewish ancestry and their spouses. The battle continued for seven years. The ministry made the absurd request that I prove my life was centered in Jerusalem. And after I did, I was told that I lived abroad according to their registry. I didn't go anywhere. I should have been given an award for surviving in Jerusalem that long to start with. Or to end with. Back to the beginning, Israeli citizens can settle wherever they want in Palestine, but I must comply with laws to prove that I was on the land, and if not, I should find my way out.

But to go out, one has to get in first. Getting into the offices of the Ministry of Interior off Damascus Gate was next to impossible. I often queued on the street for eight hours, for two or three days in a row. Some people arrived at midnight, with sleeping bags, a homeless street sight. I would wake up to queue at four to maybe make it by noon. People, men and women, shouting kids from the frosty wind or the summer heat, were sandwiched together like sardines. To avoid losing our spots, we stood like statues for hours and hours. And the fights and the harassments were endless.

The old, the sick, and those frustrated paid others to queue for them, and to profit from the chaos, a group of greedy guys would queue just to make money selling their turns, inventing new authority and rules. It turned into a business. And in reaction, the ministry distributed numbers to people at the door to secure an entry. The numbers sold for anything between fifty and five hundred dollars, depending on the season. Like countless others, I often had no choice and paid to get a number.

Still, even a purchased number couldn't guarantee a spot—it was a gamble, and if it didn't work, you were told good luck next time. The ministry had corrupt managers who were caught committing bribery, which reached down to the crooked security at the door. In the meantime, all that Palestinians wanted was to live in dignity like everyone else, get the paper done to carry on with their normal, everyday lives. This experience was so traumatizing that international news agencies reported about this injustice and discrimination. I had my first dose of trauma at the ministry at twelve years old when I applied for the laissez-passer to travel to New York. The crowds pushed at the front door as if they were escaping the closing door of a ghetto. But the struggle was to storm in, not out. Once inside, my mother instructed me to wait while she fought her way to the clerk's window. When she had made it, she was told that I must sign the documents if she wanted to complete the application. There was no way for a spaghetti kid like me to force his way through. My mother's only solution was to shout around, asking people to pick me up and have me carried over the crowd. And so I crowd-surfed from the head of one person to another, as if it was my first rock concert. I signed the application floating in the air, in gibberish, and then I crowd-surfed back to where I was.

Palestinian Jerusalemites face the ministry's uprooting policies daily. Going through these measures pushed Francesca and me to the edge. We almost packed our bags. That was it. After those seven miserable years, we contacted the minister of interior affairs as a last resort. To add pressure, I sent the same letter to B'Tselem and several Israeli newspapers. In reaction, the ministry approved Francesca's application. But by then, our dreams of having a great life in Jerusalem had already faded.

My Jerusalem was under Jewish Israeli Occupation, which aimed to tie the Palestinian identity around itself, to dissolve it from its Arab history. Kamal Boullata was born in Jerusalem under Jordanian Arab rule, and when he returned in 1984—on an American passport—for the first time since his forced exile in 1967, he witnessed a different place. It was intriguing to hear his perspective on how Jerusalem had changed, both visually and in spirit. When I worked with Kamal on photographing Christian icons in 2003, I took Lily, his partner, to Café Hillel. Later she remarked to Kamal that she was troubled because I had taken her to an Israeli café. In solidarity, she would have preferred to support Palestinian cafés in Arab Jerusalem. Anyone supporting Palestine would maybe do the same thing. Still, for me, the question was: when did we, and notably the Palestinians who remained on the land, agree to the division of Jerusalem into East and West? I was born in Jerusalem, and to me, it has always been one, a city that cannot be divided. Israelis want to see no Palestinians. Living in all of Jerusalem, for me, was and is a victory.

I have a friend, Jakub, from Jerusalem's Old City, who lived in Anatot, a guarded Israeli settlement with a history of violence against Palestinians. It was put in a prime location in the West Bank with a great view, much like the majority of settlements that occupy many hilltops in Palestine. There is one at the end and the beginning of almost every horizon. This one overlooked the desert. I asked Jakub, whose name is read Yacov in Hebrew, the same guy who told me not to speak Arabic one night because of an Israeli gang that hunted Arabs each night, but I resisted,

How can you live in an Israeli settlement?

I dropped my argument when "Yacov" said that it was his right to live wherever he wanted in his homeland. Jakub was one of those invisible Palestinians who could and would pass anywhere in Israel. Even his last Christian name sounded Jewish when read in Hebrew. He did have the perfect identity card. But this sort of existence came at a price. If his identity was revealed to his Jewish neighbors, his life would be no more.

Gilo, a settlement built over the remains of the al-Malha Palestinian village, is so well integrated into Jerusalem that its residents, settlers, consider it one of the city's neighborhoods. Gilo was built illegally after 1967, on Bet Jala land, which belongs to Palestinians. In 2007, I took a group of international artists to photograph the Separation Wall labyrinth that caged Bethlehem and Bet Jala. When we finished photographing, we went out for a drink in Gilo. Our Israeli waitress asked out of curiosity where we each came from. When it was my turn, I said,

Palestine.

She responded,

Yafe.
Nice.

I asked,

Have you been there before?

She replied,

No.

Little did she know that she was born on land Occupied by Israel called Palestine, a reality many Israelis, young and old, choose to be entirely unaware of.

Close to Gilo is Tantur, an Arab neighborhood above the Palestinian village of Beit Safafa. The hill looked over the castle of my childhood dreams. It looked deserted, standing alone on a cliff, between two roads, as if in no-man's-land, a perfect escape from Jerusalem and all its reality. The castle was a short distance from Mar Elias Monastery, built on the spot where it is believed that the prophet Elijah ascended to heaven on a chariot of fire. For years, the castle faced a hilltop, covered by a tall tree field as if a green hat rested on its top, leaving its base naturally bare. Not far in the horizon Herodium where Herod the Great built a palace-fortress, stood like a flat-topped mountain as if hit by an asteroid. This view appears a few hundred meters outside of Bethlehem in the direction of Jerusalem. The castle stands on the road where Jerusalem begins or where Jerusalem ends, depending on the direction.

The castle was the only Arab house left not settled, possessed by Israeli settlers along that long road. At the magical hours of the day, during dusk and dawn, its light glows on its old walls like burning coal. Wood boards covered almost all the windows from the outside. But there was light glowing behind one window almost every night. Francesca and I wondered who lived there. During hot days, we would often see visitors to the monastery rest in the shade of its scrubby gardens. I saw more than once people knock on its door but leaving when there was never a reply. When Francesca and I decided to leave the Old City and began looking for a new home, we almost found ourselves knocking at the castle's door.

Instead, we started our search on the hill across the road that connects Jerusalem to Gilo Settlement. The obstacles to finding the right place, in the right location, with the right price, made the task seem impossible. But we drove to Tantur's highest point anyway, and as we approached the end of the road, Francesca and I saw a villa under construction. It was built with the rare Jerusalem stone used in building since ancient times, just like those of the castle. We couldn't find the main entrance, there were many, and some were as wide as those of city gates. We stopped, and as we approached its front terrace, a cloud of dust loomed over us. Many workers were on-site cutting white stone. When the cloud dispersed, it revealed a garden path leading to a residence surrounded by green. On top of the hill, on a cold autumn day, the wind pushed us to enter the house to find shelter. Its ceilings were as high as those in the Old City. The space radiated with light that poured in from the many windows on every wall so that one can always be in the Jerusalem sky. This house was built between times, on land just like that of the Old City, transported from the past. It looked over the hills of Palestine and was situated a short walking distance from the castle of my dreams. It was there where Francesca and I gave birth to Cécile Elise Sabella.

Francesca was convinced we wouldn't be able to afford this luxury, but I believed in exceptions. We rented the house from Yasser Alyan, whose known family had lived in Beit Safafa for centuries. When we first met Yasser, I couldn't shut up about its beauty and panoramic views, even asking him whether he was an artist. He was an accountant who worked with a specialist from Germany on energy flow to help him get it right. He had designed it for three families, including his own, where each lives alone, as every residence had its own way, view, and garden.

Yasser liked Francesca and me from the first moment, and against all odds, he agreed to lower the monthly rent by half. We became friends, and one afternoon he told Francesca the history of Beit Safafa as we sat in his garden,

> After the war in 1948, the village was cut in half. The existing train tracks and barbed-wire fences became the border as a result of the founding of Israel. One half fell under Israeli military control, and the other fell under Jordanian rule. Soldiers from both were posted on each side. We couldn't see or contact our family members who lived meters away on the other side. Only after the 1967 War, when the fence came down, were our families able to reunite. Now, half of the residents in Beit Safafa have Israeli citizenship, and the other half hold Israeli Jerusalem IDs with temporary residency status. Israel can withdraw their IDs and expel them from their homes by force.

Yasser's house was on the side that gave Israeli citizenship, and his rights of ownership should be protected by Israeli law. But even owning land in Jerusalem is temporary similar to the legal status of its Palestinian residents. In 2004, not long after we moved in, Francesca finally received her Israeli identity card.

That same year, I worked on Till the End, a body of work where I collected stones from Jerusalem areas that I felt were threatened by demolition or by the change to make way for Israeli settlements and roads. I took photographs of these locations where the stones were sitting, and in the darkroom later, I printed those images onto the stones' surfaces. Each stone revealed an image of where it came from. Rooted in the land, not alien, the rocks came not from anywhere else, except maybe from outer space. They had been there, witness to everything around them. Back then, I had planned to return each stone to each spot where it once belonged, even if there would be an Israeli settlor house.

One evening, while Yasser was on his way to his house, he saw me placing the stones on the ground in a grid, looking at all of them together. He came closer to observe one of them closer, kneeled down, and said,

This is Saqqa's house.

He was referring to the castle of my childhood dreams. It turned out that Yasser was friends with Charlie Saqqa, the mystery man who lived there. I finally met someone who could help unravel the castle's history. To start with, I didn't even know that anyone lived there. When I asked Yasser how I could meet Charlie, he said,

> He rarely leaves his house. Walk there in the evening before it gets dark. He usually sits on the front terrace around that time.

The following day, one hour before the sun had set, I carried my stone with me and walked to the castle. I wanted to show the artwork to Charlie, share my attachment, and my hope that the castle remained. When I arrived, there was no one on the front terrace. I wondered if it was too dark, or not dark enough. I rested the stone on a sidewall and stood in front of the arched windows, waiting a bit. For a second, I was reluctant to knock at the door, but it was one of those moments when I knew that if I didn't do it, I would risk not getting another chance. I placed my trembling hand on the fist-shaped iron knob and went *knock, knock*. It took a few eager minutes until I heard a frail voice from behind the door,

> Na'am. Shu Biddak?
> Yes. What do you want?

In Arabic. I said,

> *I am a friend of Yasser Alyan.*
> *I'd like to show you something.*

Charlie opened the door halfway, caught sight of the stone resting on his wall, and unlocked the stubborn door chain. He limped as he took a few steps to go outside. He looked drained, a man in his sixties. We shook hands, and I explained to him where I lived and my relation to Yasser. I also apologized for taking the stone from his land without permission. The image of his house intrigued him, and he asked me to explain. We spoke about the speed at which Jerusalem was changing and its transformation to an image of itself. And that there was nowhere to escape.

I pointed to the mountain with the green hat that once covered its top. The hat was knocked off, its hill shaved, the trees replaced by a mushroom of white buildings among the rising cranes. A new Israeli colony—Har Homa. Jabal Abu Ghniem was erased. It was yet another Palestinian hilltop whose destiny was to have its land grabbed, and its name overwritten.

Charlie warmed up to me,

> The Israelis have been trying to expel us for years. They keep making it impossible for us to live here.

He pointed to a monstrous cellular tower stationed directly in front of his house that serviced the entire Har Homa settlement. The tower had been set on fire several times but was as often restored by Israeli authorities. Below the tower lived a Palestinian Bedouin family that defied court eviction orders to remain on their land at any cost. With so many other vacant fields in the surrounding area that the tower could have occupied, its real target and function became evident—to force Charlie, his family, and the Bedouins to abandon their land. The health risks of living close to cellular radiation were well known, and by living at home, they gambled with their lives.

I identified with Charlie's struggle and felt comfortable asking him about his limp. He lifted his trousers to show me the wooden leg, telling me about the car accident he had and how it changed his life. As the sun set behind Jabal Abu Ghniem mountain, and as the atmosphere turned to gold, I felt the time had come to leave. And as I carried the stone with the castle, Charlie unexpectedly invited me in. I wished Francesca was there with me to step into our castle for the first, and maybe the last time.

I followed him into the house. The hallway looked from another time, dim, with one lightbulb hanging in the center. At the end of the hall, there was a staircase leading to the second floor. I looked around, and all the rooms were closed except for two. I stood in awe, thinking of how fortunate I was to be inside. I followed Charlie into the first room to the left, which had its door half open. Inside, an elderly woman sat in a wheelchair. The windows were covered with thick curtains. The paint on the walls was faded, not taken care of for years. She was staring at flickering images on a small television with an old antenna on top. I thought perhaps the cellular tower was interfering with the signal. I said hello to her, but she didn't respond. She was leaning on one arm that rested on the wheelchair's table, with her fist pressing into her cheek. Charlie and I walked out of the room towards the staircase. On the way, I caught sight of a body lying on a bed in the second room, covered from head to toe with white sheets. Its hands were joined at its chest, as if in prayer or death. I was scared, almost believing that this was the missing body of St. Elijah, who never traveled anywhere. I kept watching for a sign of life as I slowly followed Charlie, who struggled going up the stairs. Then, I noticed the sheets lifting faintly, as if from a person taking the last breath, waiting for the grace of death.

On the second floor, everything was dark as wood plates covered the windows from outside. To bring in more light, Charlie went to unlock a rusty iron door that opened to the main balcony. The metal bar was stuck, a sign it was hardly used, and as he tried to turn it, I heard moans of agony coming from the room across. The wailing never ceased. I couldn't see the person, shrouded in darkness, but I could hear the years of suffering. Shaken, Charlie explained how he had been taking care of his aging family members one by one for many, many years.

He opened the door, and we stepped out to the castle's balcony. Before our eyes was Har Homa again. I asked Charlie how his family kept the house after Israelis settled in every Arab house on the road. He narrated,

> During the 1967 War, when Israel occupied the rest of Jerusalem, my family decided to remain in this house no matter what. My father knew that all the Palestinians who left or were forced to leave in 1948 would never return. Their homes were taken and occupied by the Jews. One day during the war, we heard gunshots. We looked through the windows and saw Israeli soldiers surrounding our house. Their orders were to open the door. But my father resisted. He held the front door with his back as they tried to force their way inside. The soldiers then sprayed the door with bullets, killing my father on the spot. They then continued their march down the road as if nothing happened. With the war raging on, we had no choice but to bury my father in our garden.

The garden lay on the other side of the hill, across the fast road that sliced the family's land and property to connect Gilo Settlement to Jerusalem. This division isolated the grave, creating two hills, making the castle stand out, as if in the middle of nowhere, in no man's land. We went back into the house and headed downstairs to the garden in front of Mar Elias Monastery. Charlie sighed and pointed at Bethlehem with his cane,

> In the past, many visitors came from Bethlehem to retreat in Mar Elias. Since Israel built the Separation Wall and

> erected many checkpoints, I barely see anyone. The army besieged the city and required Palestinians to obtain special permits to come here. But they hardly grant them to anyone.

As it grew dark, I hugged Charlie and found my way out. The castle's image became heavier than the stone I carried. I thought if all of this had happened to this house, the number of narratives hidden behind the facade of every occupied Palestinian house must be unthinkable—a reality within reality, trauma without end.

While writing these words, I called Yasser wondering about the castle's fate. Charlie couldn't withstand the pressure of keeping the house any longer from prying eyes while also taking care of his sick family. He sold it to Palestinians and moved with his family into another house not far from Yasser's, down the hill, in the valley. He died there three years later. In 2016, the train tracks that once divided Bet Safafa into two parts, separating families, came back as a new highway to connect the Gush Etzion settlement block in Hebron to the airport in Tel Aviv. One hundred meters from Yasser's house, construction of a new settlement began. He was in a battle with Israeli authorities. If Yasser lost this fight, he would have to watch as they sliced through his land, and instead of watching the sky from the mansion windows, he will have to settle with a noisy road almost built on his front door. It turned out that it didn't matter if Yasser was among the lucky those who lived on the hill and received Israeli nationalities to protect their lands. In the end, Israeli authorities treated them like the Palestinians in the valley below. And I am sure you can imagine what kind of energy Yasser needs now to work with his German specialist to find peace in his heart.

When I lived in Jerusalem, I felt I was in forced exile, detached from my surroundings and reality. Maybe Charlie and I both did. We each lived in states of isolation and alienation. Refugees at home. In 2004, Francesca and I were contemplating moving to London to pursue a master's degree. Upon announcing our plan, a friend of Francesca's who had recently immigrated to Israel from Russia shocked me with her response,

> That makes sense.
> I don't understand what you are doing in Jerusalem.
> You should leave.
>
> This is not your country anyway.

She was right about the last part—this was not my country, but Jerusalem was my city of birth. My state and its government should protect my rights, not strip them away. And indeed, Israeli IDs issued to Palestinians born in Jerusalem under Occupation have expiration dates. They force Palestinians out of Jerusalem. And it doesn't matter if you acquired Israeli citizenship. It won't secure all your rights. I mistakenly thought being a citizen would make my life easier, or at least make me stay. I had acquired Israeli citizenship to prevent Israel from forcing me to live in exile; paradoxically, I lived in exile anyway.

I remember being furious with my brother Fredo in America for insisting that his family continued to pay for his post-office box on Jaffa Street, even though he had been exiled from Jerusalem for years. I thought there was no point. When I moved to London, I also found myself instructing my brothers to keep my PO box. I had come to understand the essence of Fredo's odd request—we both hoped that we would return one day.

I never wanted to leave Jerusalem. Jerusalem left me.

9

I walked the Via Dolorosa, The Way of Suffering, up and down many times, until the day I found a sign pointing to two directions: Francesca or Jerusalem. The road towards Jerusalem was leading to eternal exile. I chose Francesca to detach from Jerusalem. Her presence was enchanting, ambiguous, cathartic if let be. Forming my bond with her felt like falling in love over and over again. In return, I promised myself to never betray her.

Life passed quickly with Francesca, like sand slipping between fingers. Our reality was of a dream, within a dream, deep into our imagination, of a tale that doesn't want to end. From the start, it was about cosmic light.

For our tenth anniversary, the bar lady leaned over the counter excited to tell us before we even picked our drinks,

> I love to see couples on their first date.

I asked her,

> *What makes you think we just met?*

She said,

> You look like you just fell in love!
> I see the spark in your eyes.

When I told her what we were celebrating, showing her our rings, she took a step back. Her excitement turned into ecstasy, calling out for all the bartenders, pouring shots for everyone.

But life does not always pass by quickly, not during the days of war. During the alleged peace talks in the 1990s, Israeli negotiators offered to give back 95% percent of the land occupied in 1967. But this 5% comes with a price, as in reality, it would consume the vast majority of West Bank land for the Israeli settlements to function like 5-megabyte computer software that required 100 megabytes of free hard disk space for it to run and function. This makes it impossible to build a continuous and independent Palestinian state, as settlements consumed the land, and their number has been growing by the day, till today.

In early 2002, Israel began constructing the Separation Wall, dissecting Palestine into many more parts, dividing its families. It was built in the heart of Palestinian land. The wall snaked around cities, villages, and surrounded houses, sometimes on all four sides. Cities like Qalqilya and Bethlehem were encircled, locked behind one single iron gate. Travel between Palestinian towns and villages in the West Bank became subject to Israeli clearance. Over five hundred checkpoints restricted and often blocked movement, paralyzing daily life. Many women in labor were forced to deliver at these checkpoints. Many died.

The land was cut, dividing communities, putting them on opposite sides. Families were split. Palestinians lived in exile in their own homes, on their own land. Jerusalem turned into a prison, surrounded not by its ancient city walls, but by the atrocious eight-meter-high concrete block. The horizon of all Palestinian cities ends or begins with the Separation Wall. Do the Israelis want to be remembered for having built the ugliest wall on earth? It is a gray bruise in both eyes, painful. Endless. Made from blood mixed with hatred. But our humanity has a long history of walls, and we all know how they end. Israelis driving on their streets hardly ever see this visual error. Israel built artificial hills, planted trees, and painted parts of the wall in earth color to make it blend into the landscape. It was easier to hide the problem than to end the Occupation. The Occupation cannot be hidden, yet Israel managed to hide a seven-hundred-kilometer-long wall from Israeli view and from the consciousness of the world.

The Second Intifada froze life in Palestine, put it in a state of paralysis. Even Ben Yehuda Street and Zion Square were deserted. When I wandered with Francesca on the empty streets, only cats were walking around, but even they seemed disoriented. The soldiers who had stationed themselves to find Arabs had abandoned their posts. There were no Arabs, or Jews left on the streets.

Killing became routine, retaliation after retaliation, that people became numb to daily reality no one wanted, and yet fought to keep, never resolve. And when death found Israelis, only a few of those who survived, or those who mourned, did not call for revenge or for the solving of the Arab problem. Instead, they saw it as a wake-up call to suddenly feel the pain of the other. But most Israelis defended the Occupation, with the plan to make it a functional good Occupation under the pretext that Palestinians had it better than other Arabs. But who wants to live under any sort of Occupation. If Africans were given a choice to be slaves in America or slaves on their native land with improved conditions, they would have rejected both. Nobody wants to be or live a slave, not here or there, and for sure, no free Palestinian wants to live under any sort of Occupation.

Photographing for many agencies allowed me to see and feel the lives of Palestinians in all of historic Palestine. I was among the fortunate few who could reach everywhere, who always found a way. But the more I saw, the more impossible it became to accept any reality under the Occupation.

A year after my kidnapping, I returned to Gaza, wondering if lighting can hit twice. I hugged Francesca, leaving her with a lingering vibration. I left in the darkness, an hour before dawn, to reach early in the morning. At Erez Crossing and Israeli army base, everything looked quiet and empty as I parked the car along the eerie concrete wall erected all along the border. But when I took my photo gear out, I heard an explosion, and when I looked around, I saw the two soldiers stationed at the front barrier continue to enjoy their chat as if nothing had happened. Seeing my photo vest and carrying gear, they signaled to me to head to the inspection area to go back to whatever they were talking about. As I walked, another explosion filled the air. This time I paid more attention as it had a whistle to it, hearing an echo of the detonation, and shortly after, the blast. Not even the birds in the sky seemed to care anymore, continuing to fly around in their no man's land. This was the period when a sense of defeat swept all over Palestine. When neither the land nor the self floating in the sky was finding any liberation.

There was no one at this hour, as was often the case during this period when it was seen risky to travel to Gaza. I bought a coffee from a machine, took a number, and sat down, waiting, listening. When the border police came from behind a glass window to call out for my number, I asked him about the explosions and whether it was safe in Gaza. He spoke without apathy that those were tank shells fired as a precaution to the empty fields of Bet Hanoun, on the other side, to deter Palestinians. Aimed to shield Israeli life, that early morning, it felt there was one shell every minute.

When I asked him about the tank's position, he pointed right behind his back. The lonely walk to Gaza was over one kilometer, through a long caged passage in the middle of a buffer zone. I was assured that I would be walking into Gaza with shells flying over my head, but it wasn't something I should be worried about. He checked my papers behind his glass window and then handed me a form from behind his hole about life and death. The only way to get in was to sign that I was entering Gaza at my own risk, relieving Israel from all responsibility for my life as an Israeli citizen. For me, that was anyway given, a moment of liberation, brief detachment, so I signed it without hesitation.

After passing my gear and myself through the X-ray in the small room next door, I headed to the locked iron gate outside, which secured a daunting concrete army complex. There, I waited a while for the soldiers whose shadows I could see in the watchtower to open the first gate so that I could traverse to the afterlife. The shadows were moving, looking at me through the dark bulletproof glass. They buzzed me in to go through the one-way turnstile, knowing that once I turned myself through the *tak, tak, tak,* there was no way to turn it back.

The road to Gaza was a crossing between two worlds. I, too, became numb to reality, later asking myself who worked under such conditions. The shells never stopped. Only now, their vibration was more felt. I walked through the corridors, alone, going through a maze, right, left, left, right, with camera surveillance on each corner. One passage after the other, listening to instructions via speakers, till another solid metal gate stopped me. To continue, I found a button for an intercom. Later, a Hebrew voice instructed me to wait for the gate to swing open but didn't say when it would. I waited a while, and when it finally did, I stepped into a locked room with another locked gate. But this one had no intercom: only surveillance, a test for one's patience.

This gate opened to the long walk to the other side, into a ghostly narrow corridor. I felt dwarfed passing its high walls, standing next to you on every turn. Later, its segments dissolved into metal grating and barbed wire, where one could see through pieces of bruised and dead land. The crinkled roof of bolted tin was perforated with bullets and shrapnel holes from previous fighting. The sounds of the tank shells continued, except now they were magnified by the deafening shiver of the tin plates that echoed back at me with their sound waves. I listened to their whistles, feeling their shiver, looking at light streaking through the bullet holes, as if each was a spirit. It was an intense sensory and visual experience, a light dance with the universe. But this performance had no ordinary end. People died.

Lives were changed forever.

I had walked this route from Erez to Gaza dozens of times—never a simple journey, a reminder of the impossible reality Palestinians in Gaza live in. They are never allowed to go out. Locked in, they live in miserable conditions, in a state of endless mourning and poverty. To this day, Gaza is a giant ghetto, a 141 square mile prison, with a limited supply of air, water, and earth. A place that made the creation of the State of Israel possible, as it sheltered the Palestinian refugees whose homeland was transformed into the land of Israel. To make it dysfunctional and safer for settlers, Gaza was split into north and south, and also cut in the middle, to protect a few thousand immigrants settlers who had built their villas in the heart of the land. These settlers lived on the beach, with indoor swimming pools and Jacuzzis, while Palestinian refugees lived and died behind fences and walls, on sand, in degraded camps since 1948.

Raed, my favorite taxi driver, was there to pick me up. He was happy to see me in one piece after my kidnapping, joking that this happened when one worked with the UN instead of hiring him. We had met years earlier and worked together many times in the past. He was the son of refugees who sought shelter in Gaza in 1948, to end up living on permanent refugee status.

I was looking into the uprooting of tens of thousands of trees during the Second Intifada. Before Gaza, I had been on the vast fields in Hebron to capture the chain massacre of the old olive trees by new Israeli settlers. This is a practice alive up to this day that saw the doom of millions of olive trees. Looking at them fallen down, one after the other, one next to the other, was like looking at a British war cemetery order. In Gaza, the story was not only about vandalism but about a military strategy of clearing out lands, erasing them to improve visibility to facilitate tank operations. This policy cut massive parts of the fertile Gaza land, desperately needed by the growing number of its people.

My first stop with Raed that day was at the dead fields and orchards of Beit Hanoun, on the northeast edge of the Strip, near to Erez. The Israeli army had just cleared it. When we reached, the trees looked massacred, crushed by bulldozers. It turned out that part of the fields belonged to Raed's family, who lived not far from there. Many farmers had their livelihoods destroyed as a result, but Raed told me they remained defiant in cultivating their land. Yet, almost every time they did, the trees faced the same destiny.

We drove around all day, jumping from one reality to another. At each stop, Raed followed me wherever I photographed to make sure I was safe. The people in Gaza, as elsewhere, were suspicious of photography, and he often stood there like a bodyguard. Everyone knew Raed, making it easy to drive around and get the job done. He knew his way around Israeli settlements, knowing the dangerous spots from Israeli snipers. Over the years, Raed's connections, sharp instincts, and the ability to sense danger made him the best fixer for foreign journalists. He helped them navigate Gaza during a period when it was constantly under Israeli fire. But what sacred foreigners now were the kidnappings, which Zoi and I were the first to fall victim to, followed by many, including the abduction of the BBC journalist Alan Johnston who was held captive for four months. For many, it was no longer a political maneuver but a gamble on getting ransom money in return. It turned into a business. It wasn't till Hamas administered the Gaza Strip in its own forceful way for the kidnapping trend to fade away.

Raed drove me to Khan Yunis in the south as the road was open that day, unlike when we had tried to pass through a year earlier. Till that point, Israel had not yet evacuated the settlements. These settlements blocked the coastline and confiscated prime agricultural fields and Gaza's principal aquifers. For security reasons, this was when the army divided Gaza into three parts. At certain intersections, the army would stop traffic on Palestinian roads to give the right-of-way to every single settler who drove in and out. The wait could be hours long. Raed and I were stuck for three hours, and he warned me not to take any photographs since Israeli snipers shot anyone who got out of the car. He recalled incidents where the army even shot at any car with an open window. In the summer, the burning heat and humidity cooked passengers.

We also drove by Al-Mawasi, where fifteen hundred Palestinians lived in an enclave, with no access to clean water or electricity. For many years, the army caged in Al-Mawasi from all sides with high fences like those used in zoos. While stationed in towers, the soldiers opened and shut the zoo gate at their discretion, frequently extending closures for up to fifty days, locking people in and out. They imprisoned the people in their own community, as if under house arrest, within the larger prison of Gaza.

Since the founding of the Gush Katif settlements, Israel sealed off Al-Mawasi residents' access to their agricultural land, and they could only go exit and enter with special army permission. And their criteria were arbitrary, depending on their mood. As a result, dozens of residents of Al-Mawasi found themselves stuck in Khan Yunis, a nearby town, without food, a change of clothes, or a place to spend the night. Only ten percent of the food and supplies essential to sustain life in the enclave were allowed in. Families cooked with thin, dried-out sticks, which kids searched for in the surrounding area. People looked sick and malnourished, no longer in touch with outer reality. I saw families who slept on sand inside their shelters, in rooms without doors or windows. They lived in darkness, as only fifteen percent of the houses were connected to electrical grids.

Al-Mawasi is on the seashore, but the fence blocked access to the sea for Palestinians. The kids I spoke to saw the sea for the first time when the army demolished the settlements. In the meantime, Israeli settlers loaded with ideology and biblical signs lived on open land, enjoying exclusive stretches on the beach. Since the founding of the Gush Katif settlements in the 1970s, Al-Mawasi had become an increasingly isolated enclave, until it was almost forgotten.

I met Zainab there, a fourteen-year-old girl who shared the story of her mother who became very ill, in need of a hospital to undergo an operation. Zainab's father applied for permission for his wife to leave and applied to escort her. The Israeli authorities repeatedly denied issuing any permission. And later, approved the request on the condition that the mother traveled alone. When she returned from the hospital, she was forced to wait at the enclave gate for days and nights, in suffering, until she died. Zainab looked traumatized as she narrated how her family later carried the mother's body from the not faraway gate, straight to the grave.

When Hamas won the elections in 2006 in Palestine under successful international supervision, Israel and the United States didn't respect the newborn democracy they had long preached for. Instead, Israel declared war on Hamas and sealed off the Gaza Strip, where Hamas had the most power. A blockade was put into place, through which only an exceedingly limited number of goods and supplies were allowed into Gaza. Dov Weissglas, the senior advisor to the Israeli prime minister, was quoted in a behind-closed-doors meeting to have said at the time,

> "The idea is to put the Palestinians on a diet, but not to make them die of hunger."

Even though Weissglas disputed this, the "Diet Plan" did become an Israeli policy, an experiment, based on the "Red Lines" document. It listed the minimum number of calories needed by Gaza's nearly one and a half million inhabitants back then to avoid malnutrition or starvation. These needs were determined by the Israeli security and the Ministry of Health by assessing caloric requirements calculated by gender and age group. Before the blockade, four hundred food delivery trucks passed through border crossings daily, whereas later, an average of only sixty-seven trucks was allowed in. As drivers waited for approval to enter the Strip, many of the products spoiled in the harsh sun. The provisions in these 67 trucks contained a high proportion of sugar and processed foods, while staples like milk, fruit, and vegetables were greatly reduced. A report from the International Committee of the Red Cross found as early as in 2008 that,

> Chronic malnutrition is on a steadily rising trend, and micronutrient deficiencies are of great concern.

Gaza was the most fertile land in Palestine. But since its hermetic closure in the 1990s, the Israeli army has kept it in ruins, a dump yard, razing most of its agricultural fields, leaving Gazans dependent on petty foreign aid and at the mercy of those powers sealing its borders. Breaking the siege became a daily battle along its borders. Incessant efforts to end it failed. Many Gazans were shot while attempting to escape through the Egyptian border by climbing over the wall or by trying to break through the gates. This stirred consciousness and outrage around the world, and in response, a fleet of ships from the Mediterranean sailed towards Gaza to break the siege. The fleet docked on the shores of Gaza, defeating the will of the Israeli navy. An act powerful enough to shake the Occupation but was not powerful enough to unsettle its foundation.

Later, another Gaza Freedom Flotilla sailed with more ships, all loaded with food and louder voices demanding the end of the brutal siege. The response was to drop marines from helicopters and raid the ships. The result was a blood bath in international waters, in the middle of the sea, far away from Gaza.

Before the start of the siege, Israel had evacuated its twenty-one settlements where 8600 settlers lived. It took its troops out of Gaza, and repositioned them at the border, closely watching the Strip with binoculars and drones, whose constant buzzing, day and night, drove everyone crazy. Israel ruled over all aspects of life, and as a collective punishment, it regularly cut energy supplies, dimming the Strip for many nights. Israel put Gaza under the microscope, controlled its behavior, turned it into a lab experiment, sucking the air and life out, testing the boundaries of people's physical and mental needs to the point of collapse.

Many reports surfaced internationally, explicitly during the 2014 war on Gaza, about using the battlefield as a testing ground for new weapons. "Battle Tested" became a selling point for Israel's sophisticated arms industry to attract and impress new merchants of war. The Dahiya Doctrine, a military strategy named after a district in Beirut and developed during Israel's frequent battles with Lebanon, aimed to flatten buildings and destroy all infrastructure. In the 2014 war, the Israeli army employed The Dahiya Doctrine, bombing many Gaza neighborhoods to turn them into ground zero. Altogether, they destroyed twenty thousand homes. They were targeted in around-the-clock F16 jet bombings, tanks, and naval shelling. During the war, there was almost no damage to Israeli property. But in Gaza, other than those completely destroyed, tens of thousands of homes were partially damaged. Two hundred thousand displaced people sought shelter in UN schools. But the shelling followed them there, and on one occasion, forty-six were killed, including seventeen children.

Israeli politicians like Major General Yoav Galant aimed to "send Gaza decades into the past." Matan Vilnai, the Deputy Defense Minister, also threatened that Israel enacts a "shoah" upon Gaza, the Hebrew word for the Holocaust.

In defiance of the Occupation and the siege, Palestinians fired homemade rockets towards Israeli settlements. But the conflict was never caused because of the rockets, as perceived by most Israelis and as portrayed by international media. Rockets were a form of resistance and not the resistance itself, which aimed at ending the Occupation. If Israel destroyed the rocket launching capabilities, Palestinians would always find new ways of resistance. Israel refuses to solve the core issue, to leave Palestinians to determine their own destiny. The Palestinians were no longer fighting for the liberation of the land, but for the liberation of the self. Defeat meant surrendering to the mercy of Israelis, submission to upper power.

But no matter what policies or collective punishments Israel employed, Palestinians imagined more and more creative tools of resistance, like the underground tunnels, and later balloons set on fire to land on Israeli settlements on the other side. The tunnels burrowed fifty meters deep into the land and stretched to eight kilometers long, as far as to the Egyptian border. Their function was to bring in the necessary supplies to sustain life. The Gaza Strip fought the blockade by taking the veins of its life and economy underground. Over a thousand tunnels became the lungs through which Gaza breathed. They were built like a maze, hard to locate. But experts knew how to navigate them. Everything was flowing through them, from milk to livestock, from cars to lions. Stuck Palestinians at either side of the border, like those who wanted to study or seek medical care out of the Gaza Strip, took the risk and crossed through. Some would never return.

In Gaza, life was risky above and below the ground. These tunnels were targeted by both Israeli jets and bulldozers. Many people were buried alive. But even those who built the tunnels were aware that they would be digging their own graves. At least one hundred sixty children were among the tunnel diggers who never returned home, even if home was just a refugee camp. They were buried before their family got a chance to see them for the last time.

I was never in any of these death tunnels. The only tunnel I knew firsthand was the Sarajevo Tunnel, constructed during the Siege of Sarajevo amid the Bosnian War. Gazans, just like Bosnians, had no choice. People risked their lives under the ground so others above could survive. Or, as Dr. Sarraj explained, many Palestinians had reached the point where they had nothing to lose.

In response, Israel and Egypt plugged the tunnel shafts with sand and explosives and flooded them with sewage. And what's worse, they fired tear gas, suffocating people wherever they were. Eventually, Israel and Egypt employed sophisticated technology that sent signals below the ground to sense any emptiness, and where they found any, everything got wiped out. They severed the veins of the tunnels, leaving Gaza to continue to bleed out.

The Palestinian refugees in Gaza live a life of paradoxes—they live on the sea without seeing it. And when the army repositioned its troops at the border, they were told they lived in freedom, without feeling it. Some Israeli soldiers who listened to their consciences joined a group called Breaking The Silence, confessing to the world the brutality of Israel Defense Forces. They took a risk, knowing they could be arrested or imprisoned, mainly because the army would typically censor what they could say. In 2014, Eran Efrati, a former combat soldier, and company sergeant turned whistleblower, began sharing harrowing stories of his personal experiences and the actions of the Israeli army. As a result of speaking out, he was arrested and questioned. Later, he defied the military he served in and declared,

> In recent days I was arrested by authorities and questioned about my research regarding the use of illegal weapons in Gaza, my mail and Facebook accounts were blocked, And I received strong hints that my life is at risk and I need to be

silent and keep low. But I'm not going anywhere. They may close my communication channels again, but that does not mean I'm not here, I'll find a way to get the information out to you, and I trust you will echo it on, go down with it to the streets, and demand your representatives, your government to stop funding the slaughter in your name, to boycott Israel and to stop the bloodshed in Gaza. The whole world is watching now, history is being made.
I'm counting on you.

Mads Gilbert, a Norwegian physician, activist, and humanitarian, volunteered in Al-Shifa Hospital in Gaza during two wars. He issued a letter while operating under endless fire in 2014. He cried to the world,

> And as I write these words to you, alone, on a bed, my tears flow, the warm but useless tears of pain and grief, of anger and fear. This is not happening! And then the orchestra of the Israeli war-machine starts its gruesome symphony again. Just now: salvos of artillery from the navy boats down on the shores, the roaring F-16, the sickening drones, and the Apaches. So much made by and paid for by the US.
>
> Mr Obama – do you have a heart? I invite you – spend one night – just one night – with us in Shifa. I am convinced, 100 percent, it would change history. Nobody with a heart and power could ever walk away from a night in Shifa without being determined to end the slaughter of the Palestinian people. But the heartless and merciless have done their calculations and planned another dahyia – onslaught on Gaza. The rivers of blood will keep running the coming night. I can hear they have tuned their instruments of death. Please. Do what you can. This cannot continue.

In this War, 2,150 Palestinians were killed, most of which were civilians, 490 of them were children. As for the eleven thousand amputees and wounded, they probably had to live without painkillers. Knowing the Israelis mentality, those won't be among the items included on the Israeli-approved list of humanitarian goods. On the Israeli side, sixty-six soldiers, six civilians, and one Thai national were killed. As for property, the estimated cost for reparations in Israel stood at $11 million, while in Gaza, billions of dollars.

Back to Raed. At the end of that long day, with a persistent headache, Raed drove me back to Erez Crossing. But destiny had it that I returned to Jerusalem this time to embrace Francesca. But this was not what Raed returned to one day. Three months later, he would appear in a documentary by the same filmmakers he drove around to sort all their worries out. They called it The Gaza Fixer. While he was on duty with the filmmakers, they rushed to see a shell that fell in Bet Hanoun. It was one of those long innocent shells fired at the empty fields of Bet Hanoun. One of them hit the center of Raed's family house, injuring fifty-six members and killing eighteen, Including five children.

This book is not about death, yet living in Palestine is. In 2002, as part of a series of raids on cities to crush the Palestinian resistance, Israeli tanks roared into Bethlehem. Around two hundred civilians, including sixty priests, monks, and nuns, and about fifty Palestinian militants sought refuge in the Nativity Church, locking themselves inside the convent. Israel wanted the militants dead or exiled. In pursuit of this objective, it placed the church and all of Bethlehem under siege for thirty-nine days. Samir Salman, a mentally disabled Palestinian man, had been the church's bell-ringer for three decades. At dawn, on the second day of the standoff, he made the short walk from his home to the bell tower to wake up Bethlehem. After being shot by a sniper, he was left to bleed to death for hours in Manger Square.

The army brought in a special crane and erected it in the square for better sniper vantage points that targeted and killed eight Palestinians inside the church compound. Some of the priests and civilians released as part of the negotiations shared horrific accounts of how the utilities had been cut off and how food and water ran out over the weeks. Starvation forced some people to strip the leaves from the lemon tree in the church's courtyard and make soup with water they found in a well. They called for removing the dead bodies of men killed earlier in the siege, which had started to decompose.

For the entire thirty-nine days, an around-the-clock curfew was imposed on Bethlehem, eased only a few hours every five days on average. Food was so scarce that when the army lifted the curfew, masses raced to the few open stores to find their shelves empty. Emergency food aid from international relief organizations was dispatched to feed hungry families.

The siege ended after international pressure, but only on the condition of a lifetime of exile for thirty-nine of the alleged Palestinian militants. Israel gave them two choices: The Gaza Strip or a foreign country. The majority chose exile in besieged Gaza. After dropping their weapons under the gaze of Israeli snipers, they stepped into the light of Manger Square, where CIA agents, Britain's ambassador to Israel, along with the Royal Military Police, watched and escorted them to their exile. They left without being permitted to see their families for a final farewell.

On the first day after the siege, when the terrible situation endured by Palestinians had finally ended, I rushed to Bethlehem on assignment for the UN's Focus magazine. I photographed priests and volunteers mopping up bloodstains in the church and the lemon tree that had been stripped to its veins.

Stepping out of the church to see Bethlehem's Old City, I passed by many crushed cars by tanks. Some were even piled. In one side street, I heard a wailing voice jumping out to me from around the corner. As I turned, I saw a man with a white beard, but had all black hair, stepping in and out of a small house door, broken, almost in tears. He was crying to anyone passing by to listen to his story. When he stopped me, I asked him what the story was, following him straight into a small, cluttered living room, without any windows. The locked air still carried the smell of blood, stains of which were scattered everywhere. The walls were perforated, the television screen had a hole, and on top of it laid a piece from a splintered skull. Sami lived through thirty-five hours of horror during the siege. He pointed to the rocking chair, and those were his words,

> My mother called us down to this place. She began to comfort my children, trying to keep their spirits up. A few hours later, about 10:30, we heard loud voices in the street and the sound of cars being crushed, mine and my cousin's. Then soldiers kicked at the door. When it didn't open, they fired through the metal shutters. There was no warning. A bullet smashed through the television and hit my mother sitting in the chair. Another struck my brother, who was on the couch. Six children and their mothers were jammed together in the bathroom. They could hear everything, but we dared not let them come out. All I could do was hold my mother's hand.

And Sami held his mother's hand, on a still chair, next to her dead son soaked in blood on the couch, locked in a room, a morgue, with all his family. His wife and her mother, his sister and his dead brother's wife, along with six children hiding in a tiny bathroom, were all trapped without electricity, and in fear of the darkness, he explained how the candle shadows added more horror to the children.

Helicopters had circled over the house that day and damaged an upstairs room, obliging them to seek shelter in this cave room. Sami called hospitals, the Red Cross, and even consulates, pleading for any help. But because of the curfew and Bethlehem a closed military zone, it was impossible. And when none of them was able to do anything, he reached out to the Israeli army. On the phone to find who was in command to carry out the two bodies, one commander finally gave him an answer,

Over my dead body.

At the end of this nightmare, Sami's beard had turned overnight from black to white.

My body had always reacted to restrictions of movement like they were pathogens, and the older I became, the more I sank into the locked-in-syndrome I had felt as a child. I was in the middle of an ocean, in deep water, suffocating, but unable to die. I couldn't push myself to the surface to breathe fresh air; my limbs were heavy, almost paralyzed. A stone pushed down into my chest, but the baby Francesca was carrying, our baby, left me no choice but to pull myself out of my abyss. This was when I boarded the rickety plane and went skydiving in Haifa to take a leap of faith. If not for me, then for my daughter.

8

When we reached the old town of Medina in Marrakech, after a long road trip from Bordeaux, Cécile was fascinated by the countless stray cats on every street corner, like in the Old City of Jerusalem. She asked me to buy over twenty cans of sardines so she could feed each cat as we strolled through the alleyways. She was ten back then and worried about Tabalu, our diva cat, which we checked in to a cat hotel in Berlin. When we came back to pick him up, the caretaker told us he had fallen in love with another cat, sleeping together all the time. It was Tabalu's first and last love so far. It took him time to recover from Lilly, which he never saw again.

Cécile loved seeing kitten photos in our family albums from the years before she was born. She wanted to know their stories, particularly curious about a kitten named Baby, who came into our lives a year after Francesca and I got married. On a rainy and thundery night, I was on my way back home when I saw six kittens thrown out onto the wet steps of the house next door to ours. They must have been discarded right after birth, as their umbilical cords were still attached, and their fragile bodies were not even wiped clean by their mother. Some were still moving in the puddles they lay in. Panicked, I looked around but couldn't find their mother, which I would find out later when I interrogated the neighborhood that she was killed as she gave birth, and the boy who had done it, had by maybe cosmic justice his finger cut off his hand that same week. I picked them up, one by one, and placed them on a piece of cardboard I found nearby.

I hastened to the house, alerting Francesca. They were all still alive. She started cleaning their bodies gently while I prepared a hot water bottle, wrapped in a towel, to warm them up. We didn't know what to do next. We freaked out. I called every animal organization in the phone book, and somehow, I was referred to Rachel, an Israeli cat expert who lived in the Jewish Quarter of the Old City. I called her, and she told me to calm down and come see her right away. With the rain still pouring, I flashed over to the Jewish Quarter. In her living room, she gave me tiny nesting bottles and kitten formula. She showed me how to feed the kittens and wipe their bottoms afterward using cotton soaked in warm water to stimulate urination. She said they had a slim chance of surviving because they had never drunk their mother's milk, rich in antibodies. Flashing back home, Francesca and I took turns feeding and cleaning them. Yet over the next week, we watched five of them gradually get sick and die. One by one, we buried them under the lemon tree.

In the end, only one kitten remained. Baby, a white kitten with a black head, lived to be two weeks old, against all odds. She was getting stronger. When I gave her a bottle, she would wrap her tiny pink paws around its nipple, suck the milk out quickly and fall asleep on either Francesca's chest or mine.

After being in the house for seventeen days with Baby, we took our first break and strolled to the cinematheque down the road from Jaffa Gate. When we came back, she was starving, meowing, and moving around anxiously in her box. I prepared a bottle and fed her. Baby gulped the milk quickly, and it came out of her nose. She was writhing around, choking. I put her in my palm and swung her upside down to help her spit-up. After she threw up, she was completely still. Worried, I put my ear on her tiny chest to see if she was still breathing. She was, but we rushed her to the vet anyway. After the examination, the doctor explained that milk had filled her lungs, cut off the oxygen to her brain, and permanently paralyzed her. He gave her the injection of death. We wrapped Baby up and returned her to her box. Francesca and I cried all the way home until we buried her next to her brothers and sisters. For a long time afterward, we felt guilty for going out that night.

For many years, I left Francesca hanging in the air. My rejection of marriage and having kids was engraved on biblical stone—

my faith was in multiple relationships. Maybe it had to do with my depression, or not wanting to be responsible for someone else's life. But kids loved being around Francesca. She had a way of calming them, and leaving them to wander in their own imagination, something she enjoyed about her work as a schoolteacher. I had never liked kids, or more so boys. I already heard too many voices in my mind, and kids disturbed my search for silence

But I didn't want to be stuck, to live in a loop and defend the same thoughts, again and again. It was only when Francesca turned thirty and knowing how much she wanted to have her own baby that I felt I couldn't deprive her any longer. When she told me she was pregnant, I jokingly asked her if it was mine. Now, looking back, she should have slapped me. But this was my life with Francesca—we were open with each other, and she always knew how to live with my insanity.

Upon Cécile's first breath, I instantly felt responsible for her. Even though I had my issues with birth and the brutal procedure of cutting the umbilical cord, I couldn't miss this unique moment in life. Afraid to look with my bare eyes, I hid behind the curtain with my camera glued to my face. I watched her through the lens as she emerged. She was calm and clean. When she was almost out, she tilted her head and looked at me. I lowered my camera and looked back at her. I fell in love.

Cécile never cried. I kept thinking about the fact that we shared the same DNA. Yet, DNA wasn't enough to establish a father-daughter relationship. We got worried when Cécile couldn't breastfeed for nearly two days after birth. But after she found her way, she didn't stop till almost four years later. Francesca and Cécile were very attached and developed their own secret language—Swiss German. I wasn't able to speak with Cécile in Arabic. Till the age of three, she only deciphered her mother's tongue. Francesca and I spoke our own version of English together, creating our own verbs and syntax. I always felt insecure about my English and didn't want to pass on an incorrect language to Cécile. My tongue was tied every time I wanted to express something to her. And when I tried in Arabic, the words that came out were rehearsed, stripped of emotion. The three of us lived under the same roof, yet we spoke and understood different languages. I felt like a foreigner at home, a stranger in my family, constantly asking,

What are you talking about?

Francesca and Cécile were not in a Swiss alliance, but we had found ourselves in an unfortunate, unexpected situation. The consequences of my not speaking Arabic with Cécile grew increasingly problematic every year, as Francesca was regularly called in to translate for us. A frustrating start for our relationship. Cécile wanted to learn Arabic, but I couldn't deliver the words to make up a sentence or convey a feeling. I felt I was an actor on stage. My bad acting did not mirror my true feelings for Cécile. When she asked me how much I loved her, I told Francesca,

Tell her:
Can you imagine the distance between here and the stars?

She looked at Mummy and said,

No.

I looked at Cécile and said,

This is how much I love you!
You can't even imagine.

The older she got, the more difficult it was for me to play with her in parks or read her bedtime stories. I rarely changed her diapers, gave her a bath, or helped her choose a dress to wear. I couldn't figure out why she cried around me until Francesca explained it to me later on. I often regretted not doing these things even though, somehow, I could have.

Cécile and I drifted apart, aware of our alienation. She became foreign to me. My presence was absent, even when the two of us were present in the same room. Francesca thought I had personal issues warming up to my daughter. I tried to correct the mistake of not speaking to her in Arabic, but I always felt it was too late, and this frustrated me. I never had any patience. I wanted change to happen right now.

When Cécile turned two, we introduced her to the YMCA, one of the few kindergartens in Jerusalem where instruction was given in Arabic and Hebrew. Cécile picked up some Arabic words, but she continued to communicate in Swiss German. It was strange to hear her shalom me once.

When we left Jerusalem for London, Cécile was almost three and a half. It was painful for her to leave her home. When the time had come to leave, she waved goodbye to almost everything,

goodbye chair,
goodbye door,
goodbye wall,
goodbye window . . .

This heartbreaking scene only stopped after Francesca picked her up and carried her in her arms, out of the house, as I closed the door. It was hard for me to watch Cécile leave. Later, she would develop a connection to Jerusalem that was so strong that we regularly returned to visit family. For years she blamed us for uprooting her, telling us this in her own way. When she was asked where she came from, she would answer,

I come from Jerusalem.

The more I distanced myself from Jerusalem, the more our city of birth found a place in Cécile's heart. It took time for her to adjust to a new life in London. She longed for return. But there was no return.

We lived in an international postgraduate house, Goodenough College. The flat that was allocated to us was small. We had no choice. Cécile's room was hardly double the size of her bed, branching out from a corridor, a punishment compared to the space in Jerusalem. The first few months were difficult for all of us, along with Cécile, who only spoke Swiss German, feeling alienated from the rest of the kids living there. She could understand English, but she never spoke it. This made communicating with her difficult.

She felt out of place. Once, she put on Francesca's shoes and climbed onto the living room windowsill to look through the barred window. The London sky was gray, making the facing residential building duller than normal. I was sitting at my desk next to the window and watched her fall into her thoughts. Cécile's eyes seemed to surrender to a landscape she saw in her mind—one I had already surrendered to. Cécile looked into my eyes, and she said,

Papa bring mi hei,zrüg i mis Land. Jerusalem.
Papa, take me back home to my country. Jerusalem.

II knew what she meant. She wanted to be at home. This was when we spoke a language of our own—the language of Exile. At last, we felt each other. That unique moment of communication animated me to make a gift for Cécile, hoping she would treasure it one day. I snuck into her room, looked through her drawers and cupboards, and chose fourteen blouses, skirts, and trousers. I picked clothes with patterns, colors, and surfaces with holes or stains on them. I cut a piece of fabric from each with scissors and photographed the squares from both sides, from the outside and the inside. I wanted to tell her that no matter what happened, she and I would always be connected, just like the two sides of a piece of cloth—there is always the other side—I will always be her father.

Using two colored threads, I stitched the cut pieces of her clothes and the photos I made of them onto the pages of a book I handmade for her. The opposite sides faced each other, creating a direct dialogue with the Other hidden in each of us.

Cécile was becoming real to me. I asked her to write her full name, Cécile Elise Sabella, and later had it embossed in gold lettering on the front cover. Inside, the cloth photos seemed as real, as tactile, as the cut physical cloth I placed on the cover. But they were images, in search of their own reality.

For the middle part of the book, I asked Cécile to make a drawing. She drew me as tall as her, dressed in a short skirt, with long black hair, smiling, playing with her in a garden, with our home behind us. My stitches penetrated the blue sky of her world, like lost flying birds, hovering above scattered flowers. I was finally telling her a story, my story, and as difficult as it was, it allowed us to join hands and escape to our world. On the first page of the book, I wrote a statement in pencil and then half-erased it, hoping that one day we will rewrite it together.

After almost three months of living in London, I was taking care of Cécile one evening while Francesca worked late. Cécile and I were sitting on a couch across from each other in our living room. I told her in English that we were going to have dinner with friends at the student house on the other side of the garden. What happened next stirred me. For the first time, Cécile replied back in English with a heavy British accent,

> Noh. I don wantoo.
> I don feeel laiyket.
> Thaayr gaarbich.

Those were Cécile's'first English words, and I had no idea where they came from. She kept speaking, and we started having a long dialogue together. I had never felt more understood by her, and I paid attention to every word she was saying. From that day onward, English became the main spoken language in our house. God bless the Queen!

Before our first Christmas in London, Cécile brought home a bunch of her drawings from her kindergarten walls. She showed them to us but hid one from me behind her back. That night, after I tucked Cécile in, Francesca told me that she was hiding a drawing of an Israeli flag. Her teacher had instructed the class to draw the flags of their home countries. Cécile told Francesca,

> Don't show this to Papa.
> I know this flag makes him sad.

In Jerusalem, the Israeli flag was unavoidable, flying high as an intentional statement to prove authority, principally when settlers Occupied a house in an Arab neighborhood. Ironically, the Palestinian flag was effectively illegal, even after Israel instated and recognized the Palestinian Authority. I never saw meaning in flags, nor did I submit to their empty symbolism, something I was hoping to pass on to my daughter. She is on her own journey.

One summer, Cécile came with me to Jerusalem. I was working on my thesis for my second master's degree at Sotheby's Institute of Art, in the heart of London, which involved on the ground research in Palestine. Given that we would stay for over five weeks, we chose to rent a house instead of staying with family. After contacting friends, Francesca found a flat for rent by an Israeli family. They were looking for someone to water the garden and take care of the two dogs.

The house was in Ein Karem, one of the few Palestinian villages that remained intact after the 1948 War. Before and after the establishment of Israel, Jewish forces depopulated more than five hundred Palestinian villages, erasing many of them off the map and settling in many others. Ein Karem was one of those in which the Jewish immigrants quickly settled in after the Palestinians started evacuating the women and children in the village, fearing they would suffer a destiny similar to that of Deir Yassin, a neighboring town, where the Jewish Irgun and Lehi underground militia massacred over one hundred Palestinians on April 9, 1948. Survivors and historical records of the Deir Yassin massacre revealed accounts of pregnant women cut open with swords, of rape, mutilation, and bodies thrown into wells. Later that day, the militia held a victory parade where Palestinian residents were loaded onto trucks and paraded through the streets of Jerusalem, after which they were all murdered in a stone quarry. A massacre etched in the mind of every Palestinian ever since.

Not one Palestinian family was able to return to Ein Karem. The residents must have felt they had no choice but to flee after hearing of the horror in Deir Yassin. All their homes were quickly settled with new immigrants. And over the years, the village became a hub for Israeli artists and artisans.

We lived in a house on a cliff, overlooking a valley covered with trees that lined its sides till it centered the sun on the horizon. The family we subleased from was renting the Arab house from an Israeli settler, who lived in the second part of the house, which had its private doorway. Only a fence separated our gardens. He could hear my conversations. One day, while Cécile was resting on the hammock to watch the clouds with the dogs, I was watering the plants and teaching her some words in Arabic. Hearing them caught the landlord by surprise, and when I was done talking, he came over, putting his hands on the fence, and asked me in Hebrew where I came from. I answered,

> *Ani bah mipo.*
> *I come from here.*

He asked,

> Where exactly is here?

I said,

> *From Bab Huta.*
> *From the Old City of Jerusalem.*

Living in the Arab house was a victory, but an unsettling one. There was no information, or record, of who had lived in the house before 1948. The people who live there today had no clue and didn't seem to care. Its memory was erased. Instead, photos of Jewish grandparents, parents, and children are now hanging on its original walls.

After the worrying failure of the Second Intifada, uncertainty and stagnation set in. While Israelis fell more and more into their paranoia rooted in fear, justifying their actions in the name of personal security, Palestinians plunged into a deeper psychological defeat, into a state of numbness towards life under Israeli Occupation. Palestinians reached a point where they could no longer imagine that they could live in freedom. The colonization on Palestinian land was clear, but what was hidden was the colonization of the imagination.

The more I lived under the Occupation, the more its effects sickened me. It made me question myself, throwing me into sudden acts to survive. For many years, I ended up performing in scenes I didn't choose. Good actors lived a less humiliating life. Driving through checkpoints was an act—only those who acted like Israelis passed without being stopped. Only Israelis had the balls to pass through military checkpoints without slowing down. I did the same. I was rarely stopped. Entering Israeli malls without "looking Arab" was an act. If caught, you would be stopped, taken aside, searched, and have your ID number registered. Getting on an Israeli bus was an act. If noticed, you might risk getting spit at and harassed. If you complained, you would get arrested just for being Arab.

I didn't want Cécile to have to act to live in her own city. In many ways, we shielded her by leaving Jerusalem. This might have been an early start in Cécile's realization of the meaning of belonging and the suffering from being uprooted. The price for Cécile feeling like a global citizen today was having to leave behind her birthplace.

Only a few houses remained in Deir Yassin after that fateful day in 1948, as most of them were flattened by dynamite during the attack. The few remaining village buildings became part of the Kfar Shaul Health Center, an Israeli public psychiatric hospital. I often wondered what kind of treatment and recovery was possible there.

Cécile's presence in my life motivated me to consciously return to my childhood to confront it. I didn't take her with me. There was no playground in my imagination for her to play in. Cécile suffered from my depressions. They scared her. Some nights, when she and Francesca would come home, they would find me sitting alone in the dark, dead frozen, unable to speak. Not even saying hello. I was locked-in again. I didn't know what was wrong with me. Or why I couldn't breathe. Each episode would last longer than the preceding one. Later on, when I could stand on my feet again, I realized I had won another battle. Yet, there was still a war in me, and I knew this war would never end. I lived examining side effects rather than unearthing the root cause.

But who really wants to face his own demons?

7

Life with Francesca passed in the blink of an eye, making me wonder if this was a good or a bad sign. But when we looked back, The Second Intifada had stolen our lives, and the Occupation was unsettling me. Being hot-tempered, my body was always on alert, ready for a fight. Maybe that's why I had been asked several times if I had ever thrown stones at soldiers. I never had, not during the First or the Second Intifada. Instead, I collected and carried the stones with me for many years until they became heavy loads on my back and chest.

One stormy night, Francesca and I drove to Mount Scopus to view the lightning blasts hitting Jerusalem. The vantage point looked over the Jordan Valley desert on one side and Jerusalem's Old City on the other. As we got off the car in the pouring rain, our feet got soaked in mud. While battling strong winds, we watched the sky above explode with sparks and thunder—an open-air trance party, gripping us with light and sound. We danced and jumped, closed our eyes, covered our ears, sometimes together, till at one point a flash almost hit us.

In many ways, this was the nature of my life with Francesca: high voltage, yet serene, navigating the extremes of life. Worrying her, she asked me sometimes.

How long will the universe keep us together?

I never imagined a life without Francesca. I feared our separation, believing it would be the mistake of my life. I saw us as the two sides of a magnet where one cannot exist without the other in the same circle of life. We had welded our unity in the Old City, behind its closed gates, forming an unbreakable bond, yet lenient enough for any change.

Ten years after Francesca and me wore the same rings, in the spring of 2007, just before leaving to study in London, I participated in

Neighbours in Dialogue, an international art exhibition in Istanbul, on a region known for non-dialogue since the dawn of time. I was working on *Mentalopia*, combining the words mental and utopia, where I felt I was living. *Mentalopia* explored cultural differences, dug into identity, uncovered national pride, and questioned our inner borders. I had asked the ten participating artists to bring postal stamps from their respective homelands. I then photographed each artist in a sideway face position, their heads detached from their bodies, looking to the west. After scanning the tiny stamps to become life-size prints later, I merged onto their surfaces the portrait of each individual artist, occupying the space not of their countries but those of others. The stamp's tiny value revealed clashing connotations like the low price we suddenly had on our heads when representing others. When I hung *Mentalopia* at the museum on hooks suspended on metal chains, it looked like the artists were confused residing in a foreign space, appearing lost.

It was there where I met Assia, at a period when I felt my body was chained, lost in its space, disoriented, floating between realities. Even though Assia was not from any Arab country and didn't speak Arabic, she woke up in me a desire, a longing to be with someone whose roots were from my land and whose language was my mother's. For me, it had all ended with Grace on the Nativity Square. I had never kissed a Palestinian girl or even hugged one. Grace was the only and last one I dared to tell I love you, and it was for our last departing words. I felt it was insane to live a life where you were born and might die there and never have the chance to be with your own people. Francesca appeared in my reality not long after my tragedy with Grace, and from that point onward, English dominated my life more, which would later tie my tongue every time I tried to speak with my daughter Cécile.

This was my personal battle, my dilemma. It added to my alienation, and I increasingly became distant from my body. I was realizing that growing up under the paralyzing physical Occupation and committing to Francesca at a very young age made my liberation struggle, both mental and physical. The realities got intertwined, and opening up to Francesca to speak about life was the only way forward.

I sat down with Francesca and told her what was on my mind and how my body felt bruised. Francesca was compassionate but felt adrift, kept listening, grappling with her feelings, as I was with mine. We were on the same page, yet each one of us reacted to its words differently. We stood at a crossroads, battling for the love we had shared for many years, but our core was strong. Breaking up was never an option or even possible. We could overcome any challenge, and with Cécile in our lives, it was natural to stay together. Each of us was on a unique journey, and living together didn't mean that we shared the same fate. Our commitment to each other was not engraved on biblical stone, but drawn by the power of light. Papers never defined one's identity or civil status. For me, both require no authorization. I accept the formality on paper, but waiting for marriage papers to feel like one, or divorce papers to feel liberated, is a waste of time.

In many ways, Palestinians did wait for signed negotiations in ink to feel liberated and to define their freedom. With its many signatures, the Oslo I Accord generated segregation in Palestine never seen before, imprisoning and fragmenting the Palestinian society. Instead of bringing peace, it brought misery. Palestinians failed to liberate Palestine with armed force, peace talks, or even by throwing stones, the weapon of choice during the First Intifada. The Palestinian struggle shifted from liberating the land to freeing the self, triggering Palestinians to feel they had nothing to lose. When their voices were repeatedly dismissed, they wore suicide vests, blew themselves up in Israeli cafés and restaurants, on random streets and bus stops. But no matter what Palestinians did to achieve independence, Israel kept the upper hand, controlled life, always blaming the other side, still finding more ways to tighten the ropes on the Palestinians in the tandem parachute jumps.

Israelis came up with endless excuses to justify the Occupation. Consecutive governments, right or left, occupied more land, built higher walls, imprisoned and tortured people, including children, and stripped Palestinians down to their underwear. Since 1948, Israel has spoken and exercised the language of war while convincing the world it was fighting for peace. Israel kept dealing with the side effects of the problem rather than ending what triggered it. The only solution was to go back to the core, to the essence of the conflict. The Occupation.

During my last year in Jerusalem, I traveled to Ireland for an art residency. I booked one seat for my flight but wasn't alone—the heavy stones I had carried on my back traveled with me. On the plane, I read Edward Said's essay: The Entire World as a Foreign Land. Before completing it, I closed the book, looked out of the window, and recalled how I felt Jerusalem was in exile, a foreign land, and how I became a stranger at home. My city of birth disappeared, became a reflection, lost in its image, entrapping me in my own space, in no space. In the air, I lost my ground and point of origin. I could no longer distinguish one land from another. While seeing my faint shadow in the window, I looked at the world and wanted it to change, only failing to realize that what needed to change was my perception of it. The world looked harsh, in despair. I was scared, and no matter where I looked, I found no escape, no exit. I was high up on a tightrope, on the edge of physical and mental collapse. I feared the harsh terrain below and dreaded standing on the land of my exile.

During the residency, I searched for images to convey my detrimental state of mind. I ended up checking out a hospice for the elderly, who were breathing out their last days on earth. I walked through its halls, passing room after another, observing how these people suffered, sobbed, listening to their endless moans of pain, living their last hours or days. But they didn't seem tranquil about imminent death. Being there, in that moment, I questioned the purpose of life. Since then, the scent of old age and death has stayed with me. I spent three days at the hospice, flattened by the suffering of the last occupants, listening to the few who still were able to speak in low, quivering voices, to tell me their story.

I looked at their hands and fingers. Many suffered from diseases that deformed their bones, paralyzing them into wheelchairs, and later onto deathbeds. Many were impaired from acute arthritis. Their fingers were dislocated, bent, as if broken. One elderly woman wore a thick gold wedding ring buried deep into her swollen finger, cutting through her skin. The only way to remove it would be by immediate surgery. An elderly man had all his fingers on both hands dislocated into a permanently locked fist position. I photographed their hands as if dismembered from their bodies, becoming suspended monuments and statutes. Their surfaces embodied an exilic landscape. Many hands had scars, violet and red clots, as if tattooed by blood under their skin. Their fragmented, decaying bodies echoed my quarrel with my life. The shape and surface of their hands mirrored the landscape of my exile, like rugged maps without center points, isolated, in search of a lost home. Regardless of where these elderly people came from, the Palestinian experience was woven, etched into their skin. Every mark and wrinkle told its own story. The scars exposed traces of personal history that went beyond their surface, and told my own story.

I photographed these aging hands, isolated against a black background. Later, the images were set in motion and projected on one wall of a darkened room so that the images seemed to float in space. On the last day of the residency, the other artists and I were asked to reflect on our participation. We sat in a circle and listened to each other's thoughts, as if in group therapy. When my turn came, I lost my voice for the first time in my life and couldn't stop tears from falling. For once, I felt my trauma rather than suppressing it. Cork and Assia were a wake-up call.

In the art projects that followed, I continued searching for unique forms to echo my states of mind. When I saw Cécile at the barred window in London, she spirited me to create photo collages that translated my disorientation. The resulting structure appeared complete, gave the illusion of wholeness, but its essence was assembled from hundreds of fragments, from a bruised self pieced together, day after day. While working on these collages, I listened to the same songs on loop until the sound dissolved into silence, enabling me to access my inner consciousness to just be.

I photographed windows from the inside and the outside to reflect how I perceived life. I was neither here nor there, not in Jerusalem, nor in London. London injected me with an extra dose of alienation, more potent than those I received in Jerusalem, throwing me out of place. I was going through a process of self-construction or more like self-destruction. Hermits sought the desert, not to find identity but to lose it. I decided to lose mine, in search of a new one, true only to me. But I became a stranger to myself, lost in my mental wilderness, my mentalopia. I felt I had no one to talk to. But when I lived in London, my friendship with Hani Zurob grew, an artist born in Gaza who lived in Paris. He switched seats with Michos on my journey into the unknown.

Hani and I communicated frequently. We spoke like cellmates, trapped, counting our days. We shared all the details of our exile, wondering about the other's thoughts and fears. We seldom spoke about the distant past. Instead, we focused on our contest with the self, on art, on breaking down inner walls. We looked for ways to crush them and melt them down. In search of our real freedom, we took an oath like two soldiers in the trenches, to never leave the other behind.

I met Hani days after his release from prison, in 2002, during the art competition Kamal Boullata was judging in Palestine. Because of a broken hand, he couldn't deliver the art set he had intended to show. Three months before the submission deadline, the Israeli army had invaded his studio, wrecked it, detained him, and put him in jail without charge for two months. Even though Hani was not affiliated with any political organizations, they accused him of belonging to Palestinian terrorist groups, but Shin Bet, the Israeli Intelligence, found nothing. During his interrogation, he was asked to collaborate with the Shin Bet, to provide them with information on the movement of Palestinian artists and on what projects they were working on. Israel has a history of being vigilant in keeping an eye on artists. In 1980, it passed a law forbidding the depiction of the Palestinian flag in all contexts, prohibiting artists from using its colors together in the same painting. Failure to comply led to imprisonment. The law was reversed only in 1993, upon the signing of the Oslo I Accord. Describing the Israeli clampdown on the Palestinian art scene, one artist was quoted as saying,

> You couldn't paint a poppy, for example, or a watermelon: they were the wrong colors. Often it was up to the artistic judgment of the particular officer in charge.

Hani refused to become a spy or a collaborator—the term Israelis used to soften its meaning. Failing to recruit him, or find anything incriminating, the Shin Bet approved his release. That morning, Hani's assigned interrogator brought him in handcuffs to a room and put a pencil and white paper between his hands, wanting a sketch as a souvenir to hang above his chair. When he asked what hand he drew with, Hani got suspicious and pointed to the wrong one. To test him, Hani drew with handcuffs a half-completed figure of a person, as if it was missing its other side. When he was done in a few seconds, the interrogator asked for the artist's signature. When Hani blatantly declined, the enraged interrogator grabbed his M16 machine gun and slammed its butt down on his arm, breaking his hand and wrist.

Hani's broken hand came from a history of brutality exercised and executed by Israeli soldiers to counter the First Intifada in 1987. They had orders from Yitzhak Rabin, the former Prime Minister of Israel and Minister of Defense back then, to break the arms and legs of Palestinians. In one incident in 1988, four Israeli soldiers were secretly caught on camera as they beat two Palestinian teens in an isolated field, one with a black sac on his face. After a round of restless kicking, one soldier picks up a sharp stone from the field and hammers it on the back of one of the teens, until he slumps over and faints into the lap of the second, who was his cousin. Then, the same soldier stretches the cousin's arm backward so that another soldier breaks its elbow with another stone. We see them taking a go at their bones, breaking them one after the other. All this takes place in just one minute of the original thirty-minute recording.

CBS recorded this horrific scene and became a tragic international story revealing Israeli brutality. It was so shocking that it set in motion many people around the world to demand freedom for Palestine. The memory of the incident is imprinted in the minds of both Palestinians and Israelis. A decade later, an Israeli TV station tracked down one of the Israeli soldiers, and he said that if he ever saw those Palestinians, he would break their bones again. On the same show, Jawda, one of the beaten teens, said he was open to forgiving them if this helped bring reconciliation.

Hani never saw himself as a victim. He found power in art, using his own body for reference. He painted the traces of his life, and the impressions that emerged on his canvas portrayed distorted figures, crippled, with dislocated joints and swollen limbs. The bodies were dismembered and reassembled, giving birth to alien form. But when his son Qoudsi was born, we encountered drawings of a boy—who looked like Qoudsi but could have stood for his father—trapped in his own space, waiting for an escape.

In their first year in Paris, Hani and Sabreen had Qoudsi. And it was not out of choice to live in Paris, even though it sounds like a treat. The sudden transition they had both endured for many years started in 2006 when Hani was granted a one-year residency at the Cité Internationale des Arts in Paris. He had previously rejected it twice, in 2004 and in 2005, because of impossible travel restrictions Israel imposed on Palestinians from Gaza in particular. All Palestinians holding a Gaza identity card were not allowed to change their Gaza residence registration when they had moved to live in the West Bank. Hani had lived in the West Bank from 1994 to 2006, possibly long enough to become a citizen in many foreign lands, but not in his own country. During this period, Hani avoided traveling abroad as Israel would allow him to leave, but he would have been deported to Gaza on the spot upon his return. He couldn't even travel to Jerusalem or visit his family in Gaza.

Hani moved to Nablus in the West Bank at eighteen to study art, and when he completed his studies, he moved to Ramallah, the commercial capital of Palestine. There, he met Sabreen, a native Jerusalemite, and because he was not able to travel to Jerusalem, their wedding plans were put on hold for years. In the end, Sabreen's father abandoned the cultural requirement stipulating that Hani must ask for his daughter's hand in the family's Jerusalem residence and blessed their marriage. In the 2008 documentary film Meet Me Out of The Siege, we see Hani on his wedding day and watch as he nervously smokes cigarettes while waiting at the hectic Kalandia checkpoint for his bride. In the end, we see her dressed in white, walking in alarm, passing by Israeli soldiers, until Hani takes her into his arms.

A year after they got married, Israel eased restrictions on Gazans living in the West Bank and allowed them to return to their updated place of residence after traveling. This was Hani's chance to accept the invitation to the artist residency, and he flew to Paris, not knowing that in a few weeks, he would find himself in a sudden exile. The Palestinian Authority was planning democratic elections under international supervision. Israel, the United States, and the European Union had agreed to allow Hamas to take part in the race. But when Hamas won with a clear majority, all the supervising parties, including Israel, rejected the results. They wanted the Fatah movement to succeed, Israel's protégé. In fact, the outcome could have been a good opportunity for Israel to reach an agreement with Hamas, which was transforming itself from a military into a political movement, a sign of their tacit willingness towards a lasting political settlement.

Fatah accepted the fallout and passed governance on to Hamas, which took office a few weeks later. In reaction, the foreign powers disapproved and suspended their aid to Palestine, effectively suffocating the economy and punishing a whole nation for exercising the democracy they had long preached for. Israel neither allowed room nor lent support for the new government to function and even jailed eight of its ministers, dozens of parliament members, and many others. Within a year and a half, and operating under pressure, Hamas and Fatah found themselves in a situation that devolved into the expected civil war. Israel's divide-and-conquer strategy worked, and Palestinians had once again fallen into the trap.

Many don't know that Israel had supported Hamas back in the 1980s, or as it was previously known as *Mujama al-Islamiya*, by officially recognizing the group as a charity. This meant the group could legally amass donations to help root itself in society by constructing schools, universities, hospitals, and other social needs. Israel's strategy was to support a rival group to decrease Arafat and Fatah's influence in the West Bank, Gaza, and even Jerusalem. Yet, to Arafat's credit, whenever tensions escalated between the two movements, he could enforce stability till his death in 2004.

As a consequence of the fallout from the election, Israel canceled Gazans' requests to change their domicile. After Hani had traveled to Paris, the Israeli embassy notified him that he would not return home to Palestine. He found himself stranded somewhere else, on hold, lost in a foreign land.

Hani's mother is a refugee from Ramleh whose family was evicted in 1948 and sheltered in Gaza, losing their home to Israeli settlers. Her father split up the children to go on two separate boats, one with the father, and one with the mother, so that at least half the family would survive. Hani grew up in Rafah, near the coast in the south of Gaza, but he hardly ever saw the sea in his life when he lived there because the sea was surrounded by the Gush Katif Israeli settlement block.

When Hani turned thirty, he landed in Paris. From the airport, it took him a while to find public transport to the city center. Never having had the chance to travel, he found it hard to navigate a foreign transportation system. In the center, he got lost for hours, underground, in the never-ending Châtelet-Les Halles station, unable to find any exit. The passages led him from one platform to another, with trains' screeching sound echoing one after another. When he stopped anyone from the crowd, they thought he was joking and continued their way. Frustrated, he turned to a homeless man to help him find his way out. The homeless pointed to Hani to simply follow the *Sortie* sign—the French word for *Exit*.

Hani later transformed this disorientation into a series of artworks carrying the same name. Trapped, Hani had to start the arduous task of assimilating into a new reality. It would take him a few years to learn to speak the language of exile. Sabreen did not want to leave Jerusalem, but joined him six months later. She maintained her hope that the situation would change and that they could return. She traveled back home twice a year, staying for six weeks each time, to prevent the Israeli Ministry of Interior from revoking her Jerusalem ID. But when she got pregnant, Hani and Sabreen delivered their baby in Paris to secure him a French passport to give him access to free movement. Sabreen named her son Qoudsi—My Jerusalem.

For their yearly trips to Jerusalem, Qoudsi traveled with his French passport. Sabreen had to renew her laissez-passer every two years at the ministry. As the boy grew older, he became confused by his father's absence on the trips home, saying,

Daddy, why don't you come with us to Jerusalem?

Cécile and Qoudsi, Palestine's next-generation, both longed to live there, at home, with their families. Hani told me that when his son turned two, Qoudsi offered him a place in his suitcase. When he learned to ride his bicycle at three, he asked his father to join him on the backseat for a ride to Jerusalem. But Qoudsi knew the fastest way to get them home. Every time they saw a carousel in Paris, he chose to ride the plane. That was the only flight they took together, but it flew in a never-ending loop back to where it had started.

On Sabreen's last visit to Jerusalem in 2013, after having lived in Paris for six years, she was notified that her permanent Jerusalem residency status was revoked. She had thirty days to appeal or leave her city of birth. They informed her that if she remained, she would need a lawyer, or two, and eventually go through a lengthy procedure, during which she wouldn't be able to travel to Paris neither. Sabreen was torn apart, was shaking, forced to choose between two exiles. The Israeli authorities forced her to sign away her birthright, dragging her to agree to a life sentence in exile with Hani and Qoudsi. Now, like my brothers, she can only return to Jerusalem on a tourist visa—once she acquires foreign citizenship. To this day, she is still waiting.

In those years, I traveled along almost every road in Palestine. I worked extensively with local and international humanitarian organizations, encountering the Intifada and its effects on everyday Palestinian life. I was there with my camera, and instead of showing misery like other photographers, I preferred to expose the beautiful side of Palestine and its people, before all else in Gaza, the city on the long seashore. I had been to Gaza dozens of times, and it was the only city in Palestine I stayed in. The first time I visited was when I was a child in the 1980s. The next time I returned was in the late 1990s. After completing my mission, I took the long walk back through Erez Crossing to reach the first Israeli security area. Leaving Erez was only possible after handing an exit slip to the soldiers stationed at the front gate. After they scanned my bags, I should have gone to the border control area to get my exit slip. I don't know what triggered me, but I walked right past it, looked at the soldiers at the checkpoint, turned my head, and strolled straight to my car. I wasn't stopped. The Gaza borders and its soldiers had become invisible to me. A year later, when I returned to Gaza, the border police officer behind the glass window at Erez looked confused, as according to his records, I was still inside. I ridiculed him, saying,

This is your mistake.
Erez is a military bunker.
Do you really think I could've just walked out of Gaza?

He nodded his head and said,

Definitely a mistake.

The bombardment of the West Bank and Gaza that started in 2001 was devastating. It hit me and all Palestinians straight in the heart. Over the years, an impossible reality emerged, one with no solution—just a standstill. This paralysis triggered me to take on the arduous task of uprooting the self in search of salvation. The question for me was where to replant my roots.

Since my childhood, there was no end in sight, and all we could anticipate was the next war. I lost track of how many I have lived through. Israel's wars seldom lasted more than a few days, or weeks, but there seemed to be no end to the Second Intifada. All attempts to calm the situation failed, and the negotiations were reset to start at the beginning again—in a never-ending loop.

My life had been consumed since the year 2000, and since then, I had been running on reserves. Francesca asserted from the outset that we should have left Jerusalem. I never lived abroad and thought the right way out was through education by seeking full scholarships for master's degrees in London. The Chevening Scholarship was the hardest to receive. To qualify, one needed a bachelor's degree, which I didn't have. My first photography degree in 1997 was not fully accredited. After academic evaluation, I was instructed to complete two years of university study to complete my bachelor's degree. I could only do it through distance learning with the State University of New York, choosing to major in visual arts. I started my courses a few months before my kidnapping in 2005 and raced against time to finish by July 2007 to make sure we landed in London before the start of the academic year in September. For the first years of Cécile's life, I carried books with me wherever we went. The readings I did for the courses were stimulating, and two art projects of mine began as assignments—thoughts transformed into concrete visuals. I was immersed in theory, adrift between words, images, and the meanings they projected.

The moment I got the news that I was shortlisted for the scholarship, I had no doubt I would get it. But a week before the interview, I started urgent root-canal treatment, and because of my incessant gag reflex during previous dental visits, the dentist had prescribed me Valium, a drug I had never taken before or needed to. I was naturally either high or low. My interview was scheduled to take place two hours before my next dentist appointment. I popped two pills and drove to the British Council in Jerusalem. Ready to go. Or so I thought. During the interview, I felt so confused. I kept rattling on. I was aware though that I asked myself,

Did I just say "children" out loud?

The interviewers got interested in what I was saying and asked me exactly how I wanted to involve children in my vision. Of course, I had no idea, and I couldn't back off or excuse myself. The more I talked, the more I heard my mouth say the word "children"—groups of children, grade schools, and educational TV shows, future generations. To back up my argument, I thought of other statements and bounced them back and forth till the committee interrupted me, thanking me for coming in, saying I could expect a reply within a couple of weeks. They heard enough. I shook their hands and left, my head down. Only after I had left the building did it occur to me that I was high or low on Valium. I was furious, fuming, not believing what I had just done to my future. When I walked into my dentist's office on the other side of town, I could see by the look on her face that she didn't think the Valium had chilled me out enough, and she sent me home to gag and relax.

Francesca tried to calm me down but almost became deaf from my shouting. I called Najwan, Kamal, Michos, and even Mother Veronica, who all thought I went insane. I wanted to call the British Council to explain myself. Instead, I sent them a fax, explaining that I had been under the influence of prescribed drugs, asking for a second chance, while assuring the committee that I was still committed to working with children.

A few days later, and in anticipation, while sitting on a swirling stool in a bar in Jerusalem, I noticed the man sitting across from me had been one of my interviewers, the one who was flown in from London. That was my chance to straighten it all out. I pulled myself together, took no Valium, and walked over to say hello. He remembered me straight away. I asked him if he had received the fax while hiding my anxiety. With a boxing British accent, he said that he didn't sense the interview had gone badly. And that he didn't see the need to send the fax to start with. Now I panicked, making me question why the hell I had sent that fax.

And so it was, a week later, I received the scholarship, and a year later, the jury was thrilled to know that I received The Caparo Award of Distinction given to the number one student in the whole University of Westminster, School of Media, Arts and Design. This was one major step on the road to reaching London, and one step further of no return to Jerusalem.

It was time for the capital of my imagination to settle on new ground. I had stayed longer than necessary in its reality. In the middle of nowhere, in my wilderness, I searched for the ability to see through images to discover hidden realities. To ease the pain of departure and of leaving my family, I looked for ways to grow my roots in the air, towards the sky. On September 4th, 2007, we boarded the plane out of Jerusalem. In the early morning of that day, while it was still dark, I rode my scooter to my parent's house to say good-bye. My mother was waiting for me outside the front door, engulfed in the darkness, hiding her tears. She looked tired, drained as if she hadn't slept at all that night. She hugged me for a long time, burying her head in my chest. She told me to come back, but I sensed she knew I never would. She found it difficult to let me go. I left on my scooter, forgetting to put on my helmet, and on the road to eternal exile, the wind couldn't even dry the flow of my tears.

The guilt I have for leaving my mother has never left me.

6

We promised Cécile that her dolls, including Nina and Isabelle, together with their clothes, were following us, packed in special boxes, flying over Switzerland to meet us later in London. She was only three when we left Jerusalem, after saying good-bye to her house on the hill. When we had moved in three years earlier, two other mansions were still under construction, spread out on the hilltop. We were the first to live there, even before the landlord. Given the house's size and grand architecture, the garbage collector once asked Fritz, Francesca's father, during his first visit to Jerusalem whether it was the Swiss Embassy or the ambassador's residence. Fritz had brought Cécile a small Swiss flag, which she stuck in the garden's soil, visible from the main street. Perhaps the amount of paperwork my studio generated, the Swiss flag, and Fritz's bright complexion and blonde hair gave the garbage collector that suspicion. Neither Mr. Fritz nor I were ambassadors.

That same year, I was showing the producer of a documentary on my work the location where I had collected the stones on which I had printed images for my art project *Till the End*. There, in the heart of the Old City, I was being asked about belonging and identity when I received a phone call from Francesca,

> Steve, guess what?
> you got a reply,
> you are officially, now and forever,
> a Swiss citizen.

I laughed. I had never lived in Switzerland. I didn't even go to the embassy to pick up an application. Friends of mine at the embassy thought I was highly qualified and had filled out a form over a drunken dinner with Francesca. The application was treated in record time. In only a few months, I received a Swiss passport. Getting it felt easier than buying a can of Coke. By contrast, after six years of marriage and living in Jerusalem, Francesca still held a temporary ID. And when she did get her Israeli nationality a year later, one condition was that she renounce her Swiss citizenship, even though this was not imposed on Jews immigrating to Israel who carried a foreign passport. We objected, and again had to consult with lawyers, and she was able to keep both nationalities. She remarked once,

> I became the Palestinian, and you the Swiss!

For me, getting a Swiss passport was a formality on paper, like when I had received the Israeli one ten years earlier. The Swiss one allowed me to travel without hassle, and the Israeli guaranteed my return home. But getting Swiss nationality didn't transform me into a Swiss artist, just as the Israeli nationality did not turn me into an Israeli one. It would have been absurd if someone had referred to me as a Swiss artist. What is identity? Identity cannot be defined by words on paper and words on paper never defined mine.

My true identity was made up of my personal views and thoughts about life, nurtured by observing its details. I never saw my identity as a label, but as a process—fluid, changing every day. Maybe this explained why I struggled when people asked me where I came from, expecting a direct answer relating to a geographic location. I wanted my answer to be true to what I felt. But in the process of not referring to labels, I became a stranger to myself, finding it difficult to relate to identity with words.

Francesca and I were cautious about where we lived in Jerusalem because the homes we built together were part of our shared and individual identities. We looked for a safe place to protect Cécile and us from the harmful excess of national and religious identity that constantly threatened to seep into our lives. People defined themselves by religion first—Jewish, Muslim, Christian. You had to belong to one, and the decision was made for you before birth. Religion was handed down like a will, becoming the first reference of one's national identity. Francesca and I were liberated from that.

We were travelers in our minds, nomads, always searching. This didn't negate where I was born or grew up. Whenever I was asked where I came from, I answered,

From Jerusalem.

Almost without exception, people assumed that I was Israeli, and their typical answer was,

So you are from Israel.

Over the years, I learned how to define myself by what I was not. I would normally continue by saying,

But I am not Israeli.

Then they would ask,

So. What are you?

They rarely associated my negation with the possibility that I came from Palestine. So, I would answer back,

I come from Jerusalem. Palestine.

They would reply,

But isn't Jerusalem in Israel?

Then I would explain,

Never forget that at least half of Jerusalem is Occupied. Not many people know this. No country on earth, except for the

State of Israel, recognizes Jerusalem as its capital.

And if it hadn't happened already, then came the question I hated the most,

> But why is your name Steve?
> That's not a typical Palestinian name.

Sometimes this would force me to say that I was not religious, but that my name is common in Palestinian Christian families, explaining that Christians made up around twenty percent of the population of Palestine before the creation of Israel and that today they have dwindled down to less than 1.5 percent because of surging demographic shifts and continuous immigration.

The repetition of these questions drove me insane when a scholar from Syria, whom I expected to know the fabric of life in Palestine, insisted that I tell the truth and stop lying about the origin of my name. We met during a trip as part of a group of Arab scholars who had all been awarded scholarships. At dinner, he repeated his question again in front of everyone, so I pushed my chair back, stood as if giving a toast, and confessed, uttering Arabic words that everyone could interpret and discern:

> *Ismi mish Steve Sabella.*
> *My name is not Steve Sabella.*

> *Ismi Khara Khara.*
> *My name is: Shit Shit.*

> *Esem marti Imsak Khara.*
> *My wife's name is: Constipation Shit.*

> *Esem binti, Iss-hal Khara Khara.*

My daughter's name is: Diarrhea Shit Shit.

Later on, I apologized for my frenzy, explaining the background of my reaction. Many of my friends thought that this problem would have been solved in general if I had said with clarity that I was Palestinian. I was saying this. But in my own way, using my language. At no point did I feel that the pronoun and verb I am, followed by a country's label, defined anyone. Adopting labels meant defending countries patriotically regardless of whether their policies were just or not.

I asked myself and others,

> *We are from a place, a city, or even a street. What if you live in a different country every ten years over the course of a lifetime. Which one do you stay true to?*

Over the years, I grew to feel proud of where I came from, and I was no longer ashamed of coming from Bab Huta. Growing up there will always be a part of who I am.

In 2004, the French consul general in Jerusalem, Régis Koetschet, invited Palestinians and Israelis to welcome Bertrand Delanoë, then the mayor of Paris. The reception was held in the consulate which was also the consul's grand residence. I had passed by the mansion before but had never been inside. It stood below the King David Hotel, which suffered an explosion in 1946 carried out by Irgun, the same group responsible for the Deir Yassin massacre. The residence was on a large piece of land, overlooking a French garden, almost a Versailles, with a panorama view of Jaffa Gate and the Old City Wall. French guards escorted us to the main hall, divided by two marble staircases winding up to an upper floor. A royal palace. I had never seen a higher ceiling in a residence in Jerusalem, sublime, a sudden reminder of Imperial France and its historical power. Live classical music played in the reception room, and after a glass or two of wine, and nibbling on blue, white, and yellow cheese, clinking glass called everyone for the consul's toast. As Koetschet's speech almost ended, surprise took me when he presented Delanoë with what he referred to as "The gift from Jerusalem." Koetschet handed him my *Palestine* + blue box, which contained the *Life Is Splendid* photo series. He announced that I was present in the crowd while continuing to speak about how the ten images of children portrayed another reality at a time when images of oppression bombarded everyone daily.

I had made *Life Is Splendid* out of responsibility towards exposing other stories from Palestine during the Second Intifada. The kids I photographed were relaxed, tanning themselves on the beach, with eyes looking to the sky—images detached from the perceived reality. The main photo was of a five-year-old-girl, whose flying hair and glittering face drew the viewer straight into her olive eyes. She could be seen without opening the box, as I had cut out a window on top, visually framing her image with the cover's blue color. People could change the order of images how they wished. The kids could look through that window into the world, and the world looked back at them, and simply observed, knowing the hardships they faced.

I wish I had done *Life Is Splendid* with Michos, as the images did travel beyond my doorstep. This time, the captured images crossed borders. A person in Ireland wrote that he wanted to give his dying friend in the hospital a trace of Palestine, a country he had long supported. One couple wished to hand out an edition of ten during their wedding ceremony in the United States. And one box flew as far as Australia.

But *Palestine +* also got its share of criticism. Simple signs and colors can become absurdly charged symbols, above all in this part of the world. Some Israelis wondered why the project's title had a cross in it, misreading the plus sign as a statement suggesting that Israel should be a Christian land. Others even thought that the plus sign stood for Palestinians wanting the land taken in 1948 back—always asking for more. Palestinians thought I chose blue because of my work with the UN. But the worst was when Palestinians or Israelis thought the blue referred to the Israeli flag. But Israel, or anyone can not Occupy the color of the sky.The only concerns I had when I designed *Life is Splendid* were aesthetic. Yet, it turned out, in Israel and Palestine, there cannot be aesthetics without politics. In a documentary on my work, the Israeli film director Avi Peretz made a remark that rang in my ear. He suggested that my portrayal of happy children was a subconscious manifestation of my desire to go back to my childhood and change it. Thinking about this, later on, I realized that past realities would always remain entangled, suspended in time.

At the end of the speech, Delanoë and I shook hands. He opened the box, flipped through the images, and was impressed—or felt pressured to say so. Seeing him walk around with a glass of wine later, he invited me to exhibit at the Hôtel de Ville art gallery in Paris. But he wanted me to show with an Israeli artist. As often is the case, a Palestinian needs his counterpart, his opposite, the Israeli on the other side. Arts institutions often feel the need to balance their decision to work with a Palestinian artist by adding an Israeli—for many, it was out of the ordinary to give Palestinians their own space and voice. These forced initiatives focus less on art and more on contrived texts and thoughts about fake co-existence and tolerance, playing it safe to avoid public criticism.

Palestinian artists who dared to go against the stream and work with Israelis were publicly criticized and slandered. Out of respect, but feeling cornered, I agreed as long as I could choose the Israeli artist. When I thought I found an Israeli with whom I could work, I sent the application through the help of the French Cultural Center in Jerusalem. The mayor's office ignored the proposal. I didn't care and was relieved the exhibition never materialized.

When Israelis and Palestinians met outside of their countries, many turned into ambassadors, blindly defending governments and all of their actions—as if they were on national duty. They rarely shared what they really thought. In 2005, I participated in a conference in Berlin, aiming to bridge the views of Palestinian and Israeli journalists. A German foundation sponsored the meetings to address the media's role during the Second Intifada and the views of each side. In one particular session, the debates were so heated that almost everyone was shouting, like politicians in a parliament session gone wrong, just short of spitting at each other. The German mediator looked helpless. In another session, I gave a presentation of my work in Palestine. I preferred to have my images tell my story in silence. Afterward, I asked the Israeli journalists a direct question,

> *How does it feel to be an Occupier? I'm sure, on some secret level, you feel happy to be on that side, and I'm sure it makes you feel powerful somehow. But you don't have to answer this question. I know exactly how it feels to be a Jewish Israeli Occupier. I drive straight through Israeli checkpoints. I never stop. I step on the gas, ignore the soldiers, or look them in the eye, and speed off.*

My statement took some Israeli journalists by surprise, distinctly Danny Rubinstein from Haaretz newspaper, who later followed up with an article titled,

I had taught myself how to look at life from an Israeli perspective and accept the rationale and justification for the Occupation. Yet, in my experience, Israelis were apathetic in acknowledging the tragic and impossible reality they had created in Palestine. Instead, the system worked to condone the Occupation by criminalizing and degrading the Other.

When Francesca received her work permit, Berlitz hired her to teach German to Israeli students. At first, she taught groups at the head office in Jerusalem. Her work quickly expanded into giving private lessons to Israeli diplomats. After getting her security clearance from the Shin Bet, she was able to teach at the premises of the Israeli Foreign Ministry. There, she prepared the diplomats for their posts as ambassadors in the German-speaking countries. One evening she returned from work, opened the door, threw her bag on the floor, and lay down on the long couch next to me. I put my arms around her wanting to know what was wrong. She told me that one of the Israeli ministers had asked how to teach her demeaning words about Arabs in German.

We both agreed on a break, a new beginning. And London seemed the way to go. Living in Jerusalem was a battle. But I couldn't drag the family to live abroad without preparation. Many things had to fall into place because my intention was to earn two master's degrees in London, one after the other. Having got the Chevening Scholarship, I still had no clue where to get the second. In a worst-case scenario, our plan was to return to Jerusalem, but we wanted to avoid having to look for another house. I asked Yasser, our landlord, for permission to sublet the house furnished for one year instead of terminating the lease.

In low spirits, I advertised the sublet on various platforms and blasted it to my UN contacts. Many came for viewings and were impressed. But no one took it—maybe our attachment to this house got in the way. They related most excuses to work being on the other side of town, not wanting to get stuck in morning and evening traffic. To come around this concern, I only looked for tenants who worked for organizations whose offices were a short drive from the house down Hebron Road. Still, I kept hearing the same excuses. Eventually, Yasser and I hired a real estate agent, who found even more candidates but to no avail.

I ran out of time to remove the new furniture, which I had kept in the house in case we succeeded in finding a tenant at the last minute. I left for London, disheartened, and asked Michos to empty the house and deliver the keys to Yasser as soon as he could. Jerusalem didn't want us to go back. Yet, to this day, Yasser and his partner Najat, and their three kids who were all born during the years we lived there, refer to it as,

Steve's House

The other dilemma was finding the right accommodation in London, where it had enough space for my studio work. I had been to London several times before and anticipated the difficulties of finding a suitable flat in the city center, as many of the apartments in London were the sizes of shoeboxes put together. And because London was expensive, the rent was calculated per week. We also wanted to minimize the horrible trips underground as much as possible, especially for Cécile. But first, we had to secure her placement in a kindergarten. The quality of children's education in London varied drastically from one neighborhood to another. But the worst part was that many kindergartens had years-long waiting lists. Finding the right housing, in the right area, with an excellent school nearby, on the same metro line as my university, all the while being affordable, was a daunting task.

I wasn't able to save any money living in Jerusalem—I still have nothing saved—and when we left for London, I was in debt to the bank which I could only pay back six years later. Francesca and I never had savings, but overdrafts. We spent our money living life. Leaving Francesca and Cécile in Jerusalem was not an option, and

I didn't want to drag them to London under poor living conditions either. They were my priority. But the Chevening Scholarship accommodated only one person and paid no extra stipends for scholars wishing to bring along their families. This meant Francesca had to find a job before we settled in London. Otherwise, there was no way we would be able to afford living there.

She and Cécile flew off in May, three months before I did. They stayed at Brian's, a family friend, who hosted them till we sorted out our accommodation. This also gave Francesca the chance to look for a job. When she arrived there, she found out that Brian's partner, Tracey, was a teacher, and remarkably, a vacancy had opened at her school. When Francesca applied, the school accepted her application promptly. The first significant obstacle was behind us.

That same May, I had to fly to France for the Jerusalem in Paris event I was organizing with Najwan Darwish at the Librairie Résistances. The French Jewish activist Olivia Zemor, who advocated the freedom and equality of all nations, ran the space. But Palestine was her primary cause. She had sold her home in Paris and secured a much smaller one, looking for whatever means possible to fulfill her vision.

I worked with her because of my belief that in life, we do what we can, nothing more, nothing less. In Paris, Olivia was a forerunner and a heard voice in demonstrations against the Israeli Occupation. Over the years, she was detained, arrested, and humiliated by French and Israeli police. The more they tried to silence her, the more people joined hands with her.

Najwan and Olivia had worked together on a previous initiative, and when she came to visit Jerusalem, he connected the two of us. I invited her to the house in Tantur, showed her around, and then we sat on the garden terrace where the wind never stopped. From this vantage point on top of the hill, we pointed to unending Israeli settlements stretching from east to west, built on Arab towns from Beit Jala all the way to Malha, wondering when this injustice would end. Olivia and I were speaking the same language and agreed on a seven-day initiative, *Jerusalem in Paris*. We discussed funding, and to help, I suggested that we contact the French consulate in Jerusalem, which had already supported several of my art projects in the past. The plan worked, and the cultural attaché quickly gave the green light.

Najwan and I invited Kamal Boullata to take part in the event to lead a discussion on *Jerusalem in Exile*, the project Najwan and I were working on, which looked into the transformation of Jerusalem into an image. But since the origin of that image can never be traced, that gave us the feeling of being lost in our own space, to live in a state of permanent alienation—in exile.

The real conflict between Israelis and Palestinians was a fight over the image, with one side being far savvier in image construction and manipulation than the other. Physically conquering the world was limited, or no longer viable, and to adjust, conquering the image of the world became the New World Order.

To prepare for *Jerusalem in Paris*, I worked on *Palestine 9 Meters*, a video of still images that I put in motion. My intention was to shake how Palestine and Palestinians were portrayed to the world. Trance music played in the background, composed by Ramallah Underground and Checkpoint 303, whose tracks infused the sounds of bullets and explosions recorded during clashes. I edited the video to appear as if it were playing on a flickering television screen. It starts with white noise, a screen with no signal, buzzing sounds, and shortly after, flickering images of people begin to appear. We see one black horizontal line moving from the top of the screen to the bottom, in a constant loop, as if the signal was not strong enough. When the station clears, images exposing unexpected realities in Palestine get interrupted. The noise reemerges until the disturbance becomes strong enough to trigger a new transmission, a new story.

In the middle of the film, the wheel of life gets interrupted by the sudden emergence of barbed wire, a military tower, and the Separation Wall that dissects the landscape, cutting it in half. This visual error is followed by hypnotic close-ups of Palestinian embroideries, rotating patterns, and shapes stitched in every color. The story ends with the images from *Life Is Splendid*, where all the effects, little by little, disappear, and what remains is a trace of the girl with the olive eyes.

I flew to Paris before Najwan, who was supposed to join two days later. But at Ben Gurion Airport, he wasn't allowed to board the plane because he didn't have the transit visa for the transfer area in Zurich. This is life with a laissez-passer—stop this person. Two days later, he found a direct flight.

Jerusalem in Paris went smoothly, and French Jewish activists did not interrupt the event or smash the windows of the library and topple over all the bookshelves like they did in the past. On the opening night, the Palestinian ambassador, Hind Khoury, gave a speech. Olivia had invited her. Khoury's attendance at the Librairie Résistances compelled police to guard the street and the surrounding area from extremists, who silenced any voices criticizing Israeli policies or called for the liberation of Palestine.

But during preparations, Olivia and I argued about the screening since the exhibition room for the video was too bright. Light flooded in through a skylight from the ceiling, like a beam from a spaceship. Because it got dark late in Paris, viewers would only see faint images on the screen, diluting the messages Palestine 9 Meters transmitted. I asked Olivia if I could cover the ceiling window with black fabric. She thought I was too demanding. But what was the point of screening an art video if no one could see it right? For Olivia, the event was the message. For me, the message was in the image.

On the seventh and last day, as Olivia was closing the library door, with stress and exhaustion apparent on her face, I thanked her and her team for the great outcome. I also apologized for any friction, telling her that, in the end, we were fighting for the same just cause. Unexpectedly, she pounded me with words, implying I was rude and that my attitude was Israeli. She ended her rant by saying,

> You are anyway not Palestinian.

It shocked me. Those were the last words I expected to hear from Olivia. She knew where I came from, my art, and my life. I could relate to the Israeli attitude, which I might have developed to protect myself in Jerusalem, but she had no right to strip me of my Palestinian identity. I was furious with her and couldn't restrain my emotions in front of Kamal, confronting her on the spot about how she wanted us to come across as victims of the Occupation, the real issue at hand. Najwan and I conveyed the exact opposite, to allow attendees to feel our victory in finding ways to face and defy the Occupation.

Back in Jerusalem, I looked at every reality to make sure the transition to London was effortless for Cécile and Francesca. I searched who I knew in London, and I remembered Mark Zeitoun. A couple of years earlier, Mark had loaned me the money to produce the *Life Is Splendid* series. He told me about Goodenough College, the accommodation where he was staying, in the heart of Bloomsbury, in London's center. I wondered what kind of education he was getting there. It turned out that Goodenough was every scholar's dream. It was not a college but a residence for masters and doctoral students from all over the world, offering subsidized rent, furnished flats, and membership in many clubs and societies funded by the college. As he said,

> If you get in, all you need to know is your Wi-Fi password, and you are settled. It's that easy.

But getting in wasn't that easy. Members were expected to contribute to the student community by giving talks, inviting speakers from their universities, and running the growing list of clubs and societies. Supposedly, the quality of the contribution was the deciding factor in accepting scholars, regardless of where they came from. Mark thought I had a good enough chance.

I traveled to London in April to check out the college and work through my long to-do list. I stayed at Mark's apartment the whole week, which was only a five-minute walk from the British Museum. I took the Goodenough tour first thing in the morning. One scholar showed us his flat, overlooking the gardens of Mecklenburgh Square and its tall trees surrounding it, separating the college's two main buildings, London House and William Goodenough-Willie G, the name of its founder. The college's gardens were bursting with white spring blossoms, like snow, and had a tennis court, a running track, children's playgrounds, and even an area with stonemasonry barbecues. We were then taken to see the grand college halls, used for the winter and summer balls, selected talks, and culture-week events. Almost every two weeks, the college invited its seven hundred members for what they called dining-in nights in its main hall, where large paintings of people hung on all sides.

The study room in Willie G was serene, framed by high windows looking over an inner courtyard covered with stretching plants from the bottom all the way up, with their leaves decorating the edges. Once a member, scholars were free to establish any sort of club or society imaginable, and the college subsidized most of the expenses. The clubs ranged from horse riding to skydiving, from the Space and Astronomy Society to the Law Society. We were told that the college even owned a private concert booth at the Royal Albert Hall. During the tour, I saw more than one stone-carved plaque commemorating Queen Elizabeth II's frequent visits to Goodenough, honoring her as a Patron of the college.

The tour ended at Freddy's Bar, where Chris Wright, the college's dean, was waiting to give a last word and then answer questions. He spoke about the college as a life-changing adventure, offering members the chance to connect on a global level, share knowledge, and turn to each other for help and collaboration. He said,

> What better lawyer or doctor could you consult with than the one you trusted and knew best from living at Goodenough?

He mentioned how strict the acceptance policy was, approving only twenty percent of applications, because, as he said, Goodenough aimed to attract only the most talented individuals. Wright's motivational speech reminded me of Robin Williams' *Dead Poets Society*. I almost pushed through the crowd to go and hug him. His words made my skin itch, made me desperately want to become a member, like everyone else around me. I was both thrilled and scared to fill out an application. Goodenough was too good to be true. After the tour, I rushed back to the apartment to tell Mark not knowing where to start,

There's no way I'm not getting in.

The biggest dilemma was finding Cécile placement in a kindergarten. On the tour, I learned about the Thomas Coram Centre on Mecklenburgh Square, not even a minute's walk from the college. It was known for its excellence, and long waiting lists—every parent at Goodenough or in Bloomsbury wished to have their child registered there. That afternoon, I strolled to the kindergarten and asked if the school still had any vacancies. The receptionist looked at me as if she wondered what planet I was living on, but she still said in a polite British way that I should start by filling out an application, to begin with. I left disheartened, believing the only real option would be to register Cécile at one of the University of Westminster's kindergartens, where I was going to do my masters, who reserved a few spots for children of sudden cases like ours. The downside was the long distance between Goodenough in Bloomsbury—in case we lived there—and Marylebone, where the closest kindergarten was located, which would require taking the underground during the horribly busy morning and evening rush hours. Neither Francesca nor I wanted to drag ourselves and Cécile around, but we had to make quick decisions based on many unknowns. Nevertheless, the Westminster kindergarten was the only viable option, and I registered Cécile there just in case. Still, we wished for this new chapter in our lives to start in Bloomsbury.

I flew back to Jerusalem; the clock was ticking, and there was no room for mistakes. I filled out the application for Goodenough and mailed them a parcel containing *Life is Splendid*, *Palestine 9 Meters*, and my art portfolio.

Before we heard back from Goodenough, Francesca and Cécile flew to London and stayed at Brian and Tracey's. It was after Francesca accepted her job offer that Goodenough notified us of our acceptance. We were on fire.

I asked Francesca to drop in Thomas Coram kindergarten by

random chance to check the application. At the reception, the same lady I had spoken with was on the phone. When she hung up, she asked Francesca how she could help her. After Francesca gave a brief explanation, the receptionist said that the person on the phone had called to cancel their child's enrollment, who happened to be in Cécile's age group. But out of fairness, she could only consider Cécile if we had already filled out an application, which I did. The receptionist offered the vacancy to Cécile. Francesca was simply there at the right moment. Fire, fire, fire!

The allocation of flats at Goodenough was random. Once a contract was signed, it was like a Catholic marriage. Changing it wasn't possible, and scholars only found out where they stayed on the day of their arrival. This worried Francesca and me, knowing how vital space was for both of us. Most of the flats looked basic, with dated rundown furniture, but those overlooking the garden were the nicest. Next to Willie G, away from the dorms, was a separate building that housed three spacious flats. One on each floor. Those were a dream to get.

One afternoon at the beginning of September, the three of us arrived at the Willie G reception carrying six large bags. We were told that our flat was on the first floor, meaning it wasn't one of the three dream flats. But we hoped it would at least face the garden. There, we took the elevator up, dragged our bags out, took a left, and walked down a long, narrow corridor with dorm rooms on the right and restrooms on the left, then we turned left again and walked down a shorter corridor, going through swinging doors, looking left and right for our flat number: 134. Our destiny was waiting for us to unlock its door. Francesca crossed her fingers, Cécile skipped, chattering some words in Swiss-German, and I wished with all my heart that it wouldn't be too bad.

The door opened inward, straight into a two-square-meter box of a kitchen. In the corridor connecting the living room and our bedroom was a door to Cécile's room. It hardly had space for a bed and half a cupboard. All the furniture looked old and bulky, bought at Argos, a cheap British catalog retailer. The dark stains on the sofa were the type that resulted from years of use and no cleaning. And God knows what else. The walls were a pale yellow, like those in clinics and hospitals. And no, there was no view of Mecklenburgh Square Garden, but of a dull building, occupying the view from every window in the flat. We dropped our bags, took a defeated breath, and digested the downgrade from living on top of a hill, down to a cell.

This wasn't a problem of luxury. Space always played a major part in my psychology, affecting my health. But there was nothing we could do because to the college, being selected was already enough, and I was too embarrassed to complain and request any change.

The first weeks hit us hard, and Francesca and I suffered. Residing in that space felt like a prison sentence, again, sucking the last pockets of air after leaving Jerusalem. One morning, I went straight to talk to the warden. I gathered my strength and knocked at her door. I opened up to her, gently clarifying how space affects me, carefully choosing my words. She had listening ears but was firm about the rules.

That year Goodenough weathered many changes. Major General Andrew Ritchie, the new college director, who had been appointed a few months earlier, was reshuffling all the departments and services at the college, from catering to the appointment of a new priest for the chapel. The Major General accepted this appointment upon retiring from the British Army after thirty-four years of military service.

By now, Goodenough was affecting my relationship with Francesca. We never came to see the flat as our home. We could not relax there and just be. Living in dullness, our talks always repeated themselves—stagnation set in. And I felt our only way out was through the front door or out of the window.

When the warden was replaced, I spoke with the new one, and she was more sympathetic, promising to help find a solution. Not long after, she found another couple who had requested a change and suggested we switched flats. Etai and Eliza were from Israel. We had met them briefly during one of the dining-in nights. We were eager to see their flat, but it turned out to be smaller than ours and had a cockroach problem. There was simply no point, as they also disliked ours.

The college mainly accommodated single scholars, and Willie G, where all the families were housed, had a few family apartments. The last option was to pay attention to when a family left and ask the management before they allocated it to a new resident family. Bending the rules, the new warden offered us and the Israeli family alternatives. We saw two other flats, but both of them were worse than ours. A month later, we heard that one of the dream flats in the building next door was becoming available. I hurried to Laura's office. But it had just been taken by Etai and Eliza.

Exhausted, frustrated, and disappointed, I dragged myself to Willie G Bar where I also worked as a barman twice a month, as part of a contribution to the college. Amir, from Israel, was on shift that night. He was also on a Chevening Scholarship, studying army strategies at the Imperial College in London. He had worked for the Israeli Counter-Terrorism Bureau, and we often quibbled before our shifts over a shot or two of whiskey about the conflict, agreeing and disagreeing on diverse issues. We had an open dialogue, unusual between Israelis and Palestinians, which usually starts or ends on eating hummus together. Or not.

But that night, after another conversation, this Amir was like the other Amir, who drove the fancy car to the Dead Sea, with an installed radar to identify and smell Arabs from three kilometers away. Only this time, this Amir had an upgraded radar,

You are what we call "Palestinian Light."

In the past, Israelis had remarked that I couldn't be a real Palestinian. Did they expect me to have a long beard, wear a keffiyeh, and not have my own voice? I had never heard this term before and asked Amir what he meant. With a smirk, he said, almost tapping on my shoulder to tell me that there was something good about me,

You are like Coca-Cola Light. A low-dose Palestinian.

If I was going to be compared to a fizzy drink, he should have definitely labeled me a raging Swiss Red Bull.

5

One night in colorless London, Cécile put on high heels, hung a fancy bag over her shoulder, and rambled around the house pretending to talk on my phone. Then she sat down on the couch opposite me with her legs crossed, lowered her voice to say,

> Daddy, you're strange, but I won't tell mummy.
> Let's keep it our secret.

She was only four back then and had just started speaking English a few months earlier. I asked her why she thought this way. Her answer was vague, she played around, but I felt it had to do with my depression. She had often seen me chained by my thoughts to the blue couch or flat on my bed, under the cover, without movement, caving in to piercing silence.

In London, I couldn't relax, slow down, finding it difficult to adjust to the city's hectic rhythm, which heightened my sense of alienation and disorientation. Exile hit me—no longer a mental state of mind, but a physical reality. I was not living under Occupation anymore, but my depression still reached a record low. I was sure this depress-ion was masking another ailment, and to get to its roots, it was vital to delve into my psyche further. I was sinking, living in a suspended state, unable to reach the surface, or go down to any ground to push myself up.

London moved in crowds, was full of signs, *dos* and *don'ts*, many written and displayed like orders. I felt that personal freedom and individuality were an illusion. Everyone seemed to struggle, dragging on. In the underground, travelers were trapped in their own worlds, lonely, rarely communicating, as if everyone else was invisible. I often stood at the platform's cutting edge, past the safety line, watching mice scurry along the charged tracks disappear when they felt the breeze pushed by the approaching raging train so that they were not torn apart. I would close my eyes to feel the wind blow against my face until it struck with a vengeance, warning to step away from the blasting thunder about to storm in.

Cécile often warned me to step away from the edge. I didn't want to burden her with my emotions and political views. Yet, it was inevitable that she would see me get agitated when I watched the news from Palestine. I would stand up and curse at the TV in Arabic—probably the only Arabic she heard me utter in the early years of her life that was not stripped of emotion. But in my heart, I felt blessed for being able to withdraw Cécile from a life under Israeli Occupation, saving her from the humiliation of always being treated inferior. I didn't want her to get hurt or to be in the wrong place at the wrong time.

When I was nineteen, my brother Paul and I hung out in the Old City. One rainy night, while heading home walking on Via Dolorosa, we heard shouting voices in Hebrew, one after the other, and then all together,

> TISHKAV AL HARITZPAH!
> TISHKAV AL HARITZPAH!
> TISHKAV AL HARITZPAH!
>
> LIE ON THE GROUND!

I looked down the road and saw a squad of Israeli soldiers. Some were on their knees with guns aimed at us, while others rushed towards us in combat stance. Paul and I panicked and dropped flat onto the ground, face down, telling each other we were about to get fucked. We had no idea what was happening. When the soldiers reached us, they grabbed our hands and put them behind our backs. This position pushed me to the ground, soaking my face in street water. I lifted my head up to breathe, and then a soldier put his boot on my face, pushing it back down to the ground. I couldn't breathe as he kept his foot on my face, cursing at me in Hebrew.

After subjecting us to a body search, they grabbed each of us by the arm and pulled us up. Then, more soldiers arrived with other Palestinians they had arrested around. They bundled us up like prisoners of war, commanded to walk in a row with our hands on our heads, between two groups of soldiers. They lined us up with our faces against the wall at the first station of Via Dolorosa. We were searched again, one by one, while they checked our IDs. When they found zilch on Paul and me, they let us go.

Apparently, an Israeli yeshiva settler had been stabbed in the Old City that night, and the soldiers were searching for the attacker. Days later, a stone was placed at the stabbing scene in memory of the killed settler, as is the custom when any Jew is killed in the Old City or elsewhere. The names of dead Palestinians are only engraved in memory.

The feeling of submission escorted us for years. Paul said he wished he could glue his ID to his forehead, frustrated by the number of times he was stopped each day. That night, I promised myself I would not be degraded by soldiers without resisting. This was why, back in 1996, I was furious with the Israeli soldiers who dragged me into the dark corner on Zion Square, threatening to beat me. But during the Second Intifada, the last thing any Palestinian wanted was to be forced to lower their trousers and lift up their shirt. The pretext was the search for suicide bombers, but the humiliation of men and women alike was not enough. After stripping, Palestinians were to turn around, slowly, with their arms spread wide open, like in a penguin dance. Many incidents were caught on video by news agencies, which then transmitted the image of defeated Palestinians around the world. Or maybe, it was the defeat of the Palestinian image.

I almost fell victim to a strip search once during a cloudy spring day in 2003. I was hired to photograph the land terracing in Hebron. At that time of year, the terrace fields exploded with white blossoms. I was with a local driver in a jeep with a West Bank license plate, meaning it could not drive on most of the West Bank streets, reserved solely for Israeli vehicles. To punish Palestinians, Israelis also cut off access to many Palestinian towns with barbed wire and massive stone blocks. A strategy practiced up to this day. The checkpoints were everywhere, and getting from one destination to another meant traveling through remote, unpaved roads.

Just as I was telling the driver how taken I had always been by the stepped stone terraces, an Israeli army jeep emerged out of nowhere. The driver stopped the car, placed both of his hands on the steering wheel, and froze in his seat. Over a loudspeaker, the soldiers ordered him to turn the engine off. I had my photographer jacket on, and coiled wires from my flash and battery wrapped my chest. I knew I would be taking a risk stepping out of the jeep looking like a suicide bomber. I was also worried about making any sudden moves to hide the cables. Israeli soldiers, known for having loose fingers on the trigger, often shot Palestinians without justification. The soldiers stood in front of their jeep, with their guns pointed, and asked the driver to come out first, slowly, and stand in front of his vehicle with his hands high in the sky. There, they ordered him to unbutton his shirt, unzip his trousers, and then turn around with his hands still in the air. There was no way I was going through the penguin dance. When the driver finished the performance, they yelled,

LO LAZUZ!
DON'T MOVE!

When the soldiers called for me, I stretched my head out of the open window and yelled in Hebrew that I was on duty. No, I was not going to get out of the car. I had to come across to them as Israeli in a flash, equipped with a combative attitude, or I would have to go through the same humiliation. The only penguin dance I would perform might be, maybe, on a dance floor. When the soldiers thought I was one of them, they asked what I was doing there, and when I explained, they finally let us pass. After we continued our way, the driver turned to me with eyebrows raised. My confidence and refusal to submit to Israeli soldiers alarmed him. We both knew I was taking a risk. But what choice did I have?

In 1995, while studying at Musrara, I worked for a couple of weeks at the Holiday Inn Hotel in Jerusalem, close to the Israeli Knesset, the week when Yitzhak Rabin, Israel's Prime Minister, was assassinated by a Jewish Israeli. They assigned me to room service. During an overnight shift, I got an order from a room on the top floor. I took the elevator up and knocked at the door. A man with a hoarse voice replied. When he opened the door, he stood in front of me in his white underwear. I recognized him at once—Ehud Barak, The Ramatkal, Commander-In-Chief of the Israel Defense Forces, and Israel's Prime Minister a few years later.

In a rare understanding of how miserable life had become in Palestine, one year before Barak took office in 1999, he said in an interview in response to the drastic situation and lack of any personal security in Israel,

> If I were a Palestinian at the right age, I would have joined one of the terrorist organizations at a certain stage.

I never served in the army or fought in any wars, but my body had been shot by bullets a thousand times. One of Palestine's biggest mistakes was accepting the weapons Israel had authorized the Palestinian Authority to carry as part of the deceptive Oslo Accords. A few years later, the weapons gave Israel the pretext to attack Palestine using air and naval forces to inflict unimaginable damage, mainly in the Gaza Strip. Since then, Gazans had been subjected to living in a state of war. In the 2014 war on Gaza, without any sense of morality, the Israeli army demolished many tall buildings in the already crowded Gaza, giving residents seconds to run for their lives before they see their homes disappear in the air. Had I been Arafat, I would have collected all the weapons and thrown them into the sea. What Palestine needed was not weapons.

Goodenough had an unusually high number of Israeli scholars than other countries, as if the management accepted any application from Israel, whereas only two or three Palestinians got selected per academic year. Scholars referred to others by nationality—ranging from Japanese to Kenyan to Mexican—until they learned the correct way to pronounce each other's names. During my stay at Goodenough, and given the large and changing number of international scholars, I had to introduce myself to a new person all the time, forgetting again who was who.

My problem was my poor memory for names and faces. As a professional photographer, I had photographed thousands of people, and when I got home, I deleted all their images from my head to empty my mind. But after a while, I could no longer discern between faces, making it difficult for me to remember if I had met someone before. I even struggled when I watched movies, often unable to distinguish one character from another. The problem was so annoying that even after having dinner at someone's home, I would forget their names and faces. And then, after being reintroduced a few weeks later, I had no clue.

A good enough idea would have been to glue my ID to my forehead wherever I went. I had run away from Jerusalem, a city with an overdose of identity and ideology, only to discover I now lived in a place characterized only by identity and identification. During one of the first dine-ins, Cécile and I looked for a place to sit, but all the chairs and benches were occupied. Everyone in the hall was speaking in one breath, like in an angry beehive, and for sure, it did not sound British English. After waiting, we found a corner and sat across from a family who turned out to be from Israel. The mother already knew who I was, identifying me as "Steve, the Palestinian." Out of curiosity, she asked me in English where in Palestine I came from. I replied in Hebrew,

Ani meh Yerushalayim.
Yerushalmi.

I told her, "I come from Jerusalem—a Jerusalemite." She paused for a second, trying to make sense of my words. I explained that I had no issue with correctly stating this in different languages. In Arabic, I would always say,

Ana min al-Quds.
Udsi.

But in London, I also encountered some reactions from members of the Arab community who wondered why I didn't refer to Jerusalem by its Arabic Al-Quds name in English. Their rationale was that if an accord was to be reached, as part of a two-state solution, Jerusalem would become the official capital of Israel, and the part of Jerusalem where Palestinians lived would be called Al-Quds. This would present the illusion of two separate capitals sitting side by side, on the same land.

I was at Goodenough in December 2008, when Israel launched a three-week-long war on Gaza, killing over fourteen hundred Palestinians, the majority of whom were civilians. On the Israeli side, six soldiers were killed, four from friendly fire, along with three civilians. Israel's excuse for starting the war was to stop rocket fire from Gaza. Gazans were fighting to break the hermetic siege imposed on the Strip since Hamas's election in 2006. Halting the rocket fire or ending the blockade would have never solved the problem because they were not the actual reasons for igniting the war. The rocket fire was not the resistance that Israel sought to eliminate, but a form of resistance. If Israel had squashed it, Palestinians would always find other forms of resistance to fight the unending oppression caused by The Occupation.

Glued to the TV, I desperately waited for the war to end. But breaking news came in of a shelling that killed twenty-one members of the Samouni family, part of a larger Israeli attack on the eastern side of Gaza. I wanted to break the TV, as I once did when I threw our set with goliath fury from the Old City rooftop into the lemon tree's courtyard. To calm down from the shock of this horrific scene, I stormed outside to breathe some fresh air and smoke a cigarette. I had quit five years earlier, but the week I moved to London, I found myself heading to a kiosk to buy a pack. In the reception area, I saw Christina, a physician and violinist who was getting her master's degree in music and with whom I had become good friends. She saw I was distraught, my hands shaking. She sat me down on the couch. I vented to her about what I had just seen on TV. Lior, from Israel, joined the conversation, wondering why I looked agitated. I told him,

Did you hear about what just happened?
I am still shaking.

He said,

No. Tell me.

After describing the scene, I said,

Can you imagine? An entire family was wiped out in Gaza, vanished from the face of the planet.

He looked at me, and in cold spirit, he said,

We should be thankful that the entire family is dead.
This way, no family members have to mourn.

Christina's jaw dropped when she heard Lior say this so casually. He might have spoken without thinking, but I was familiar with this kind of raw, unedited Israeli reaction towards Palestinians. Many Israelis see Palestinians as inferior, something else, an enemy not worthy of any compassion.

This prompted me to tell Christina a story from a previous conflict in 2006 of a young girl from Gaza whose family members were killed after a bombshell hit them while they picnicked on the beach. A local news crew arrived on the scene and taped the girl on video, in tears, crying hysterically, calling out for her dead father's body buried in the sand. Then she ran to check the dispersed bodies of other family members, dismembered, one by one. This devastating scene was yet another on the list of those inscribed in the collective memory of Palestinians and others. And no, not even in Palestine did people erect any monument in their spirits.

In response to this war, the siege of Gaza, and the absence of an answer to the question of Palestine, Goodenough scholars often invited international speakers to shed light on issues that mattered during the Arab Culture Week always scheduled during spring. In the spring following the 2008 Gaza War, the week started with a lecture by the political scientist, activist, and Professor Norman Finkelstein. A well-known academic from the United States, who long advocated an end to the Israeli Occupation and for the creation of a two-state solution. His book, The Holocaust Industry, published at the end of the second millennium, provoked global controversy. Finkelstein's parents were Jewish Holocaust survivors. His plight was that Israel dishonored the deaths of Jews by always waving the "Holocaust Card" when anyone dared to criticize its policies. He called for the obvious that no country should be immune to international law. Many times, respected human rights organizations reported on the war crimes committed by Israel. Still, nothing was done to bring it to justice, even after the International Court of Justice ruled that the Occupation, including that of Jerusalem, the settlements, and the Separation Wall, were illegal.

Finkelstein's superior knowledge on the Palestinian-Israeli conflict is unparalleled. He is knowledge-drunk, an academic with true authority, equipped with universal morals. He uncovered the fabrication of history constructed by the most respected authors on Israel and Palestine by digging deep into their footnotes and busting them in public. Critics find it challenging to argue with him, or prove him wrong because Finkelstein confronts them with facts, the truth—and this truth does not have multiple angles. It is either right or wrong. The Holocaust can never be justified. Period. Similarly, no one can justify slavery, rape, torture, or the Occupation. Anyone who justifies the Occupation is like someone justifying rape.

In one of Finkelstein's lectures, several pro-Israeli students who became emotionally agitated repeatedly interrupted him—yelling and crying. They compelled him to silence them and explain,

> Every single member of my family on both sides was exterminated. Both of my parents were in the Warsaw Ghetto uprising. And it is precisely, and exactly, because of the lessons my parents taught me and my two siblings that I will not be silenced when Israel commits its crimes against the Palestinians. And I consider nothing more despicable than to use their suffering and their martyrdom to try to justify the torture, the brutalization, the demolition of homes that Israel daily commits against the Palestinians. So I refuse any longer to be intimidated or browbeaten by the tears. If you had any heart in you, you would be crying for the Palestinians.

But people in the Arab world also criticized Finkelstein, including Palestinians, who accused him of not having a clear stance on Israel and Palestine because he wouldn't take sides and specifically say he was pro-Palestine. To this, he responded,

> I am not pro-Palestine. I am pro-justice.

I had heard of Finkelstein before but hadn't yet had a chance to read his books or listen to him speak in public. This was not the case for the Israelis at Goodenough, who saw him as a threat, an enemy, a Holocaust denier, a self-hating Jew, a pro-Palestinian. Since there were many Israelis at Goodenough, they worked in concert to block his lecture and censor the content of all the other Arab Culture Week events. And it worked, revealing an Israeli bias within the college's management, agreeing with the Israelis by default. The Arab scholars had to work much harder to convince the director and the dean that they wouldn't invite speakers who would spread propaganda, but those who could provide another critical perspective. Living at Goodenough felt like living under Israeli law and logic. The college became like UN meetings during wartime. Each Goodenough member came with a standard statement to make, maintaining the status quo—useless. Israelis, regardless of what political camp they came from, often acted as if they represented Israel, defending and legitimizing its actions, almost at any cost.

When the Israelis heard Finkelstein was coming, they rushed to the Major General to cancel his visit. Many scholars found the Israelis' objections unjustified, and a few scholars hung Palestinian flags in solidarity on their room windows. Finkelstein had been invited to speak at Oxford, Yale, and many other serious universities. Refusing to give him the stage at Good-enough was absurd. But Goodenough became a battleground, and the Major General sent general emails to the scholars more than once to calm the situation. Canceling a talk was against the ethos of the college. He had no choice but to agree to Finkelstein's appearance, but to maintain order, he did so on the condition that the event was offered to members only—unlike all the other talks, which were open to the public.

An hour before the highly anticipated event started, I came across Anat, Lior's partner, in the Willie G reception area. She approached me, being The Palestinian Light, to understand her wounds. I listened to her, not in concert with why she felt hurt and threatened by Finkelstein's talk at the college. She said that the Arab scholars lacked sensitivity when they invited a speaker who called for her death and Israel's destruction into her own living room. My reaction was to clarify that Finkelstein was not giving the talk in her living room, but in the college's hall. I asked her to come to his talk, voice her opinion, share her concerns, raise her hand, and say whatever was on her mind, or her soul. But as often is the case, we prefer to defend old thoughts rather than challenge ourselves to explore new ones. Anat declined.

I was running late for the talk. I had already asked my friends to reserve a seat for me in the front row. At the door, scholars selected by The Major General were stationed to check our IDs, one by one, as if by military order. No one could attend from outside the college, and this censorship felt like an imposed curfew. Failing to block the event, none of the Israelis attended, even though they all claimed they were pro-peace. And they even expected the director not to attend neither, an act many deemed an insult to an invited speaker on that level.

Shortly before the talk began, the director snuck in and sat in the back of the hall. In the front row, I faced Finkelstein during his one-hour presentation. I had never heard anyone speak with such clarity and authority about Palestine and Israel. His arguments were all based on hard to refute historical documents, including sources from within official Israeli archives—challenging to question. Listening to him was like seeing a puzzle finally solved. I admired him for his dedication to a cause so far away from him since he lived in the United States. But justice is blind to distances and not bound by geography.

When Finkelstein said his last words, I felt an orgasmic rush. I stood up, along with everyone else, including the director, and clapped without end. Once again, I wanted to hug a man for his words like those of Chris Wright. Only then did I fully grasp why all Israelis feared him.

But later, the director prohibited the hanging of the Palestinian flag, forcing one Palestinian student to take it away. He announced that any future talks concerning Israel and Palestine had to be approved by him. This censorship pushed the Arab scholars to fight for their rights even more, but their proposals were often rejected based on maintaining order.

The Israelis had lost the Finkelstein case but subsequently won many others till they had it right.

There is no doubt that the Holocaust was a dark chapter in the history of our humanity—a must for all of mankind to learn about. I never understood why the number of murdered Jews had been questioned. The death of even one person in a gas chamber was one too many. One winter, on a cloudy and rainy day, during a road trip with Cécile, traveling without a destination, we found ourselves close to Auschwitz-Birkenau concentration camp in Poland. We decided to go there. As we passed through the town of death, Cécile and I agreed to skip lunch. I told her what happened during the war, preparing her for what she was about to see. She didn't stop asking questions, and I couldn't find the right answers. When we reached Auschwitz, everything seemed disorganized at the entrance. Visitors looked confused, not knowing where to wait or when their tours would start. It shocked me that we had to buy tickets, that there was an admission price, a value assigned to witness humanity's sickening past, when it was stripped of all its morals. After a tour like the one we were about to take, anyone with a conscience would have donated far more than the fixed price at the door.

You could only enter on a guided hectic tour, organized by language, so we chose English. But the tour didn't offer the chance to absorb the spirit of the place, in silence, without the tour guide's loud voice. At many stations, I wanted to slow down, to listen to my trembling inner voice.

On the second part of the tour where the train tracks led to the shacks and army barracks, we could walk freely. There, I held Cécile's hand as we made our way from the gate along the train tracks till the crematorium, the very end, reflecting on history and atrocity, on Self and Other. We looked at the ground and saw two pieces of wood splinters slashed from the wooden tracks. We each picked one up. They looked like monuments, and we both cherished one, where mine became later part of the glass and light installation, All That Remains.

We sat on a stone platform to rest near the crematorium, next to a group of young Israeli boys and girls wearing white shirts with Israeli flags wrapped around their shoulders. The group's guide asked them to imagine that moment in history. I was waiting to hear the slogan that I grew up seeing on top of the Wailing Wall in Jerusalem, and then it came,

> Lo Nishkach. Lo Nislach.
> We Will Not Forget.
> We Will Not Forgive.

I sighed, took a deep breath, pondering how Palestine, the land and its people, had also paid the price for the Holocaust. I left Auschwitz with a permanent scar etched into my skin.

All my life, I despised anyone who apologized to me when they mentioned Jews in conversation, presuming I must be sensitive. For me, being a Jew is just like being a Christian or a Muslim or anyone else. But the trap that Israel wants the whole world to fall into is criticism of Israel is criticism of all Jewish people. By that logic, you could be transformed instantly into an anti-Semite. In such conversations, I was compelled to clarify that my struggle was not with Judaism but with Israel's policies.

In reality, Palestinians became anti-Zionist, not anti-Jewish. For most of my life in Jerusalem, Palestinians didn't hate Jewish people but hated what they were doing to Palestine. Today, it's even clear that not all Zionists are Jewish. And that not all Jews are Zionists. There are even Arab Muslim Zionists. But the Jews in Israel also fell into a trap, believing that Israel and Zionism represent every Jewish person in the world. Israel does not represent every Jew, and because of this fact, as Norman Finkelstein states, it should stop calling itself a Jewish State.

During my stay at Goodenough, my life was again mirrored in my art. The time had come for a battle with Israel to settle accounts. I prepared for a visual confrontation. The struggle on the ground was affected by manipulated images Israel portrayed to the world. In this war of representation, Israel had the upper hand. But, I was savvy with image construction and in creating visuals that alter perception. The military defeat of the Arab World by Israel was quickly followed by the collapse and defeat of its image. The Arab world could no longer generate images of value, allowing others to generate its image. In reality, the Arab nations are now fighting for the liberation of their image.

I looked for six Israelis who had served in the army to invite them into a new negotiation room, one they were not used to as the peace conferences were failing, one after the other. As a starting point, I had all of us strip down to our underwear. Only then did we agree on the scene of the battle—in front of the Separation Wall. There, we would be photographed in our underwear, and later on, our images would be displayed as life-sized prints. Six Israelis would stand in a horizontal row against a long concrete wall, and one Palestinian would stand on the opposite side, on different ground. The images would then be turned to face each other in a decisive visual confrontation. I wanted my image to pose a threat, even though it would stand alone:

Settlement—Six Israelis & One Palestinian.

4

Since Francesca and I found each other, we remained entangled in the air, in our own tandem jump. What tied us together were the strings of love that kept us secure, never feeling pressured to land, aware that each of our actions affected the other. Our destinies became intertwined, hooked, enabling us to speak openly about our fears and worries in life, and the more we talked, the more we delved into inner turmoil.

In London, I often asked Francesca if I had captured her in my reality, and she always said she defined her own. I wasn't as gentle with her as I had been in Jerusalem. I was fighting my inner war, and with the speed of the descent, the ropes got stretched, and the distance between us increased. I fell into myself, and even though Francesca tried to lift me up, I became heavy, making it difficult for her to rescue me. This bruised our connection, and both of us were struggling to mend its gaps.

Goodenough was not home. Its maze of corridors locked me in my physical and mental exile. One night, Francesca came back angry after a meeting at the parents club at Goodenough, which she co-managed with Yuval, a psychologist from Israel. He asked her about our flat, and whether we were happy with it. She vented to him, expressing how space was affecting and limiting us. He told her,

> To feel better, remember your house in Jerusalem, and then you will appreciate what you have here.

His attitude infuriated her, and even though she didn't need to, she sent him photos of where we lived.

Back in Jerusalem, we often heard Israelis, including the intellectual elite, on TV, radio, and on the street, degrading Palestinians and labeling them as subhuman. Politicians, including prime ministers, spoke without filtering their thoughts, using the most derogatory of terms. I even remember that during the Second Intifada, a Knesset member stated on TV that he justified the killing of Palestinian children because they would become future terrorists anyway. If these same politicians spoke that way in any European country, they would either resign or go to prison. But in Israel, they praise inciters and pat them on the back. Dr. Mordechai Kedar, a scholar of Arabic literature at Bar-Ilan University, spoke out a day after the bodies of three Israeli teenagers were found, killed by Palestinians. He said in a public radio interview,

> Terrorists like those who kidnapped the children and killed them—the only thing that deters them is if they know that their sister or their mother will be raped in the event that they are caught. What can you do, that's the culture in which we live. . . . I'm not talking about what we should or shouldn't do. I'm talking about the facts. The only thing that deters a suicide bomber is the knowledge that if he pulls the trigger or blows himself up, his sister will be raped. That's all. That's the only thing that will bring him back home, in order to preserve his sister's honor.

I wrestled with his words for days, wondering who would want to study with a professor who justified rape. Then again, Yigal Amir, the Jewish Israeli terrorist who assassinated Israel's Prime Minister Yitzhak Rabin in 1995, had studied at Bar-Ilan University.

Professor Benny Morris, Israel's premier historian, said the following in a Haaretz newspaper interview in 2004, towards the end of the Second Intifada,

> The bombing of the buses and restaurants really shook me. They made me understand the depth of the hatred for us.

> They made me understand that the Palestinian, Arab and Muslim hostility toward Jewish existence here is taking us to the brink of destruction. . . .
>
> Palestinian society . . . is a very sick society. It should be treated the way we treat individuals who are serial killers. . . . We have to try to heal the Palestinians. Maybe over the years the establishment of a Palestinian state will help in the healing process. But in the meantime, until the medicine is found, they have to be contained so that they will not succeed in murdering us. . . . Something like a cage has to be built for them. I know that sounds terrible. It is really cruel. But there is no choice. There is a wild animal there that has to be locked up in one way or another.

If Palestinian society is sick, then the direct cause is the Occupation Virus. Not only it destroyed the self, but it restricted and hijacked the imagination. If the Palestinians have reached the point where they can no longer imagine a life in freedom, how can any land get liberated? All Israeli authorities work in concert to ensure that Palestinians felt trapped, regardless of where they lived, including those who came to be labeled as Arab Israeli, who make up twenty percent of Israel's population today.

The cage worked. I have met Palestinians born in the diaspora who felt they were under Occupation despite having never set foot in Occupied Palestine. This impression had to do with the power of the Occupation, which started with the land and then shifted to occupy the minds through the colonization of their imagination.

The Occupation feels eternal, which is how the Israeli system wants it to be. Over the years, the system generated images of defeated Palestinians and the defeat of all Arabs by extension. Their circulation was controlled to the extent that people fell victim to constructed images of and for them. The battle between Israelis and Palestinians became a battle of images. Today, the Palestinian image requires not only visual liberation, but also a tremendous amount of visual correction. Only then, reality begins to change.

In 2009, I was invited to give an artist talk on *Settlement* at the Academy of Arts in Berlin, where I met Micha Ullman, an artist from Tel Aviv. Ullman's parents had immigrated from Germany in 1933, just as the Nazis were coming to power. A day earlier, I had visited his public art installation on Bebelplatz Square commemorating the Nazi book burnings, which began the year they left. One can only see the installation through a thick glass window cut flat on the ground around the cobblestones. Looking down, you saw an underground room, many empty white bookshelves. I told him how I liked it when the viewers drowned their heads in darkness to see the light. Our friendly chat led us to subjects on Jerusalem and exile, on image and reality. I said,

> *Jews wrongly assume that they have returned to Jerusalem. When the Jews were forced into exile two thousand years ago, they took Jerusalem with them, in the form of a mental image. This image has escorted them through time. The Jerusalem that Jews want to return to today is no longer the same Jerusalem of the past—it was forced into exile. How could Jews feel at home when what they returned to was only an image, an imagined place constructed by religious ideologies, by media, by Israeli government-issued Aliyah brochures to encourage colonization. In reality, the Jewish claim of having returned to the homeland is an illusion. The fact is, all Jews are still in exile. And the same is true for all Palestinians who developed their own mental image of the Palestine that once was. Today, Palestinians and Israelis are fighting over an image of a place that doesn't exist. To find peace, we have to free ourselves from living in the image of the past.*

But living in images and the real Occupation cannot be compared. Not living its physicality, I now felt my life was held hostage by the image of the Occupation. Under Occupation, is a state of mind every Palestinian is born with, generation after generation until the Palestinians became the Jews of the second half of the twentieth century.

The Israeli on my back has absolute control over my fate, attached to me in a never-ending tandem jump. I am like a prisoner serving a life sentence for a crime I didn't commit. I would not be able to survive without the jailor's ropes and presence above my body. The only option to reassert command over my life is my right to self-determination, to end my life. From the moment I was born, I carried with me a secret suicide vest. But I didn't want to die, and for sure, I will kill no one.

The Israeli historian Benny Morris searched for a cure, and this quest motivated me to find my own. The search for one led to my collapse more than once, but I refused to capitulate to war, grief, and death. Instead, I looked for another way of living, one where my destiny and imagination were mine.

Francesca suggested I speak with a psychologist, for sure not Yuval, but I knew that would be useless in my case. If anything, I needed a team of psychologists. I didn't believe in therapy or prolonged prescribed drugs. They only dealt with symptoms and side effects, were cosmetic, and masked the real problem. To counter the virus invasion meant delving into the darkest points of the self. But the more conscious I became of the urgency to do so, the more drained I felt; even walking short distances felt like climbing up a mountain, paralyzing me, locking me in my surroundings again. I wanted a cure, a way out, and this was only possible if I faced the root cause of my disorder.

Settlement—Six Israelis & One Palestinian required all six Israelis to strip down to the core. I wanted to remove the cosmetic layers coating the Israeli-Palestinian image battle, to stop treating the side effects. Israel stretched the Separation Wall like a 720-kilometer bandage to cover up the Palestinian problem, but that would never solve it. Neither was the Palestinian reaction, which called for the decrease of checkpoints, better traffic regulation, and easing the siege of Gaza. Both sides continued to fail to see the bigger picture of liberation.

In London, I no longer shied away from identity or wanted to escape into my own world. After fifteen years of self-interrogation through my art, I finally confronted my Occupier face-to-face to reach a final settlement. I stood alone, for myself, confronting all six of them, but also confronting my own identity. I labeled myself Palestinian, aware that resisting The Occupation will continue till the last standing Palestinian. I was standing for all the Palestinians, yet as an ambassador, my role was not to represent ideology but to get rid of it.

Hagai, an environmentalist, was the first person I wanted to approach about participating in Settlement. We had spoken before at Goodenough on occasions, and since he handled the Middle East Club, aimed at bringing together Arabs and Israelis, I hoped to convince him. I attended none of the club's gatherings, despite Hagai's reassurance that they went beyond the surface. They offered members of Goodenough discounted memberships at the Cannons Fitness Center. Its access was below street level, hidden from sight at the far end of London House. At the bottom of steep stairs, Cannons looked like a former military bunker. As you entered, you caught sight of a three-level down swimming pool with blue tiles all around.

One freezing night, to escape the cold, I rushed into the steam sauna. Closing my eyes for relaxation was not really my thing, so I kept watching the water drops condense into moving paths on the foggy glass. After turning over the sand timer twice, I ran out of breath and stepped out to sit on the marble around the pool. By chance, I saw Hagai and thought this would be ideal for bringing up my proposal. He was swimming with athletic synchronized rhythm, wearing goggles. Impressed, I walked to the other end of the pool and told him,

> *You're an excellent swimmer.*

He replied,

> I had to learn how to swim just in case the Arabs throw us into the sea.

I wanted to tell him that if Palestinians were thrown into the water, the majority would drown since they don't have access to the sea. Instead, I said it was a good joke. Then, he continued with,

> You know, today at the Middle East Club meeting, I was surprised that the Arabs who attended didn't understand how afraid Israelis are of that happening. We live with with this fear.

I jumped in the water and swam towards Hagai. I wouldn't swim far at sea, but the deep water in pools no longer scared me. I said,

> *The State of Israel actually survives on creating this paranoia. If you take the fear out, the State of Israel will cease to exist. It is the strongest state in the region, and it has nuclear weapons. If you're going to be thrown into the sea, trust me,*

> *it wouldn't be by the Arabs.*

Hagai said he wanted to live in peace but couldn't because of groups like Hamas. Unsurprisingly, he didn't know that Israel had supported Hamas since its birth to counter Arafat's Fatah. At that point, I realized it wasn't the right moment to talk about a sensitive idea. A few days later, on a midnight stroll around the garden, I saw him smoking under the streetlight in front of its chained gate. I went over. Hagai was intrigued and agreed to participate before I even reached my point. But when I mentioned that we would all strip down to our underwear, his face went pale, and he fell silent. I could tell he felt cornered and changed the topic. When I got home that night, I wrote to him to clarify. He replied,

> I totally agree with what you said about how people from both sides need to meet and get to know people on the other side. That's exactly my inspiration and goal for the Middle East Club. I invite you once again to come one time and see for yourself. It's not about debates. It's about us. Individuals.
>
> Regarding the project, I had two thoughts. One practical—we can all have the same underwear so we keep on being equal. The other is that by having six Israelis and yourself, the project becomes very personal, very "you." If there were six Palestinians, then that can be understood as one nation in front of the other. But having just yourself there makes it (to my view) more: "Steve and Israelis", or "how Steve sees the Israelis." This is not good or bad, it is just different than two nations.

I replied to him, how can we be individuals if we wear the same underwear? We are different nations, but we are equal. By each wearing his underwear, this stresses our freedom and individuality. Two emails later, Hagai decided to commit himself.

Yishai was the second Israeli I spoke with. He wasn't a member of Goodenough then, but I had seen him at college events in the past. He was always on alert, reminding me of the security chiefs at Ben Gurion Airport when he walked or gestured. To me, he came across as one of those ambassadors, speaking for Israel and Israelis. I was cautious, suspecting a conversation could end up like an interrogation. But one evening, on my way to Willie G, I bumped into him while exiting the garden, and we started to chat. Yishai wasn't on my list of Israelis to approach, but I casually asked him if we could meet over the next few days to discuss something, agreeing to meet at Freddy's Bar in London House.

When we met, we sat in a quiet corner facing each other. I quickly learned that he had worked as chief of staff for the Knesset Speaker and a clerk for Chief Justice Aharon Barak of the Supreme Court. He was about to start a master's degree in economic development and intended to go for a Ph.D. in law.

I handed him a two-page document on the objective and waited for him to finish reading while slowly sipping my hot cup of tea. As he lifted his eyes off the paper, he said no. He had his political career to worry about. We spoke about bodies and scars, about images and their layers from the past. I said these bodies must communicate directly with each other, without any foreign mediation. We could no longer live as victims seeking constant sympathy and solidarity.

As we kept talking, he opened up, saying that whenever he turned on the radio in his car and heard anything in Arabic, he perceived it as noise, distortion and quickly changed the station. He was ashamed that he met Palestinians for the first time in London, not during the thirty-three years of his life in Tel Aviv—ironic for two nations living on the same land. I kept listening, giving him space, but when he justified the construction of the Separation

Wall, I asked him why it made Israelis feel more secure. The dramatic decrease in the number of suicide bombers was his answer. Like many Israelis, he maintained that Israel's growing sense of security would eventually lead to the wall's dismantlement. I pointed out that there are long-term psychological effects, which only lead to resentment, continued resistance, and more war. In the end, I couldn't convince him to participate, but he did offer to help me find other participants.

One misty night, while smoking a cigarette outside, I saw Itay lighting up, not far from me. Even though he and Eliza got the dream flat, I didn't hold that against them. We set off talking about philosophy, his field of study, which led us to counter *Settlement*. I asked him to participate, but when I mentioned the underwear, he lit another cigarette, exhaled a large cloud of smoke, and said, more firmly than Yishai:

Absolutely not.

At first, I thought his rejection was ideological, but then he took me through metaphysical realities about being insecure with his chubby body. He paused for a second and then said his friend Shachar might be interested.

I called Shachar, and he proposed that we meet at Hummus Bros in Soho. I agreed, knowing too well how often engagement between Palestinians and Israelis was reduced to sitting together and wiping hummus. We arrived at the same time, coming from opposite sides of the street. He had long hair, like mine, and wore a black trench coat and polished shoes. As we shook hands, I asked him if he was a model. He chuckled, saying that he only knew computer models as he worked in IT. While waiting for the hummus to land on our table, I changed my mind to hand him my text, preferring to keep the conversation personal and casual. Shachar listened to me attentively, his elbows resting on the table and hands joined at his chin. I sensed that something was worrying him, that he didn't trust me. Eventually, he shared his concern about the image of six Israelis versus one Palestinian, asking me why the number was uneven. For him, the Israelis would look as if they had been condemned to death, awaiting their execution, and wondered why I didn't want to make it six against six. I responded,

> *Your remark gives Settlement another layer. I'm not looking for a stand-off, a shootout, or to present two equal sides. The conflict was never equal, and yet it is always reported that way. But look at it this way, six against one—you stand on the stronger side.*

My argument got to him. As we continued talking, he revealed that he was also worried about the images possibly being misused, asking me to guarantee that they would only be published in this context. I said,

> *What is the point be of showing them out of context? It would have been way easier to hire models to make the project, but I wanted real Israelis, soldiers who had served in the army, with scars, with history.*

We based our agreement on trust, without the need to sign any documents, and shook on it. This small gesture made me realize that all the past peace negotiators wasted their strength crafting empty sentences rather than finding novel ways to build trust and mutual understanding. A few days later, Shachar texted me with the message,

> You can count me in.

Yishai also helped set up a meeting with Oren, a friend of his who lived with his wife at the International Student Hall, a block away from our Goodenough Square. The International Hall was like a labyrinth, with glass and metal bridges connecting the separate building sides. It required a Ph.D. to figure out how to ring Oren's bell and get to his flat. When I finally did, I apologized for the delay, as he and Aliza welcomed me in for tea.

We spoke about breaking down cultural differences, border issues, and national pride, topics I didn't discuss with the other Israelis. They listened with concentration, trying to construe where I was going with my narrative as they had no clue yet. Yishai had kept it as a surprise. But when I mentioned the underwear, their faces dropped. I remember saying,

> *I want my statement to come out of the work itself. I collaborate with you by choice. When Palestinian and Israeli artists collaborate, I often see it as artificial, lacking substance, generating cheap texts, embracing fake coexistence. In many ways, the artists get censored, or censor themselves, falling indirectly into clichés and propaganda.*

Oren wanted to speak with his family in Israel before agreeing because he was aware that his image would stand as a symbol for many others, just as my image would.

A week later, Francesca, Cécile, and I went out for dinner at Hare & Tortoise, a popular pan-Asian restaurant on Brunswick Square. As we sat down, Yishay entered, along with his wife and two kids, and sat next to us. They were Goodenough members. After a few minutes of chat, Yishay was quick to suggest we join the tables together and asked me what I was up to. I hadn't considered him, believing that a man in his forties, with kids, and studying for a Ph.D. in education would find posing in his underwear inappropriate. My words came out rehearsed, like an ambassador dictated by limited choices of expression. I felt they lacked genuineness, but Yishay felt the spirit of my search, agreeing to participate before I even invited him. I realized my mistake in prejudging others.

I met Matias, a chemist, in an Italian café in Camden Town Market. I arrived a bit late and found him waiting for me, reading a book at the back of the café. When he stood up to shake my hand, I was momentarily intimidated by his height and realized it might be a problem when photographing him among the other Israelis. I showed him my work on my computer, and he was impressed by my *Till the End* stone series, which led me to talk with him about the Occupation. Matias expressed himself like an autobiographer who was not at terms with his past, using words layered with guilt and doubt. He dominated the conversation and spoke about his background and the period he served in the army, spent stopping children and controlling daily life in the West Bank. Deep down, he also wanted a way out, a settlement to free himself from the Occupier, a label he couldn't escape either.

Yoni was the last Israeli whose destiny became tied to mine. I was introduced to him by a mutual friend Rula, a Palestinian from Nazareth who lived in London who briefly briefed him. He was doing a Ph.D. in Oriental studies at Cambridge University. We spoke on the phone, and before I even explained anything further, he confirmed that he wanted to participate. His quick reaction made me suspicious, compelling me to follow up with more details in an email. We later agreed to meet at his favorite pub off Russell Square.

Yoni spoke perfect Arabic, which was rare for an Israeli, but this naturally garnered more mistrust than friendship. Palestinians were suspicious of his Arabic, suspecting he worked for Israeli Intelligence. He complimented my Hebrew. The language was not a barrier between us. After several pints of beer, we exchanged stories, and he shared how his love for the Arabic language led him to fall in love with a Palestinian girl. It was an adolescent affair, just after high school, and where they knew, as he disclosed, that going public was never possible. So it ended before it started.

We got drunk, no longer sure if we were speaking in Arabic or in Hebrew—and we never talked about *Settlement*.

In our settlement, context became content—one part being that a Palestinian managed to strip down six Israelis, seeing it as a major victory. Many wondered how I was able to do it. Because of a camera error, we had to strip not once, but twice. And the only answer I could come up with came from a postcard I saw hanging on the wall of a London pub:

> If You Want To Change The World . . .
> Start With Your Underwear.

3

My life was always in my art. And art always captured my life. But, Francesca never ceased to be the spark shining on all my work. Present, yet hidden under layers of images. This made her feel invisible at times. The way I saw it, the absence she perceived was only on the surface. Everyone knew how obsessed I was with her, how much she arrested me.

Being on the same wavelength gave us the power to penetrate unexplored imagination, to push it further by breaking invisible barriers set only by the individual self. I felt enlightened by her presence. But during our first year in London, she became more entrapped in the canvas of my life. The thought of waking up one day and not finding her next to me, or Cécile, pushed me to get up. But waking up each morning itself was difficult; everything was dull, walking fatigued me, and my back hurt me day and night. I preferred to go nowhere, sinking into my bed longer each day. One autumn day, Francesca and Cécile dragged me out for a walk in Victoria Park.

The path to the pond was covered with a bed of leaves. The leaf piles at the edge of the lake looked like small mountains rising out of the earth. Walking over them as I held Cécile's hand felt like stepping on hollow, empty ground as if the land had disappeared. As we reached the pond, Cécile let go of my hand and ran to the swans. The water's edge around the entire pond was covered with tree pollen interspersed with feathers and other residues of life that found their way into the stream. We watched as they slowly moved forward, creating the most captivating compositions on the surface. Later, I transformed the images I took into *No Man's Land*.

We picked up a bunch of leaves off the ground and looked at them closely. At first, they all looked the same, but Cécile couldn't find two that were identical, even from the same tree. Looking closely at their surfaces, she realized they were all unique.

In the land of my exile, the view from the barred window in my Goodenough cell looked the same every day. When I watched Cécile climb onto that windowsill, wearing shoes that didn't fit her, feeling out of place, I saw the view differently. I photographed her standing there, from different angles. Then I shot other windows and their views of my immediate surroundings. I collaged them together, making the windows appear photographed from both sides, simultaneously exposing interior and exterior worlds. They revealed new mental scapes that carried my unsettling states of mind. I was neither here nor there—not in Jerusalem, or in London—but lost somewhere in a sea of thoughts. Even though I perceived *Settlement* as a self-empowerment mode over my image as a Palestinian, I could still not feel true liberation. I was torn apart, without a sense of gravity, disoriented, but hyperconscious that I would always be Occupied, nailed, chained, seized in an image that would never find ground. It seemed my destiny was to live suspended, in the image of under Occupation, in a permanent state of exile. Locked in my reality, I was certain there was no exit.

But in the three years we lived in London, something was shifting as I withdrew from the world when I sat for hundreds of hours to collage images, just like Mother Veronica had when she painted the icons. In conversation with myself, I dug deep into my psyche to mirror the state of mental exile I was going through, calling the art series *In Exile*. The windows I collaged looked into my past, and in the process of layering them, I reflected long enough until I found ways to place the past beneath the layers. Collaging cut images helped me glue the fragments of the self together. I became more stable—the glue was holding. The stones on my back were getting lighter. My depression subsided. Change was happening, and my altered state of mind enabled a space where new roots could grow in my relationship with Francesca. I was able to be present again.

But it was inevitable that the hidden layers of my past and

their residue would quickly emerge again. The past cannot be hidden. I became aware that my exile was a symptom, a side effect, and not the cause of my disorder. It wouldn't be until a trip to Dubai in 2010 that the glue would dissolve, allowing for dramatic change, shaking me to the core.

I landed in Dubai, the land of the blooming desert, with ecstasy in my veins. It was my first trip there. I let the city's vibration guide me from one reality to another. I was excited by my new show at The Empty Quarter Gallery, which sold out before it opened, about my art shown on the cover of a prominent magazine, and *In Exile* destined for auction at Christie's.

On the day I landed, I had four surreal encounters that led to mystifying connections. When I count the most important people I met in my life back then on my fingers, four of them appeared on that special day.

I met the first of them late that night, on the terrace of a villa lit with torches as pathways around the garden. I had been invited to an exhibition after-party. Sitting on a long couch, I talked to the gallery owner, who asked what compelled me to make art. My answer grabbed the attention of somebody sitting alone nearby, listening in. When the gallerist left, she turned to me. The fire surrounding us made her eyes glitter like stars. Entranced, I traveled through them to distant galaxies, and when I returned—I was forever changed. Straight off, we began talking with the ease of unfiltered words. Speaking to her was like a whisper in the wind. Feeling no gravity, I referred to my depression and exile in the past tense for the first time in my life, saying that my passion for making art was over because there was no longer an inner struggle fueling it. She spoke about transcendence and how, through the power of the mind and the heart, there were no limits—she was like an alchemist with words. She was different, hypnotic to listen to, and in that moment, I knew she would become a new light in my life.

The Muse.

As she was about to leave, I told her about my problem with remembering names and faces. She found it amusing, asking if this would happen to her too. But there was no chance. I memorized her face, like a sculptor who sees a masterpiece from a distance. Her charm was like a new drug, entrancing me to go through multiple realities. But I didn't give her my number, and hugged her goodbye, this time without any promise, wondering if I would ever see her again.

She left me in honest dialogue with myself. I headed straight to the bar and ordered a double or a triple shot of whiskey. There, I bumped into a tall woman, dressed in white, which matched her long white hair, wearing sunglasses at night. She was rolling herself a cigarette, and while I waited for my shots, we found ourselves talking. Christa spoke English with a British accent that revealed a hint of German. When I introduced myself, she recognized my name, quickly connecting it to my exhibition at The Empty Quarter,

> Oh, you are the painter without the brush who takes photographs instead.

I didn't know whether this was a compliment. Her confidence and charisma intrigued me. Christa then spoke about a memoir she had written, The Road to Miran: Travels in the Forbidden Zone, an area I felt I was on, telling her I was also conceiving a memoir one day. Christa was an artist-turned-art historian. I didn't know then that she would later work on writing the study for my first monograph, covering my art from the beginning till that point, and where two years later, we would travel together to the room where I was born.

While walking with Christa the next day, arm in arm, through the Art Dubai art fair, we bumped into Jeanno, an artist between two realities, born in Kabul, but she lived in Berlin. Jeanno spoke with words stripped of nostalgia or melancholy to make it easier for her to move ahead when talking about her homeland. We felt connected. I asked Jeanno if she would like to see my work at the magazine stall, and she came a few hours later. While I was signing a few copies, I saw her emerge from the bustling crowd, her eyes catching mine. When she arrived, I pulled out my laptop and asked her to show me what she was working on. She spoke about Erased Memories, which consisted of images she had taken on her first trip back to Kabul since she fled in 1978 with her family. Upon her return to Berlin, and after developing the film, a mechanical error in her camera caused black and white streaks. She was curious about the error, about the light and darkness that obscured her images, which, just like the memory of her past, were missing details, a reminder that there are no mistakes in life.

That night we went to a party together on the seventieth floor of a building whose elevator had just sixty-eight buttons—this is where my relationship with Jeanno would exist later, in another dimension. We went out on the terrace, stood side by side, our shoulders touching, and observed the night sky. We understood each other without having to speak, as if we had grown up in the same neighborhood, to the same family. That year, I would end up living on the same street as Jeanno in Berlin, by complete coincidence, or perhaps by cosmic intervention.

As Jeanno left the magazine stall, a lady with long red hair and a silk scarf around her neck approached the booth. The magazine's publisher introduced me to Karin Adrian Von Roques, and after a few minutes of honest chat, she vanished, leaving me with the feeling that we already knew each other. Just in hearing her first few words, my impression was that they went beyond the surface. In three years, she would knock on my door on a very fateful day to find out she was The Angel of Death.

The next morning at the art fair, while walking with Christa again, I saw The Muse coming in my direction, her eyes exploding with glitter. I stopped her. This time, I chose to bypass serendipity. I asked for her email address, and as she wrote it on the tiniest piece of paper imaginable. She asked me what I was working on now, and I said,

Nothing!

She wondered why,

I feel as if I have healed myself. And since I only create art out of depression, there is nothing left to mirror.

She laughed and said with a smile that embraced the universe,

Then why don't you mirror what you feel right now?

It hit me right there, like lightning. Just like I had always traveled to the darkest side of my mind, I could also travel to the other side and mirror all the beauty that was already there.

I flew back to London vibrating, shaking. I let the euphoria burst into art. This time there was no isolation. Instead, I jumped through the windows of my exile to land onto trees, with the earth below me and the sky above. I shook my camera like a mad man, like prisoners shaking during interrogation. The movement caused blurry images. The universe was collapsing in on itself, disintegrating. In part, the images showed trees, as if uprooted but still standing, now thriving in another location, defying their own reality. I had been injected with adrenaline, blood flowing through my veins, struck by lightning over and over again, in an erratic state of euphoria. This new spark altered my consciousness and made me aware of the possibility of change. In that state, to become more malleable, I broke my bones, crushed them, to allow a new self to emerge. I looked to the sky and planted my roots in the clouds, to always remain free and in transition.

I shared my new state of mind with The Muse, who was back then studying esoteric psychology. In her first email to me, she wrote,

> Carl Jung said that there is an alchemy when two individuals meet and connect; like a chemical reaction, they form a new substance, and so it was with our chance meeting.
>
> I look forward to witnessing this beauty unfolding, which actually has its genuine beginnings in you! We, on the outside, who brought it to your attention, are a mirror to all that is beauty and light in you.

The Muse was another sign from the universe. I got addicted to her words and waited for her emails every day, where our conversations shifted between her reality and mine. The Muse was also in a state of inner turmoil, inflamed, and together we combined energies to piece our puzzles. She was in transition, battling her own identity, straddling her unconscious and conscious mind, exploring the blurry distinction between the two.

But only a few weeks after Dubai, my ecstasy dispersed when I read a text by Edward Said that woke me up, shedding light on how exile was an oscillation between melancholy and euphoria. My euphoria was only an injection, and that like all addicts, when its dose became insufficient, I would panic and look for a stronger drug. I knew that the moment the effect faded away, I would have to go through a novel process of salvation—I would have to face the pain of stitching my wounds for real healing.

I emailed The Muse explaining what I was going through, how I felt occupied by my thoughts and constructions. She replied with this quote by a poet,

> All changes, even the most longed for, have their melancholy; for what we leave behind us, is a part of ourselves. We must die in one life before we can enter another.

The layers from my past were reemerging again. There was no escape—the glue was dissolving, and I had to face them soon. The Muse was quick to write back,

> These dark nights of the soul, which you have already gone through and will continue to go through, interrupted by alternate states of happiness and euphoria or peak experience, which are enmeshed in the fabric of the glue that you have used to hold your psyche together, are part of the melancholy journey we all go through in life.
>
> If you have experienced depression, see it as your mind's defense mechanism against expressing true rage or sadness. The points where you plunge the lowest are moments of ego death. I think a great many artists and people, for that matter, who unfortunately decide to end their lives, misunderstand this state as a call to end their physical existence. By doing this, they are mistaking ego death for physical death. It is actually a call for you to radically reexamine your shadow side and end its stranglehold over you. If you can get through these periods with the help of a supportive guide, you will come to see that it was an act of grace that brought you to your knees, to make you self-aware. You have already translated this self-awareness into art, and I think you will continue to do so.

Three months after Dubai, during the summer, I flew from London to Berlin for the opening of my exhibition at the Academy of Arts showing *In Exile*, as part of my nomination and acceptance of *The Ellen Auerbach Award*, which included the publishing of a study on my art in which I thought Christa was a perfect match. In Berlin, and as my euphoria was running out, I feared the next collapse. One day, near twilight, I strolled through the Wall Park in Prenzlauer Berg, where the Berlin Wall stood, dividing the city into two parts. I walked east, down a bustling street lined with cafés, known for its buildings with pastel facades. At that hour, the sky was burning with color, vivid like the graffiti I had just passed on the long wall stretching across the park's hill. The sun cast a long streak of light, creating a strong shadow, a contrast visible on the buildings on either side of the street. I kept on walking, charmed by the trees on the two sidewalks, their branches converging as one looked at the far end. I stopped at the first intersection, took a moment to look around, and with my eyes, I climbed up to the balconies of the building in front of me. There, I felt I could breathe fresh air after living in the contamination in my Londo exile. I grabbed my phone, called Francesca on the spot, and in the moment, I said,

Bombina!
We are moving to Berlin.
Trust me.
You will not regret it.

Berlin was the answer to empty London. Francesca and I learned how radical situations sometimes required radical solutions. Complaining about misery was a waste of energy. We had the power to change our reality, and we were on the same wavelength as we have always been. In less than three weeks, we were in Berlin. London was in the past tense.

During this short period, Francesca applied for teaching positions at three private schools, all of which offered her jobs.

And for Cécile, we found a private school offering an English and German curriculum. Berlin was welcoming. This time, none of us, not even Cécile, hesitated to say goodbye. All that was missing now was finding a home.

When Francesca and Cécile left for Berlin, I stayed behind to pack and hand over the keys. I put our memories into forty-two boxes, labeling the box that had my old keys, including the one for my PO Box, "Jerusalem."

By coincidence, The Muse was in London. This was our first chance to see each other since our first encounter. We agreed to go out and meet in front of Angel station. When she appeared, she looked as anxious as me, not knowing where to start. In our email communications, we had dropped our masks, and now we were standing face to face, feeling a bit bare. A few hours later, on Upper Street, our galaxies collided, resulting in a bond that hypnotized me, sending me miles forward on my road to liberation.

The Muse's presence, in body and mind, was therapeutic. She once wrote,

> That is how I come to accept our reality. We've rarely met in physical form, but our energetic connection is strong. I can free fall in my mind and know that you are there with me.

Whatever The Muse gave me, I mirrored it back. In one of her emails, she summed up perfectly the nature of our symbiosis,

> I choose to visualize the healing and joy that you have brought me through the metaphor of an ocean wave. First we met—the tide gathered, the momentum built, and then as it grew into a glorious wave, soaring and crashing, we experienced the ecstatic high of the union, and the wonderful conversations that followed, and then the gentle end as it dis-

appeared back into the ocean.

During Francesca and Cécile's first days in Berlin, they stayed with Ruthe, a friend from Haifa who had left Israel nineteen years earlier. We had become friends three years before our move to Berlin after I joined a group of international artists to participate in her 2007 art project Challenging Walls, which projected images of everyday life on both sides of the Separation Wall to create window-like views to the other side.

Francesca found out that Jan and Ayelet, Ruthe's friends who lived across the street from her, were leaving their flat. When I arrived, we set up a meeting to see it right away, hoping that we would get a lucky strike. Jan and Ayelet had decided to return to Israel but didn't know when. They were looking for someone to transfer their contract to eventually compensate them for the kitchen they had installed, a common practice in Berlin, and buy all of their furniture. When we visited the flat, we could imagine it being home—struck by its high ceilings and squeaking wooden floors. We agreed to take it, not bothered about buying the furniture, even though none of it was to our taste—we thought of that as the price we had to pay to get in and take care of it later. But a week later, we called and declined the offer because the house was missing a room.

For the first six months in Berlin, we settled like nomads, and we lived in bizarre sublets in the east and the west. Finding a flat with the right size, price, and location required months of searching—it was everyone's nightmare. Cécile had to leave for school a few times from hotels. We even stayed at the Academy of Arts, taken in as art refugees, when the director heard that we lived in a hotel. Then Jan emailed a new offer, which we declined again because his departure date was never set. But we always said no with a heavy feeling. We continued searching, never finding any suitable space. Francesca and I had agreed never to make the same mistake as we did in London. We were fixed on finding the right home, the main reason we left.

Even though Jan lived on one of the most coveted streets in the desired eastern side of Berlin, he was having grave difficulty finding someone to take his flat. When I picked up his last call, all he asked for was compensation for the kitchen since he had shipped everything else to Israel. He wasn't happy about it, but he had no choice.

After being stranded for too long, and seeing how that affected Cécile, Francesca and I agreed to take it—the decision was final. Jan was bitter with us. When he cleared out the flat, he unscrewed each and every light bulb and even removed their sockets, leaving the electrical wires dangling from the ceiling. When we had our meeting to pick up our keys, we entered the new home in darkness. The landlord used a flashlight to show us around, but we could hardly see a thing. The next morning, when we went back to see it properly, I looked out of the window for the first time, and it suddenly hit me. It dawned on me that I was looking down at the same spot where I had fallen in love with Berlin, making that call to Francesca.

Sometimes, we fail to see what's there, right in front of our eyes.

2

On a snowy day, during one of Berlin's coldest winters on record, we moved into the new flat. When we unpacked, the box I labeled in London "Jerusalem" was missing, and in it was my key for the PO Box. I never found it. A few weeks later, the street I had fallen in love with was getting unearthed, receiving an overhaul infrastructure, causing a vast hole stretching from its beginning to its end. For the next three years, our flat overlooked a muddy construction site. Every morning, we woke up to the sound of trucks pulling in and out, beeping, to a view of meters long pipes and cables, next to mountains of stones desperate to be cobbled back together.

Since leaving Jerusalem, I had been rebuilding my home, brick by brick. But when I would go back to visit, I would feel ravaged the moment I landed in Tel Aviv and exited the plane's door. I could see a toxic fog coming towards me, and since I couldn't re-board, I knew I would have to tolerate more contamination. I no longer had any patience for the Occupation, the stagnation, or the suffering. Even Francesca lost her citizenship for living outside of Jerusalem. We were never informed that she had to live in Israel for three years after she received it.

When I was there, I was tortured by seeing my parents, since I couldn't help as they got old and sick. Guilt hovered like a cloud above my head. What made me return was Cécile, who felt her roots were from Jerusalem. But resenting my city of birth disturbed me, was not natural, and to live in serenity, I determined to envision a renewed bond with Jerusalem.

Back in Berlin, it would take me weeks to recover. I would share my frustration with Jeanno, whom I regularly saw since we lived on the same street. The glue holding the self together was dissolving, and the old me was still holding it together instead of just letting the self adjust and transform. Memories of Jeanno's past ad mine became intertwined, empowering our connection. When I told her how I had glued my fragments of self together as a sign that I was more stable, she responded,

I like the idea of fragments and glue, so flexible.
No structure can exist forever.

Jeanno told me her life story in fragments. In 1978, at five, just before the war, she had to flee Kabul carrying nothing. Unlike Cécile, she didn't have the chance to say goodbye to anything. They cut her hair short to make her look like a boy to facilitate her escape. When she showed me a picture, I really couldn't tell it was her. Jeanno ended up staying with her aunt in Delhi, who later took her to Berlin. Her brother wasn't as fortunate as her and was stranded in the beginning, along with their parents, in a refugee camp in Pakistan. After three years of effort, her family was able to make it to Berlin. But when Jeanno saw them, she told me,

I felt like a stranger to myself.
I couldn't speak.

Her tongue was tied—her native language replaced by German. By then, her family had lost their house and land, and from all that past, only thirty family photos remained, the last thing her mother grabbed before leaving home. When I met Jeanno, she was like me, delving into images and the realities they create, looking for answers. To come to terms with her history, she was an artist on a mission to scrape away the pain, layers of nostalgia, which had come to coat those thirty images over the years. We both lived with lost homes. In the same year I left Jerusalem and uprooted myself, Jeanno returned to Kabul for the first time to search for her roots. Jeanno cried as she told the story of visiting her lost home on that trip, after thirty years. She had no idea who occupied it but mustered the courage and knocked at the door. After explaining who she was, the Afghani occupiers still welcomed her in. Over a cup of tea, she asked them how they came to live in her childhood house. It turned out that her parents had managed to reclaim the house a few years earlier, and this Afghani family now living there bought it from Jeanno's mother. On the spot, Jeaano called her mother right then and there, screaming in disbelief, in tears. And those tears came flooding back as she retold me how she felt at that moment. All I could do was hold her hand, and listen, let it all out.

When Jeanno returned to Berlin, her mother offered her a share of the sale, but she declined it, not wanting to put any value on her uprooting. Instead, her mother gave her a piece of land in the south of Afghanistan as a remuneration. When I asked Jeanno what she wanted to do with it, she said she would open it to local farmers.

But two years into our friendship, and given its intensity and beauty, a fight led to the most unexpected, a fracture in the heart. It was then when I learned that deep connections are dangerous because when injured, they are almost impossible to heal. I felt only another cosmic intervention could bring us back together.

A few months before our fight, we had been invited to speak at TEDx Marrakech together. Given that none of us contacted the other, I prepared to step on the stage alone to give a separate talk. But, two days before our departure, Jeanno emailed me, saying that she had decided not to go. I hoped her decision was not connected to what had happened between us and urged her to attend and deliver her talk, ending my words with,

> *Jeanno.*
> *Maybe once we are high in the air,*
> *we will find our words again.*

She never replied. I boarded the three-flight trip into the unknown alone, but it turned out we were on the first plane together. When we saw each other while boarding the second flight in Munich, we both wondered how we had gotten there. In the one minute we chatted, she clarified that she was attending because she had adjusted her schedule and had nothing to do with me. Jeanno came over on the plane, where we spoke for a few awkward minutes, and then she returned to her seat. We didn't even see each other after we landed till the third connecting flight, from Lisbon to Marrakech. It only had a few passengers on board, almost empty. I was assigned a window seat at the very back of the plane. After I sat down, I noticed Jeanno walking up the aisle as if towards me, doubting she was making an effort to clear the air between us. But she put her bag in the overhead locker and sat in the middle seat, right next to me. I said I was glad that she came over, but she hadn't done it on purpose—this was her allocated seat in the empty plane. I didn't believe her until she showed me her ticket. As the plane ascended over the gray clouds to the blue sky over Africa, the frost that covered our hearts dissolved. As we landed, we held each other's hand and hit the reset button.

One afternoon in Berlin, we sat in a café, and she showed me images from Three Fragments from Jerusalem, made during her residency in the Old City a year earlier. In one photo, she appeared using tweezers to remove a single layer of white paint peeled away from the ceiling of her room. In the solitude of her space, she shared how she watched pieces of dangling paint fall through the air. For Jeanno, the shapes of the changing fragments looked like puzzle pieces. The negative spaces they left behind became like a map terrain, transporting her to her lost home in Kabul. She collected those brittle pieces of dry paint, memory, and placed them between the pages of books. The fragments were like those inside my Old City house, which had many rooms painted in different colors. And where after every summer, the walls started to peel, creating shapes, fragments, and contours that puzzled the eye.

The inevitable cycle of peeling would begin again, and we would paint more layers on top. Over the years, the colors merged, and one layer dissolved into the other. I grew up staring at those fragments dry, and peel off, and turn to dust as they made their dive through the air. I would always found pieces on my bed, or the dust that remained of them. For me, the fragments were like hidden archives that recorded the passage of time and its changing realities. Their layers unveiled palimpsests as if each was a handwritten manuscript that had been erased and written over but still bearing visible traces of its past.

I saw these layers as the last physical residue of my past, what I really had to come to terms with. They were visible traces that I could see and touch. I got up and stood on my chair in the café, gesturing to Jeanno about how hundreds of them would look on a huge canvas, or sandwiched between plates of glass suspended in the air in a grid, as if looking at a colored map, the universe, land from below, like joined islands of discontinued geographies of unknown worlds, floating in the air. The light passing through the transparent glass fragments would mirror colorful shapes on the ground, making the fragments flow between image and reality, between memory and its reality.

On those newly found maps, there was a direct passage between Jerusalem and Kabul. The borders dissolved as each fragment was connected to the other. Collaborating on this expedition with Jeanno would have allowed me to rediscover my Jerusalem.

Our next step was to find an institution to endorse it, which would enable us to travel to Jerusalem and start collecting. But no matter how hard we tried over the next two years, we failed to find any support. Jerusalem–Kabul in Transition would remain a reality that matters only between Jeanno and me. Envisioning the dream allowed us to transcend our points of origin, to find new routes towards home.

I felt Jeanno's pain on the loss of her childhood home. It was a year earlier when I had rented the Occupied house in Ein Karem in Jerusalem from the Israeli family. This house belonged to a Palestinian family who, in all likelihood, had been forced into a refugee camp and then condemned to a life in exile. For those thirty-eight days, I struggled with my identity, the Palestinian Right of Return, and morality. I would often think about what Najwan Darwish said in the documentary *Jerusalem in Exile*,

> I can't understand how a nation can take the land of another. Who could live in someone else's home, without a problem, not even on a psychological level? Isn't it surprising that the people who live in these houses don't think about who used to live there?

When I took my first step to enter the house, I felt the Arab tiles on the floor shatter under my feet. I stood still for a moment, thinking of the original owners and how they would feel should they ever return. The kitchen at the far corner of the house looked frozen in time, as if untouched since 1948, with its old stove and one single wood shelf with large pans dangling from it. The Israeli who was guiding us through each room answered all of my questions, but when I asked if he knew the identity of the original owners and their fate, he had no clue.

That night, lying in an Israeli bed, under white sheets, Francesca and I spoke till the early hours of the morning, listening to crickets chirping outside as if calling for someone, in an endless recital. The next morning, I felt compelled to photograph every detail of the house, confronting its history. I became an obsessed visual investigator, collecting images, searching for clues, for any trace from the past by looking at the present, at what was still visible.

I photographed the wood-framed portraits hanging on the wall, showing the Jewish family tree of grandparents, parents, and children. I photographed the antique cupboard decorated with wood carvings, which looked dated to the original owners because of its size. Once it was there, it remained where it stood.

I photographed broken bottles, the broad silver spoons in the drawers. I photographed the children's drawings on their bedroom doors and a dinosaur figure on the shelf. I flipped through the pages of all their books and was surprised when I found a published photo of mine. An image of mine was already living, present in this house. I photographed the patterns on the floors and ceiling, their shoes, the contents of their bedroom drawers, their wardrobes, and their clothes, along with their storage boxes, the views from their barred windows, the wood ladder in the garden resting on a lemon tree, even the worn-out hammock Cécile liked to sink into to watch the sun disappear in the valley behind the trees.

I felt like I had violated the space and that it could be justified. I wanted to use the images in my work but was ashamed, despite knowing that I could justify my actions and that many would perceive it as a victory against the Israeli Occupation. When I returned to London, I questioned my ethics further. The line between right and wrong seemed blurry. I asked myself,

> *Do I have the right to go through their belongings?*
> *Was is it right to rent a stolen house?*

In the end, I emailed the Israeli family about what I did and what it meant to me.

I didn't know what I was going to do with the colored digital images till four years later when I realized that the fragments could be used as bases to print the photographs on. I returned to the house I was born in, and others in the Old City, to collect colored peeling wall fragments to later spread black and white photo emulsion onto their fragile surfaces, to make them light-sensitive. I was curious to see the resulting alchemy after the bases merged with the images, which I transformed into black and white negatives to print them later in the darkroom.

I had to inspect how to access many more homes, knowing that many people would find me and my intentions suspicious. When I lived in the Old City, my own home was under threat, like everyone else's. I did not trust any strangers to enter the house. This concern came from the countless stories of Palestinians losing properties because Israel would dismiss ownership documents that dated back to Jordanian, British, or Ottoman rule. There is even a reference book written by a notorious lawyer on the complexity of ownership loopholes in this small part of the world. For decades, fanatic Jewish Israeli settlers succeeded in snatching up properties in the city's Muslim and Christian Quarters. Some houses were sold by greedy Palestinians who would flee the night before the settlers burst in to drape long Israeli flags like banners over the house's facade. Some of these sellers were later targeted by Palestinians and killed for being traitors. But whether the sellers escaped or slaughtered, that wasn't the end of the story. Around-the-clock settler security personnel, armed from head to toe, escorted every member of the Jewish families, turning these settled homes into army bases and the neighborhoods into sites of unending confrontation.

I traveled to Jerusalem not knowing where to start, wondering what I would tell random people when I knocked on their doors to collect dust from their walls. Because they were brittle, I wanted to find as many fragments as possible, in different shapes, sizes, and colors, and to protect them, I placed them between glass plates.

My first destination was the Old City house, where I headed straight to the inner room on the second floor to reach the two alcove windows just below the ceiling, one at the left of the main arch and one at its right. Because they were far up, my father stored his antique and leather books in them, but it also meant that we never really scrapped the old paint off when we painted a new one. I climbed up the wooden ladder my father had built, and with a sharp scraper, I started peeling into the hidden layers.

The more layers I removed, the more colors I found of all the paint throughout its history. I recognized the light blue and orange of my childhood but was surprised to also see traces of pink. The pieces I found there were a celebration of colors fused into each other, painted by many hands over the years, including my own. I felt like an archaeologist, digging, collecting what everyone else was throwing away. I asked many people in my neighborhood, friends, and strangers to help me locate more fragments. I called house painters, asking if they had jobs in the Old City where I could join them. To my surprise, they took me seriously, even though what I wanted was virtually worthless from their side, but from mine, they were visually priceless.

I heard my neighbors were renovating their house, a few doors down from our place, at the base of the hill. I rushed straight over to find their front door open. I was in the house before, and I could hear the echo of their voices coming from their dark inner rooms, almost like caves. When they welcomed me in, I walked through the rubble and saw them gathered inside. They had just started peeling the paint off the walls, skinning it in stripes and patches. I started peeling alongside them, and it felt like I was peeling my own skin, looking deeper into the layers of my self. Each violent tear exposed what was hidden beneath my scars. I peeled and peeled till there was nothing.

While searching for more homes with a friend, I saw a sign in front of an old house warning about its imminent collapse.

There were red tapes all around. But, I could see from below the ceiling of the rooms rich with old paint. We ducked under the red tapes and entered the forbidden zone. Narrow dusty corridors with steep stairs led us to find ourselves in a small courtyard with stone arches on opposite sides. Only stray cats lived there. The building was abandoned because of thick cracks that fractured the main pillars, a sign of pressure from the weight above, or the soft land below, caused by previous earthquakes that turned Jerusalem into rubble. Jerusalem was always built on the remains of the old. As I peeled, I collected the last traces of a centuries-old house that would soon disappear and turn into dust. We wandered from room to room, remained long enough to rescue every fragment before the imminent collapse.

One day during my trip, the son of a baker I knew in Bab Huta overheard me talking about old paint with the owner of our local grocery store. He invited me to look at the bakery, run by his family from generation to generation. It still carried on the custom of cooking meals in a wood-burning oven for customers who brought in their own food pots. I remember going to pick up our pot when I was a child offering the baker a portion of its contents. We entered the bakery by descending steps straight to the pit where the Farran—the person operating the oven—stood next to wooden peels, in assorted lengths and shapes. The baker's son took me to the backside, where I had never been before. The walls were black from the oven's smoke as if burnt. He wanted to take me to the attic. The ceiling was a hidden treasure, covered in many layers of paint dating back to old times. The moment I touched their surface, chunks of cyan and yellow fragments fell off and turned to sand, requiring me to remove each piece like a surgeon. The fragments were brittle from constant exposure to heat, yet this was precisely the fragility I was searching for. The baker's son started helping me by taking the fragments and placing them, like bread, onto wooden trays. Except those trays were not going to any oven, to be burnt under fire, but to be exposed by light, carrying us to our past and future.

I became known around the Old City as The Dust Collector as many people heard about it. I was invited into many homes, and the more I peeled, the deeper I dug into myself, the more I understood the essence of what it meant that exiled people become free not when they deny their homelands, but when they come to terms with it.

I waited on purpose until the end of the venture in Jerusalem to collect fragments from the room I was born in Via Dolorosa, The Way of Suffering. Christa had flown in from London to continue her research for my monograph, the origin of my art story. I knocked at the door, standing one step away from my first home, where my attachment with Jerusalem began.

My deceased uncle's wife came out, together with two of my cousins with whom I hardly ever spoke. Their family had been disconnected from mine since my parents left the shared house to live in Bab Huta. My aunt recognized me,

> You are the son of Emile and Espérance.
> I remember you.

After a brief chat, I asked her for permission to go to the room I was born in to collect the fragments in case anything was dangling. I was relieved when she said that they always made the room dirty and led me straight there.

Christa was taken aback as we entered, to find out later that she was aghast as she took her first step, as if she had traveled back in time. She has her own story to tell one day. A white sheet divided the room in half to cover the wide bed on the back from the second half, which was a living room. The furniture looked like Aunt Marie's, from another century. The walls were full of Christian icons, symbols, rosaries, and Saint Mary statues with Christmas decorations around, but they didn't look like they only celebrated the last Christmas. Like a shrine, there was hardly any empty space left on any wall. The television was on, and choirs were performing in Christian camps set in Lebanon or Syria. It was too loud, but my aunt and my two cousins seemed not to care, as if they had gone deaf from listening to these voices religiously.

Christa was hesitant to drink her tea when my cousins brought it in. She took notes instead, excusing herself. She asked if she could smoke a cigarette or two, and my cousin Antone offered her one. Out of nowhere, he asked me,

Are you the one who married the Jew?

I wondered where he got this information from and asked him what he meant. It turned out that he had misread the article Danny Rubenstein had written about my wedding in Bern and the Hava Nagila mishap. I tried to explain, but he nonetheless found more truth in the written word.

After drinking my tea, I asked for a ladder. Christa watched as I started peeling and noted how the process resembled the peeling of an onion: the removing of layers until there was nothing. I was aware of this being my chance to dig into my wound, straight to the source. I mapped out my past into each fragment. The peeling got rid of the toxic residue I had been carrying with me for years. I handed each piece I removed to Christa, who laid them on the floor. Standing on the step of the ladder, the distance between me, the fragments, and the history I embedded in them became clearer, like the solving of a visual puzzle. I was letting go. Now, the fragments carried history for me. And I could finally let go of the stones on my back.

I placed hundreds of fragments between dozens of glass plates, carrying extra bags with me back to Berlin, making me look like I was smuggling archaeological findings. I was worried about the paranoid Israeli security at Ben Gurion Airport, who were even suspicious of pieces of paper, checking each sheet individually by using the most sophisticated X-Ray scanners. But these scanners would never be able to detect in these fragments the many layers of hidden history.

In the taxi, on the way to the airport, I closed my eyes, and a sense of triumph overwhelmed me. The residue that I had carried through the years was dissolving. I was no longer in exile, feeling that whether one was born in Jerusalem or elsewhere, one is always becoming a citizen of planet Earth.

Floating in my world, waiting in the long security screening queue before check-in, I listened to loud trance music, not even realizing it was my turn. The security officer nudged me by the shoulder to grab my attention. I took out my headset, apologized, and handed her my passport. She asked me where I came from. I answered in clear Hebrew,

> *I am a Jerusalemite.*
> *But I live in Berlin.*

Less than a minute later, she wished me,

> Bon Voyage.

I carried my fragments with me and flew home to find the fragments in one piece.

Back in Berlin, I went to the darkroom right away. I transformed the color digital images I took in the Occupied house in Ein Karem into black-and-white negatives. I brushed the light-sensitive emulsion onto the fragments to make them like photo paper—except this paper wasn't blank.

When I developed the photos, the images dissolved in the

fragments' color, bringing them to life by alchemy, like magic. They looked like real unearthed objects, like relics from the past, some like cave art, all of which originated from the digital images I photographed, transforming them into artworks that could never be replicated. If an archaeologist were to look at the pieces, they might assume that they were unearthed artifacts. Yet, upon careful inspection, the archaeologist would find that these fragments are created by an illusion.

I traveled to London, carrying three originals to show them to Dr. Venetia Porter at the British Museum. She had acquired before one of the *Till the End* stone series for the museum's collection, which had been made using a similar photographic technique. Among the three I carried was the fragment with the photograph of the kitchen, the one that looked frozen in time. It was a Masterpiece. I was struck by how much its visual spoke of Jerusalem, homeland, Occupation, exile, and return, among many other connotations beyond my personal narrative, and beyond the surface of the image.

I told Dr. Porter that I had achieved with the fragments what I aspired to achieve with the stones, feeling liberated. She put on her glasses, examined them, and warned me to take care of them since they almost fell apart when simply looked at. I left the museum contemplating our conversation, and as I was looking for my card to exit the tube station, one box slipped from my hand, and The Masterpiece shattered into pieces under the feet of the crowd. It quickly turned back to dust.

Working on the fragments and their layers in the solitude of the darkroom made me aware that Jerusalem cannot be reduced to a few symbols, to a set of keys, or a PO Box. Nor can Jerusalem be contained in any image.

The journey of life is a journey of images. The study of history is the study of images, in all their shapes and forms. While researching on image and imagination, I stumbled upon a passage by Georges Didi-Huberman that put my thoughts into words that could not have been more clear,

> We need pictures to create history, but we also need imagination to re-see these images, and thus, to re-think history.

1

My bond with Francesca, my Jerusalem, is older than time. Maybe we are the last lovers left alive. Since the beginning, we were two spirits flying together between the pages of time. She was never on the back seat in my quest for liberation. Like co-pilots, we traveled to many destinations to discover new territories of the self, in a forever adventure of renewing the self to be what it wants to be.

The beauty of all beauties, the hiding snow-white between realities, has always been The One. After the first spark, the exploding light created a nuclear bond, fused our cores, transforming us through the trembling power of love into One. Before, I never gave it a thought that she was The One because I always felt she was so, a great sign I was living in the moment. And who wants to wake up from a beautiful dream to recount its details before they vanish? I was aware I lived with Francesca like in a dream, floating between reality and the free imagination.

One summer, a friend gave me an old book she found in a flea market in Berlin, thinking I would like it. *Awareness* was the first book I read where I never marked a single sentence. I read it at one go, and when I did the second and the third time, I made sure I made sense of every word. *Awareness* by Anthony De Mello, written in unparalleled clarity, was so good that I believed it should be taught in every school in the world, calling it The Book of All Books, the one that has the power to transform all your realities, attuning you to the symphony of the universe. And there, everything is beautiful. Feeling the change it did to me, I sent many books as gifts to all the people I love, especially Francesca and Cécile.

That same summer, during the Fête de la Musique festival in Berlin, in which the street we lived on became the center for it, Francesca and I were partying outside with the crowd until the police stopped all the festivities abruptly because one neighbor had complained about noise at ten pm sharp, sending thousands of people home. Still in the wave, Francesca and I looked around us and invited whoever we danced with and whoever our eyes randomly caught to continue the techno party in our house around the corner. Maybe twenty people joined us. Among them was a DJ who brought along many drinks. Also among them was a man in his fifties who looked attuned to the symphony of life. The art hanging on the walls intrigued him, commenting with clarity on the black and white alchemy of the fragment paint pieces from Jerusalem. We talked about image and imagination, illusion and reality, about puzzles and the power of love. His sharp answers intrigued me to wonder who he was, and when I asked, he said,

> I am an artist of the soul, the heart.

When I inquired what this really meant and what materials he used in his art, he said,

> I paint with words.
> I have a healing clinic, and I help people by drawing images of their words, re-ordering them, and then project them straight back into their sight. This allows them to see their reality better. And from there, they can change it.

Elated, I told him,

> *Do you know The Book of all Books, the one that changes all realities?*

He asked me which, but because of my issue not remembering names or faces, I said,

> *Awareness, but I forgot this moment who had written it.*

And with another smile that embraced the universe, he said,

> It's by Anthony de Mello.
> But there is another book which I believe is The Book of all Books.

Since I have been obsessed with the clarity of *Awareness*, believing that it should replace the law as a reference system from what *is* right or wrong, to what *feels* right or wrong. It taught me to pursue aware actions, become a better human being, rather than seek absolute awareness. This should be the prime expedition in our endless pursuit of global citizenship. I was really curious which book he had in mind, mostly because we came from different worlds. I couldn't wait for the answer,

> The Way to Love.
> And it so happens that it is also by Anthony De Mello.

Francesca and I went clubbing on one of those long weekends in Berlin that started on Friday and maybe ended on Monday. For the first twenty-four hours, thunder hit Francesca's core and mine, and with every whip, it pushed us galaxies apart. We whipped each other with the intensity that could make the blind see. Again and Again. No matter how much we tried to align ourselves back, the light of our awareness was very dim. This was when I learned that trying was the weakest word, or action, which has failure embedded in its essence, as one tried something till it didn't work out. We were shouting, consistently screaming, sending vibrations to everyone around in our cosmic fight. Had I been the owner and saw us in that state, I would have kicked us out and denied us entry forever. Enraged, we sank deep into the darkness of our souls, lost in the chambers of our ego-mind.

And with the blink of an eye, The Love Fairy suddenly appeared from the smoke on the dance floor. That was what Francesca instantly called her, just when I wanted to tell her the same the moment The Love Fairy revealed herself to us. I couldn't see the color of her eyes. They were in every color. Her hair flowing like the river of life, glittering in endless beauty. She wiped Francesca's tears and said,

> Don't cry here and now.
> You can cry tomorrow.

She hugged both of us, very tight, and yet it felt light in her magical presence. Her lips brushed Francesca's and mine while she placed her hands on our hearts, saying that we were exploding with light, not accepting any reason for this cosmic fight. She mirrored our inner beauty back, to consciously look inside, and feel life. And when we turned into One Heart, while the three of us hugged in this parallel universe, she said one word before she left, and we never saw her again,

> B e a u t i f u l

Shortly after our new home in Berlin in 2010 found us, the Arab World exploded with euphoria, a word the media used to describe the emerging reality of the so-called Arab Spring. It all started in a Tunisian market, when a struggling street vendor, Mohamed Bouazizi, set himself on fire in front of the governor's office, protesting against poverty, constant provocation, and the corrupt regime. Little did Bouazizi know that he would change the course of history four weeks later. After nationwide demonstrations that grabbed the world's attention, the pressure forced the dictator Ben Ali to flee to Saudi Arabia on one dark night in January. Bouazizi's story triggered almost all the Arab nations to interrogate themselves, undergo an awakening that spread like a domino effect from Morocco to Kuwait and beyond. The change was happening quickly, firing up the people's imagination, and nothing was capable of stopping it.

I already had set myself on fire a year earlier, but I was careful not to associate my artwork with the revolutions, pointing out that my states of transition, euphoria, and beyond euphoria, which I had turned into art series by the same names, coincidentally preceded the blaze of the Arab World. They reflected my battle to break free from my own fear in my pursuit of self-liberation on all levels.

But when the Tunisian dictator Ben Ali fled that night, marking the sudden end to a decades-long brutal regime, two voices rang out that touched me along with millions of others. The second voice came from an older man interviewed on the street after news spread about the fleeing of Ben Ali in his private jet. With watery eyes that could move a stone and heartfelt peace of mind, while stroking his white hair with the palm of his hand, he said in sheer disbelief,

> Harimna, harimna nantazer hazihi al-lahza at-Taarikhiyyah.
> We have aged, aged, waiting for this historic moment.

But the first voice came from another man wearing a training suit with a phone in his hand, who ran out shouting into an empty street at night, the moment Ben Ali escaped. He was caught on video by a passerby, yelling and repeating in a raw emotional state, again, and again, and again,

> Ithararna.
> Ma'adsh fi khof.
>
> Ben Ali hrab. Ben Ali hrab. Ben Ali hrab.
> We are liberated.

Fear no longer exists.

Ben Ali ran away. Ben Ali ran away. Ben Ali ran away.

The man who snapped the video could be heard crying behind the lens. During the first live broadcasts of both scenes, several newscasters found themselves in tears on air, unable to make a sentence. Al Jazeera News aired the videos over and over again, at the top of every hour. They became instant icons, not for the Tunisian revolution, but for the pure elation of what happens when freedom is *felt* rather than *said*.

Their voices became every free person's voice, a wake-up call, an alert, a celebration, recapitulating the long-anticipated personal liberation from oppression, from agony, washing the frustration with joy and euphoria, which many people felt after living too long under control.

Every morning when I woke up, I turned on the news to get my ecstasy, listening to them, primarily the first one. They became my new self-prescribed drugs. When I mentioned them to Kamal, he interrupted me, saying that he turned the volume all the way up whenever they appeared. For weeks, I spoke about them to whoever would listen, expressing how change can only really start from within.

Right around then, I flew to Paris. One night, Hani and I were invited for dinner at the home of collectors, Gamal and Najet, whom I met a few years earlier and who never stopped supporting my art voyage. They lived in a historic building across from the Dôme des Invalides, the large church where Napoléon Bonaparte was buried. We arrived early, so we took a walk around, allured by the blissful atmosphere painting itself before dusk, transporting us to parallel realities. It felt like something striking was about to happen. We stood on a small arched bridge to take in the moment as Hani smoked a cigarette while we watched the sun disappear.

Gamal's doorbell was shining, and as he buzzed us in, we entered an antique elevator to go all the way up to find him opening the elevator door to greet us and welcome us straight to his house. On the spot, I saw my *Euphoria* artwork, the collage of explosive trees like fired-up neurons, hanging in the long corridor. And around the corner, *In Exile*, the collage of windows and all possibility, was hanging above the mantelpiece in the grand living room facing windows looking over the sky of Paris. As we sat down, Gamal wondered how I was doing. There was only one thing on my mind. I said candidly, gesturing to stress every word,

> *When I die, there will be two voices in my head. The second will be of the man with white hair who cried as he said "Harimna, harimna", and the first will be of the man who shouted "Ithararna. Ben Ali hrab."*

Gamal listened, but I could see that he was waiting anxiously to tell me something, but waited till I let it all out, or maybe because I never knew when to shut up,

> The old man with the white hair was my wife's teacher in Tunisia. And the first one is our dear friend and is joining us right now.

I thought he was teasing me, and then the doorbell just rang. I looked at Hani and asked him to pinch me, and in a couple of minutes, there he was—the icon, the voice of all voices. As he entered, he introduced himself as Abdennaceur Aouini. This time, I didn't hesitate to hug a man who inflamed me.

Bouazizi and these two voices moved millions into the streets to self-interrogate themselves. On Cairo's Tahrir Square—Liberation Square—the world watched as the Egyptians forced out another dictator, Hosni Mubarak. It took just eighteen days. The will of the people, who fought for real felt freedom, compelled the most powerful countries in the world to side with them. But democracy was the last thing those world powers wanted for the Arab World—it wouldn't have served their interests. It has always been easier to control dictatorships than to work with elected governments, which are more likely to follow the will of their voters. Colonialism only changed form, enabling the colonizer to no longer be there on the land, but could instead set a proxy to conquer the new system, and by extension, people's imagination.

In Tahrir Square, the Egyptians fought for the liberation of the self, and their image, which had been captured and defeated by brutal systems. Reclaiming their image that night was their real triumph. The next challenge was to maintain control of it, mainly because the next regime would want to reconquer that image to show the world who indeed had the power. As always, in the end, the people pay the price in their strife for freedom so that others later can live in it.

Wars proved that physically conquering all the world was impossible, but today it became possible to dominate collective consciousness. We live in the colonization of the imagination era, which is far more dangerous than colonizing anything in reality. And I came to an awareness that what was stopping the liberation of the land of Palestine was because people were Occupied in their imagination without knowing, or feeling it.

When the image of The Masterpiece dissipated to dust in the London Underground, I realized I had also been stripped of the power I thought I held over images. This piece no longer exists, but a photograph of the original artwork exists, the only evidence of its past materiality. My experiment transformed a digital image that can be copied infinitely into a unique piece of art that cannot be replicated. When I left the darkroom and saw the result, I believed I had cracked a visual code, gaining power over images, controlling what happens in the darkness of the camera apparatus, and later in the darkroom. But, it turned out to be a visual dilemma. In the end, the image won because the only proof that the artwork ever existed was now through its digital image. This made me reflect deeper on the applied apparatus to focus on the image of the Israeli Occupation and the free or freed image.

What came first, the world, or its image? My visual research explores the genealogy of the image, studying its history, navigating the unseen light, traveling through images to discover their hidden realities. And if the world has always been an image, as philosophers have repeatedly stated, the search reaches infinity. I wondered whether I was creating or unveiling something already out there, waiting to be found, revealing light palimpsests never seen before.

My relationship with the image is like being on a space odyssey, in search of understanding image formation and the origin of light. And since the image is part of the imagination, unlocking the visual code will allow me to see beyond my own reality.

As long as I didn't resolve my paradox with the Israeli Occupation, of the Israeli on my back, the virus would become more toxic, and its living residue would continue to suffocate me. We are all born free, but at the moment we get detached from the umbilical cord, we become bound, tied to an infinite number of other attachments. Life after that becomes a process of liberation, about our endless resolution to free ourselves from everything. I wanted to enter a state of holy silence, find the silence between my thoughts so that I can listen to my heartbeat, and later transform its vibrations into art. The only way to free myself was to unbuckle, take a leap of faith, and release myself from the Israeli on my back, knowing the price will be my life. Living under Occupation was never a reality I was going to submit to. And since such surrender was not in my nature, my fate was sealed. All I could do was have faith that I would have power left in me to survive after the impact.

I unbuckled from my never-ending tandem jump, from always being suspended in the air. I crashed. I didn't plunge into the sea to hit rock bottom and push myself up to the surface to breathe fresh air on my own for the first time in my life. Instead, I hit the solid ground, smashing into razor-sharp barbed wire, slicing me into pieces. I was torn apart. I couldn't move. It felt as if all my bones had broken, crushed, splintering through my skin. I found the free land I had long been looking for, but now I was alone, somewhere, waiting to catch my last breath.

I fell flat on my bed in Berlin. Day after day, all I could do was stare at doors, hallways, and windows leading to nowhere. There was nothing anyone would be able to help me to stand on my feet. I lived in isolation, a hermit at home, in a cosmic desert, awaiting my death sentence.

Kamal and Hani knew I was fighting my last war. When my silence lasted weeks, and then months, I received a one-sentence email from a worried Kamal saying,

> Just when the caterpillar thought the world was over,
> it turned into a butterfly.
>
> And never forget the real prize.
> Francesca and Cécile.

Hani dropped me a line echoing Samuel Beckett words,

To be an artist is to fail, as no other dare fail.

I didn't have an antidote to the venom. The slow process of draining the poison from the virus paralyzed me. Even when I rested my eyes, I couldn't find any way in my dreams.

And on the day of all days, standing on the edge of all edges, not looking at the sky, but deep inside my darkest point, Karin Adrian von Roques, The Angel of Death, knocked on my front door by random chance. As she sat down in the living room, I told her that she had come by chance on that day.

I had never spoken to a curator and art historian like I did with Karin, exposing what most artists hide. She asked me what gave me energy and what I had faith in. I said,

In Nothing.
Maybe In Art. But since my process became contaminated, I lost my faith in it. And with it all my energy.

I told her that I had no back-up, no God to rescue me, that it was game over. Then Karin shared her wisdom about inner light and truth. Her words reminded me of Mother Veronica's philosophy of faith that I had learned on the Mount of Olives. But unlike Mother Veronica, who lived in the convent since she was five, Karin was a nomad, always in transition, moving forty-six times, living in seventeen countries.

My power to create new realities was no longer present or became hidden. But she planted a seed in me that flourished the moment she said goodbye at the door. We spoke about death and life, about art and history, about exile and freedom, about Self and Other, about the beginning and the end. I drew for her how I transformed the problems in my life into visual dilemmas, which, once solved, or decoded, allowed me to see the bigger picture. I had been stuck in my chamber, in my own mental space and darkness for a long time, unable to solve my next puzzle.

She said I needed guidance, but not just from anyone. It would have to be from a special person who would be conscious of how I perceived life to help me visualize, code a way out. As she spoke, The Muse, who I was no longer in touch with, flared in my mind. The Angel of Death was a guiding star.

In the morning light, acting on her lead, I got in touch with The Muse so we could visualize my way out of the shadow land in my cosmic desert. The Muse was already like a chip in my mind, the only person who had my elixir.

To steer me in the right direction, I explained what was going on, and she nailed it down, seeing the bigger picture, that I saw my art and life as one. She cited the example of autobiography authors whose writings could never represent their whole lives—their texts and my art expressed only a small part of who we were. This was when I recognized that my art and I were not one. For the next few days, I was in a crisis of transformation, realizing that art, the long-time vehicle of my liberation, was now holding me hostage. I decided that the only way out was to divorce myself from my art, to live separate lives, so that it wouldn't affect me when such words echoed,

I bought a Steve Sabella. I sold a Steve Sabella.

I was not for sale. My art was. When a work of art is born, it has a life of its own, separate from the artist. From that moment on, my association with my work changed. I freed myself from my art, as much as I freed my art from my life story. I unriddled how to be part of my art, and apart from it

I saw The Muse as the Master of Chambers, helping me navigate my mental maze and darkness. She handed me keys, and it was up to me to find the doors they unlocked. I told her that I felt I was being shot at from all angles on the battlefield, that I didn't want to live a lifetime of fighting, of digging trenches, of constantly stitching my wounds to prepare for the next confrontation.

She asked me to close my eyes, relax on my couch, and then imagine I was alone. Somewhere. I chose the desert, the dry landscape all around the Dead Sea. She asked me how I was feeling,

> *I am exhausted, powerless from the constant fighting.*
> *I don't know how much longer I can survive.*

She told me to imagine two people walking towards me and then to describe them,

> *They are coming from a distance, slowly, towards me.*
> *One of them is radiating with light, and the other is engulfed in darkness.*

She said to ask each of them what they wanted from me. I was silent for a minute, and when I opened my eyes, I said,

> *The one with the light wants to save me, but he is too weak.*
> *The one with the darkness wants me to die.*

This was when The Master of Chambers turned things around.

> You have perceived it wrong all along. You are tired because you have been running from the person in the darkness when he wants to help you. You should surrender, accept your death, and allow a new Steve to be born from the cocoon he has been stuck in for so long.

I listened to her, understanding what needs to be done. I had stayed longer than necessary in the darkness of my soul and could not accept the changes in me. Fighting my own death had been exhausting—I was scared of a new reality. I had been the main obstacle on my road to liberation.

The next morning I woke up feeling light. I broke the invisible mirrors around me, going through the realities of my creation. Leaving the past behind unprocessed was not going to fix anything. The only real way out was to re-order the pages of my past and come to terms with their reality. Once and for all.

The Ascension Church Bell Tower flashed back to my consciousness. Except, for now, I extended it to become the tallest building in the world, stretching high up into the sky. Then a man, full of life—who looks exactly like me—walked straight into the building's elevator across from the reception desk where people regularly came to deposit stones they carried in a backpack to leave empty until the bag gets full again. In the elevator of life, the man pressed the button to go up to the last floor. The elevator opened to a round view looking over planet Earth, giving anyone an objective look. As he stood there contemplating his life and why he was called there, two people dressed in white approached him with a leather book embossed with letters written with light,

The Life of Steve Sabella

The man got informed that I was in critical condition and that I was about to die. They asked him to accept that when he left the room, he would adopt my life, become me, and continue my life and his from that moment on, embracing both.

This state of acceptance, of loving the self, the fusion, and the detachment transformed my past into data, archived memories, transformed into an encyclopedic reference. I became the protagonist of my story, where the story no longer controlled me, but the opposite. It gave me the power to call in painful memories without hurting myself, to feel real emotions from the past, and not sink between their sharp waves.

I sat down and sifted through each and every page in The Leather Book. I read how I stitched my wounds with the barbed wire I fell into in my last hours, making me stronger than ever before. All the poison dripped out of my veins. I found life between euphoria and melancholia, between exile and home, between my reality and free imagination.

As a child, I pointed a flashlight into the well of my Old City house. Today, I look into the dark well of my life and see my own light mirrored back. Every time I fall into the darkness—my darkness—I remind myself that liberation always comes through the search for inner light.

One day in Berlin, I looked from my house windows down onto the street below to watch construction workers laying pipes, pushing wires and cables in a hardcore operation. They had to temporarily relocate the street lights very close to our windows, making them glow at night like long candles with constant flames. Francesca and I often played music, turned the couch outward, and sat facing our light reflections. This was our moment to talk. One night, she told me,

> Your river might not be flowing as strongly as it used to when you were younger. Maybe it can no longer move rocks downstream. But, look at it this way, now your river is wider and deeper.

One night, I told Francesca about The Muse and how she saved my life. Deep down, Francesca was relieved that I got better, yet I felt she was hurt. It was my turn to be there, and Francesca has her own story to tell. But in my myth, she has always been The

One.

Once we flew to Dubai on separate flights for my exhibition *Independence*, a series of images of Francesca and Cécile that I had photographed on a remote island showing their exposed bodies as if disintegrating and reforming. When we traveled back, we boarded separate planes. Yet, we both arrived home at the same time to open the front door.

Home has always been where Francesca is. As the workers cobbled the street back together, Francesca, Cécile, and I decided to go on a new road trip—from Berlin to Zagreb, and then return via Vienna and Krakov. We listened to an Arabic song on the trip, and Cécile was happy when I translated some of the words. But it turned out she already knew many of them. There was more Arabic in her than we both knew. We got lost on the way and found ourselves on a bridge to one of Croatia's islands, so I booked a humble bed & breakfast on my phone to spend the night. When we reached our destination, the landlord was outside, smoking a cigarette. He came over, leaned towards my window, and explained that he had made a mistake and no longer had the room we confirmed. He asked us to park where we were and invited us inside his home to figure out what to do. We followed him straight into his living room and sat around the massive wood dining table, where his partner was busy preparing some complicated dish with steam coming out of the kitchen. The three of us felt that something was about to happen. He excused himself to fetch a folder, and in the meantime, his partner offered us drinks and put out cookies for Cécile. When the landlord came back, he sat down and began searching through the folder with one hand, making phone calls with the other, and maybe a third one to smoke his cigarettes. After a while, he said that he had found us a better place and asked us to follow him in our car. Concerned, we drove behind him for quite a while. It seemed like we were heading in the wrong direction, and we had fallen into a trap.

But when we reached the destination, it was like a scene from A Thousand and One Nights. A mansion on two levels with outdoor terraces sat on top of a high pointed cliff rising from the sea below. It had its own winding stone staircase going around the ridge to the beach all the way down. The view was endless, in any direction. The water in the secluded bay below sparkled in colors, again, I have never seen before.

It took no power to surrender. We loved sitting on stones as if hanging over the cliff's edge. Cécile giggled as visitors climbed all the way up from the winding staircase to find a locked gate and a sign that read,

Private Property

But, we often let people go through to reach the upper road. At one moment, when the sun was at bay, the three of us ascended down the winding staircase to reach the barrier separating the sea. At the secluded bay, the atmosphere was out of this world, reflected in still, silent water. When it got dark, Francesca and Cécile plunged into the clear water, and I plunged into the moment. My whole life flashed by. The pain disappeared. I was finally present elsewhere. And right there. I felt every mistake and failure I made in my life was absolutely necessary to discover the light being where I was at that moment. And there, I felt complete. I cleansed my imagination, declared my independence, had a rebirth to be born in every moment in life—an act I believe every Palestinian, every Israeli, and every other Citizen of the World should do so that we all become One Heart.

In my moment of love, peace, and serenity, of light, I watched Francesca and Cécile in the water and felt the bliss of their presence. Just then, Cécile's words echoed in me, and in them was the power to make the blind see again, transform any reality, and live attuned to the never-ending and forever changing cosmic dance:

Imagine if it was the other way round,
dreams were our reality
and reality was only
a dream.

0

This is not the end of the story but the beginning of the story. There is an Other in all of us. Each Other. The time has come to stop drawing borders and start drawing our future. And the future is now. We are a speck of nothing in the equation of the universe. Yet, from nothing, everything is possible. The state of darkness is the state of all creation. We can all rise from ground zero, and zero is a great place to start, hit the reset button, and begin a new chapter.

Writing is a way to go home. Painting is being at home.

Those were Kamal Boullata's words. Through the power of drawing reality, I found my home. Only beauty emerged when one delved into Kamal's world to listen to razor-sharp words, words that always came out from the heart. Kamal had a distinctive voice, the tone of a Master narrator. You seldom wished to hear the end of his stories. He was true to himself, and one word that echoes in me which he always said with energy,

Forward.

And the only way forward in our journey of liberation is forward. Kamal passed away not long ago in Berlin, where he had lived his last eight years, and against all the odds, he was laid to rest on a Jerusalem hill looking over the Mount of Olives, near my father's grave. I was fortunate to see Kamal two weeks before he departed. After the night I visited him with Michos, who was in Berlin by chance, I flew to Jerusalem, our city of birth. He looked young, energized, inspired, speaking about ongoing projects. His words were vivid, transporting us into many worlds. Since we first met, Kamal shared his knowledge without conditions. Kamal was an outstanding scholar who added to the layers of history new threads that weave the past effortlessly to the future. He based his theory on observation enriched in being in the moment. And there, he never wished to be in the center, choosing to wander over the peripheries of life. But life found more than one way to push him naturally to the center.

One cannot speak to Kamal without details. During a visit to his house, I heard him suddenly get loud, laughing on the phone with the poet Adonis. I thought a star fell down from the sky. The matter was that they spotted one missing comma in a poetry book they were co-editing. This was a great lesson to pay attention to the delicate and vibrant fabric of life.

Kamal was an expert on the literature of the soul, on the language of life. Every conversation with him was about essence, about true being. As for his art, his visuals are mirrors of pure light, transparent like the soul. Kaleidoscopic. Always changing. They capture your vision upon first glance, and the deeper one looks, the closer one reaches a central point, one that resides in the self. And once there, it becomes inevitable to see Kamal's clairvoyant colors float in an endless rhythmic dance.

Kamal inspired many in his life, and I do feel his journey has just begun. His departure is not a loss but a reward to all humanity. They forced him to leave Palestine, but Palestine never left him. And Jerusalem was always at the center of Kamal's heart. Seeing how he lived his life, he was one of my beliefs that to be born in Jerusalem, or anywhere else, means one is always becoming a citizen of planet Earth.

Just before the Coronavirus engulfed our reality, I was one out of forty people from all over the world chosen to be part of a co-action creative group to counter extremism through arts and culture. Our first encounter was in Venice on that weekend when it drowned, was in a state of emergency. And that's how we all felt about the state of the world, weeks before the virus invasion. On wide whiteboards, we started drawing a new image of the world as we imagined it. Our second encounter was in Brussels, and our mission was to transform this imagination into reality before we headed to Washington, D.C., to decide on the action. None of us argued, agreed, or disputed. All of our conversations started with an and, where everyone contributed, adding to the bigger picture, which we all solve together. The *I* was silenced, replaced by what *we* can do to create a world based on global awareness.

The shared stories, visions, and honest words transformed many of us. I had one hour to spare before my trip to the clouds, finding myself strolling aimlessly around the streets of Brussels. But the universe has no wrong answers. The sun was shining in the blue sky, warming the cold street corridors. I looked at the sun with my eyes closed, accepting its rays and whatever they carried with them. And then I felt a new state of freedom, that as long as there is one person left who imagines a better world, life has a chance. And there is more than one person. There are many, all waiting for their ideas and dreams to be weaved together by cosmic light. The seeds are all out there looking for the right ground to flourish. And they can with the blink of an eye. Until then, the ground we are all looking for is wherever we are, and the seeds are right there in us.

I was in a state of bliss. And the moment my canvas found me in the light-room, I transformed that state of bliss into Everland inspired by when we were divided into groups during one morning session and asked to invent an imaginary home on an island, to draw it together, and then give it a name. One idea led to the other, from Noland, to the inverse of Neverland.

Everland is the land of Palestine, with roots stretching everywhere. And like never before, Palestine has fallen off the map of the world—sidelined, lost its center. *Everland* is a photo collage of Palestinian embroidery, a tradition passed from generation to generation by women who sew patterns and motifs to reveal their heritage, ancestry, and place of origin. Palestinian embroidery is proof of presence that no power can uproot from the people's imagination, a celebration of collective identity and narrative that gets renewed, awakened every time we see or touch its beauty. But given Palestine's history, the beauty pierces the heart. I remember my mother and sisters engaging with it when I was a child living in Jerusalem's Old City. The process was one of meditation where one spends endless hours traveling from one tiny square to another, feeling invited to explore the self and its truths. Given the richness of colors and shapes, one inevitably enters a state of trance.

Everland is not stitched with cotton, wool, or silk, but with digital threads weaved on a new fabric of life, on the fabric of light. And if the light falling on the earth is always new, how can we stay the same? We are creatures of light. And the light shines in all the colors of the world, creating the threads of our life. And it is up to us how we weave them together. Every time *Everland* will be on display, its nine squares will be put in a different constellation, including their orientation to any side. This way, *Everland* will always have endless possibilities, creating a new visual, forever changing.

Everland celebrates all the beauty that comes out of Palestine, a place where everything gets disrupted. Yet, the collage enables the cross stitches to penetrate deep into new borders, creating unique designs, connections that look as if they represent every other culture to reveal the spirit of the world. We are all from everywhere and nowhere. Poetically, we are all from elsewhere. And that nowhere is the everland we are all searching for. Getting there is an extraordinary journey of endless discovery.

Kamal described my work for the foreword of my monograph as a dream. But Kamal's last words were a dream within a dream. I dedicate *Everland* to the spirit of Kamal Boullata, who left us with two books, treasures, whose titles alone reveal the greatest symphony of life:

There Where You Are Not
&
Uninterrupted Fugue

We are all interconnected by visible threads of life, part of a much larger picture, which we all contribute to together. And if we are to remain in the cosmic picture, we must inject into ourselves the image of a better world, and this time not keeping the vision still in its dream. We are in the era of essence, imagination, and hard work, like never before.

Imagine, is the strongest word I know. It has the power to change all realities. We live in an era where the power of the free mind and imagination is controlled and contaminated, also like never before. Possibilities and infinity are interconnected. There are infinite possibilities. And imagination, like infinity, cannot be measured, which gives the imagination limitless power. And the same power is in all of us.

And as you read my endings lines now, I recall Brother Robert Wise, my first mentor who taught me about the essence of life when I wanted to suck all the air out in the horrid mouse experiment so that I feel life first. Wise taught me about computer models, how to code, create the software from scratch. Now, I code resorting to the mechanics of light that has embedded in it all the secrets of life. Through the lens of art, through the lens that leads to the dark chamber in my camera, I was able to design new realities, and in the process, I designed a new self that updates every day. My relationship with the image is like being on a space odyssey, in search of understanding image formation. And since an image is part of the imagination, unlocking the code allowed me to see beyond my reality.

Wise saw how I looked at problems from multiple angles. I always thought there is a solution at the other end of every problem. Focusing on the problem only magnifies it, while looking at the solution opens windows of possibilities.

We should hit the reset button, reorder our program, reset its data memory to allow for a rebirth to happen so that life always feels like a new beginning, a new order.

The world we put together will never be perfect, but in life, we should all do what we can to make the world a better place, nothing less, nothing more. A great way forward is not to fight what's there but to create what's not there.

In the world of art, there is no reality, only imagination. As long as there is one Palestinian left who imagines a free Palestine, the Occupation has no chance. The time has come for the language of life. My awareness of life intensified when I learned the be in Berlin—to just be, and let be. I learned to process life without filters. To look at reality and see it as it is and then go deeper and beyond. We can only be do this when we focus, eliminate all clutter, noise, and distortion in our endless journey inwards, towards the soul. And because the soul does not like to be lied to, I quickly learned to be honest with myself and focus on things that matter.

Palestinians will continue to resist till the end, till the last Palestinian. The fighting has shifted from one of liberating the land to one of liberating the self and the colonized imagination. Freedom is a universal truth. We are all born free. No freedom council like the UN, or governing bodies like the EU, or governments like that of the United States, and definitely not of Israel, get to decide who is free or not. Palestinians should stop waiting for arbitrarily set dates to obtain their individual independence. Independence day is today, and everyone should declare it.

Israel was established to create a Jewish nation so that the Jewish people could have a state of their own and control their own destinies. Palestinians will not accept anything less than the same. Would you live under any sort of Occupation?

Many Palestinians feel that Israel has the right to kill them, that the international community has failed to force Israel to comply with international law. Instead of facing the consequences for its crimes against humanity, Israel benefits from protection. Israel has isolated itself, creating fake peace and spreading the propaganda that Palestinians do not want peace. But there has not been any real intention to ever end The Occupation. Israel's governments expanded it strategically so that it would never end.

Ilan Pappé, an Israeli historian and social activist, stated in an interview,

> The endgame is still implementing the initial Zionist program of having as much of Palestine as possible with as few Palestinians in it as possible. It may sound like a tactic, but in Israel, this is a strategy if not an ideology—namely part of life in a daily routine of continuing to oppress the Palestinians. . . . This is a source of income for many, many people in this country. Ultimately, it is not a state that has an army and a police force; it is an army and police force that have a state.
>
> The last Israeli attack on Gaza has to be put in a longer historical context. It is just another point in a long history that probably stretches back to the very beginning of the Zionist project in Palestine in the late 19th century. Zionism in essence, is a settler colonialist project, very much in the same mould as such projects in Africa, Australia and

the Americas, the only difference being it has not as yet completed its ambitions.

Around six million Palestinians live in the diaspora today, another six million live within Israel's borders, and almost four and a half million of them live without the right to vote, without a voice. In polls asking the Israeli public if they preferred a democratic or a Jewish state, the majority chose the latter. Israelis do not want a bi- national state with equal rights for all its citizens, but they also reject the establishment of an independent Palestinian state. Therefore, they choose The Occupation.

The Jewish people know better than anyone else what it means to be persecuted and targeted because of their beliefs, the way one looks or thinks, or even just is. Israelis do want peace, but they want it while expanding settlements and controlling Palestinian life in the name of their own security. Real peace comes when we see the other with respect, as an equal.

History has proven that peace on colonized land starts when the colonizer publicly acknowledges what it has done. The first step in finding peace between Israelis and Palestinians is for the Israeli government to give an apology from the heart to all the Palestinian people.

Israel should apologize for every tree they cut down, every village they erased. For expelling natives from their lands. For settling in Palestinian homes, for stealing their property. Israel should apologize for the millions of stranded refugees and for not allowing the vast majority to ever set foot on their land again. Israel should apologize for trying to erase Palestinian culture, for fragmenting Palestinian society, for injecting fear into Palestinians and Israelis.

For fabricating history. Israel should apologize for twisting international law, for subjugating millions to live in open-air prisons, for using Gaza as a battlefield and testing ground for modern weaponry. For degrading Palestinian life. Israel should apologize for all the people, including the children it has killed. For murdering their dreams. When Cécile and I talk, we often start with,

Imagine . . .

For many years my life was held hostage by The Occupation, but in my dreams, I was always free. Once I learned how to change my own consciousness, my imagination became my reality to live reality as a dream.

As for liberating the land of Palestine, I leave it to our collective **imagination.**

Lightning Source UK Ltd.
Milton Keynes UK
UKHW040824210421
382278UK00013BA/992/J

9 783949 392047